CANDLESTICK

NIGHT FAC OVER LAOS

JAMES P. "PAT" HYLAND
JD, MA, CW4, USA (Ret.)

LUMINARE PRESS
WWW.LUMINAREPRESS.COM

Candlestick, Night FAC over Laos
© 2017 James Patrick Hyland
www.jamespatrickhyland.com

All rights reserved. This book or any portion thereof may not be reproduced or used in any manner whatsoever without the express written permission of the publisher, except for the use of brief quotations in a book review.

Printed in the United States of America

Cover Design: Claire Flint Last

Luminare Press
438 Charnelton St., Suite 101
Eugene, OR 97401
www.luminarepress.com

LCCN: 2017952310
ISBN: 978-1-944733-37-7

*In loving memory of my father, Herb (1912–2005),
mother, Bernice (1918–2005), and only brother, Tom (1942–2016)*

This collection of simple tales is dedicated to those who were sent into harm's way in the U.S. military, in any war, action, police action, or engagement, at any time, and at any place. In talking to others who were in these different places and served doing different things, I have learned that every person's war was different, but always very personal. Few had anything funny happen to them.

Fewer still have had the love and support to be able to tell personal stories to release the demons.

This book is also dedicated to those who have shared or are still sharing my life and who have supported me all the years since September 1, 1970, my DEROS (Date of Estimated Return from Overseas) from Southeast Asia.

Finally, I dedicate this collection of stories to my U.S. Air Force pilot training class, 69-07 (The Magnificent Seven) of Laredo Air Force Base, in the land of the big BX, with special thanks to my Section Leader, Banks Prevatt.

CONTENTS

Acknowledgements xi
Forward xiii
Life in the Air 1
The Great American Dream 3
Goodbye, Kansas 4
The Telephone Call 6
Trolling for Gunfire 8
The Letter 11
Nightmares 12
Officer Training School 14
Laredo: The T-41 15
Laredo: The T-37 16
A-1 Down 20
A Hospital:
    A Sobering Experience 35
Laredo: The T-38 37
Bulat 41
Another Surprise 44
Super Spooky and the Green Goblin 46
The Thunderstorm Ride 58
Getting an Airplane Assignment 61
Five Days Without Food 62
Prisoner of War Training 65
We'll Be Running Down the Mountain When
    We Come 74
Trying to kill the Beetle 78

Combat Crew Training	81
Reality Check	85
Jungle Survival School	88
Jungle Boy Marksman	90
Dead Bodies	92
Sleeping with Jungle Rats	94
New Fish	100
Goodbye to Steve	102
"Volunteers" Needed	103
Waiting in Saigon	107
Taken for a Ride	108
The Mysterious Major	113
Leaving Saigon	117
Bottle Busters	119
Mad Minutes	121
Getting Started	122
Truck Killers	124
My Dollar Ride	125
The Aircraft	129
My First Court Martial	131
Me at Snake School	139
The Crew	145
Flare or "Candle" Missions	149
Fighter-Bomber Missions	150
Lima Site 20	160
Aircraft Commander Combat Check Ride	163
Navy Air Strike—Almost	167

Cousin Roger and I Tackle R&R in Bangkok 169
Fatal Target Focus 176
Blind Bat—Crew Count 177
Food Poisoning 180
Boondoggle to Hong Kong 184
My Second Court Martial 187
Blinded by the Night 190
Parachute Panties 193
Paper Bombers 195
My First R&R in Hawaii 196
My Second R&R in Kansas 199
Other CTOs 203
Runaway Flare Pallet 209
Courage 211
The Bank Job 212
Mu Gia Interstate 221
An Arclight Encounter 224
A-26 in the Weeds 226
Court Martial Number Three 230
The Bob Hope Show 246
Taping Records on Nights Off 247
Days 250
The Outdoor Theater 252
Mustang 254
Officer of the Day 260
The F-4 GIB and New Year's Eve 264
The Chinese Highway 268

The Russian Talkers 269
Blotting Out the Stars 270
Chief Navigator in a Party Flight Suit 271
Author before a night mission in Laos, 1969 278
About the Author 279

ACKNOWLEDGEMENTS

This "book" of memories is the result of my desire to have my children, Candi, Kelli, Chris, and Jenny, understand a little more about their crazy and sometimes weird father. My parents, now both gone, told me on several occasions that "Vietnam" significantly changed me in ways they could not understand.

Although I started to write down some of these stories several times shortly after returning home, I didn't get very far any of those times. Vibrations in my head and bad dreams always resulted and writing more merely increased the pain. I was having enough trouble just keeping myself going on a civilian track without poking the tiger snarling in my head. My unjustified and always present anger was enough to frighten me from making things worse by writing things down that stirred those juices.

Many friends helped me along the way, until I could finally sit down and put some of the stories in my head in writing. My friend Roger Beattie always encouraged me to start. My Army National Guard buddies, Larry Willer, Carl Austin, Mike Jackson, and Darrel Linenberger gave me the courage to face my demons. Lisa Coalwell helped me get started toward setting out these stories in a way that we hope is both clear and understandable.

Along the way, and none too soon, I met and married my soul mate. She gave me the daily peace and loving support that I needed to get these simple stories on paper. Even though she didn't understand the reasons for my anger and confusion, she understood enough to know that I was in pain and needed her personally administered balm. With her help, I worked harder at getting my stories and thoughts on paper. When I did, the nightmares stopped. I owe everything in this book to my wife, Leslie.

FORWARD

I wish I could write. I also wish I could play the piano, but five years of lessons as a child destroyed that wish. Like dancing, which my mother insisted that I learn, was another of those wishes that never materialized. I went to the Soviet Union, the USSR, in 1965 as a university student in a summer language immersion program in Russian. I vowed to keep a diary setting out every minute of every day in the belly of that evil empire. I knew even then, as a 21-year old Kansas boy, that those 10 weeks would be an experience of a lifetime. I wrote 2 whole pages in the first 2 days and thereafter only made short jottings of interesting things—like "Boiled tongue again for breakfast. That makes 10 days straight."

This collection of memories, which my children tell me get better every year, is the best I can do. Now, I can look back at most of these incidents and laugh—something I wasn't able to do before I started this final version. Sometimes, when other things get under my skin, I will wake up after a Candlestick nightmare, sweating and shaking, and wonder again why these memories still haunt me. But that's getting better knowing that my wife is sleeping there beside me and I'm not going out again tomorrow night for another four hours of getting shot at in the dark.

There's not real meaning to this collection or moral. It just happened, hopefully as I have tried to describe. Even if it happened one way and appeared a different way in my head, this is the way I remember that year in Thailand and Vietnam. Sometimes I remember better than others and sometimes I get to make a story a little better in the telling than I really remember it. But that's the way things sometimes happen.

Pat Hyland
Springfield, Oregon
April, 2017

LIFE IN THE AIR

While I was flying the plane as Aircraft Commander, I'm not sure I was scared, in the traditional sense. I was not afraid of being shot at, shot down, or killed. I was not afraid for me. I was afraid of failing, of letting my crew down, of making the one disastrous mistake that would engulf the plane in flames and cause each of us, all ten of us, to die a slow, falling, meteoric-burning death.

I was apprehensive about finding myself alone in the jungle with only my pocketknife after a bail out caused by enemy anti-aircraft artillery (AAA) fire. I sure didn't like the idea of being 200 miles from safety through areas of Laos that had been a part of a military free-fire zone for years. Laos at that time was an area where enemy soldiers freely roamed and bragged about doing really atrocious things to captured American pilots.

Maybe I was afraid of returning home a changed person, or going back to a wife who had also changed while I was gone, or re-entering a world that had gone crazy with drugs, anti-war rallies, campus shootings, and hippies throwing blood or spitting on soldiers, sailors, marines, and airmen coming home. Maybe it was a lot of things—things I didn't know or understand.

Those thoughts hit me hard during the day, waiting for the mission to start at night. Days off, when the next mission was one or two days away, were hell. I wanted to get into the cockpit as soon as possible and get back to doing what I was trained to do and good at. But at the same time, I wanted to stall as long as possible, or not go out on the next mission at all, to avoid the fatal mistake that caused me nightmares.

But I wasn't built that way. I couldn't avoid my role and responsibility. I volunteered for every available additional flight that was posted. If a pilot wanted the night off, I was the first to volunteer to take his mission. Someone sick? Pat will do it! Someone on R & R in Australia? Pat will take that mission. Most pilots flew about 125 missions in their year at Nakhon Phanom Royal Thai Air Force Base, which we called "NKP or Naked Fanny." I flew 165, night combat FAC (forward air controller) missions over Laos, plus I flew 15 or 20 trash-hauling runs into South Vietnam to get parts or supplies, have fuel tanks foamed, or any other excuse, because life on the ground was complicated.

But life in the air—after finally peeing on the tire of the C-123 as my last and final act on the ground, then getting into that ugly airplane and getting it and everyone in it safely aloft—was relief. Now, I could breath again. Now I could think again. Now I could do my job—to call in and direct airstrikes to kill trucks on the Ho Chi Minh trail (we called the "Trail") and to bring my aircraft and 9 other crewmembers home after our nighttime mission.

Suddenly, everything was simple. Fly! Get back to NKP! Have a beer!

In the air, I became invisible to anyone I didn't want to see me. I became invincible to every enemy gunner shooting at me. On many nights, I had enemy AAA gunfire coming at me from everywhere below, 37mm, 57mm, and sometimes 85mm rounds, but I could fly that airplane right through all of it. I danced on flak (a WWII name for exploding AAA rounds, also called "shrapnel"). My situational awareness was so sharpened by what I was doing that it was like being outside of the airplane, looking down, and taking in and understanding all of the information that was happening in and around the airplane. I became one with the aircraft, to the point that I could feel components inside and out vibrating and humming. I knew the instant anything changed from that normal operation. I was everything within that aluminum skin—a true FAC.

But on the ground, I worried—it wasn't so easy.

THE GREAT AMERICAN DREAM

I didn't set out to be a pilot. I didn't want to be a part of the war in Vietnam. I didn't want to join the military and submit myself to the whim of officers who I believed were in the military because they didn't have a choice or because they weren't too smart. I had already heard that all the bright boys and Senator's sons had managed to occupy a military slot somewhere safe in Toledo, Jacksonville, or Tucson. I had watched TV most evenings and listened to Walter Cronkite explain very patiently just how bad the Army and Air Force were doing in Vietnam. I read the newspaper every day and tried to avoid reading the number of Americans killed the day before in the jungle, way over in Southeast Asia. I didn't want any of that. I had wanted to be a lawyer since I was knee-high to a fireplug. Dad was a lawyer. Granddad was a lawyer. I wanted to be one too and live the Great American Dream.

I had married Vicki Kay McBride a year before she graduated from Kansas University. I was a year older. I graduated from KU with three majors (Russian Language and Literature, Slavic and Soviet Area Studies, and International Relations) and a very low grade point average. The year was 1966. Now I was in KU Law School, with professors in three-piece suits, students in coats and ties, lots of arguing back and forth between students and professors, and lots and lots of time in the law library stacks reading and doing memorandum briefs.

Married life was new, but life at the university was growing very, very old. I ended my first year of law school, again with average grades, necktie rash, a frustrated ego, and a very bad case of cabin fever. After Vicki graduated in June, 1967, we were both ready to either bolt away from dreary Kansas or cut each other's throats.

GOODBYE, KANSAS

We decided to try Washington, D.C. for the summer. We drove there in my 1964 ½ Mustang with very few personal things except clothing. I had applied for summer school at George Washington School of Law at American University and Vicki had started sending out resumes for jobs. We found a third-floor walk-up apartment in city center with one bedroom, a small kitchen, and a living room at the back of the house. Rent wasn't much and we could catch the bus just down the block to our jobs. With a few minor problems during our summer there, we survived pretty well on our own and began to enjoy the interesting parts of the city.

Near the end of the summer semester, I decided I couldn't take any more college crap, so I informed KU Law that I wasn't coming back for the 1967 fall semester.

I had a job at the American National Bank of Silver Springs as a teller, so we decided to move into Chevy Chase to be nearer my bank. The bank was located on the ground floor of a high-rise apartment, where we found a studio apartment (a one-bedroom was too much for us to afford). I could ride the elevator down to work every morning.

Vicki found a job with the General Services Administration in the heart of D.C. Since I usually got off work earlier than Vic, I would often ride the bus downtown to wander through the various Smithsonian Museums until she got off work. We'd ride the bus back to Maryland and stop sometimes on Connecticut Avenue at one of the many ethnic restaurants for a quick bite of dinner (neither one of us knew how to cook, so it was lots more fun eating out). We were beginning to get to know each other, while sharing an adventure away from our small-town homes in Kansas. We were beginning to have some fun together, working each day instead of studying, and exploring Washington, D.C. We weren't getting rich with our entry-level jobs, but we had enough after rent to eat out a few times each month.

Life was getting better.

THE TELEPHONE CALL

One day after work, I got a phone call. On the other end was Arnold Fuhrken, who announced he was the president of my hometown draft board and he'd heard I had dropped out of college.

Washington, Kansas, my hometown, is the epicenter of small-town Kansas gossip. It really wasn't a surprise to me that Arnold knew about my plan to take a "temporary" break from law school. But what did surprise me a great deal was his further announcement that since I had a low draft number (65, as I recall), I had better either get back in college to keep my draft deferment for attendance in law school or enlist into the military.

"If you don't do one of those options pretty soon," he said, "I will be compelled by law to send you a draft letter." I thanked Arnold, asked about his wife and family, listened politely for a short time, finished the phone call, and promptly staggered into our small studio bathroom and threw up.

In just a few, short minutes, life had gone from better to being a draftee foot soldier in the Army, carrying an M-16 in the jungles of Vietnam and getting my proverbial butt shot off.

I immediately contacted all of the recruiting centers in D.C., trying to find myself a cushy (and safe) military job. Needless to say, every other mother's son was trying to do the same thing. There were many draft numbers coming up and too few cushy jobs to go around. I couldn't find a place for me in any military unit that wasn't accepting just foot soldier enlistees. I was trying to avoid that. Since I had always wanted to fly, just like my Army Air Corps Dad, I applied to the Air Force and the Navy for a pilot-training slot.

Several weeks later, I got another call from Mr. Fuhrken (although it had been "Arnold" earlier, it was now "Mr. Fuhrken," because he held my life in his hands). He asked how things were going in my enlistment process.

"Fine," I said. "I should hear back in the next week or two from either the Air Force or the Navy about my pilot-training applications." He said that was fine, and that he'd call me back about then.

Now I was in for it—making up stories about how either the Air Force or the Navy was going to offer me the greatest job in the military in just a few short weeks. So I hung in there, trying to find some way I could serve, not get shot, and make my parents proud. Flight training was my highest hope. Any available slot as anything but a foot soldier, jungle bunny, beetle crusher, Army draftee, M-16-carrying private would suffice. But I couldn't find anything.

TROLLING FOR GUNFIRE

Very early in my missions as a FAC, while I was still a *copilot, we were flying in the beginning of the monsoon season. Monsoon was when it rained every day, with outrageous downpours, heavy lightning, and toad-choking flashfloods, all through Thailand and Laos. Our target trucks were few and far between on the Trail, which was in eastern Laos along the North and South Vietnam western borders and spread out eastward toward most of South Vietnam. The 606th Special Operations Squadron, my unit at NKP, was tasked to be truck killers. We carried parachute flares for special missions to help ground-fighting units, hence our call sign "Candlestick." But even as we flew for three or four hours over triple-canopy jungle and river basin plains, we would see only one or two trucks on the Trail through the rain showers and fog.*

We tried to avoid the thin rain clouds that formed around us, since our C-123 was painted green camouflage on top and midnight black on the bottom. We flew with all of our lights off, which we called "Black Out." But a black aircraft, without lights, silhouetted against a white cloud, even at night, made a very clear target for the enemy gunners below. These missions were stressful because we had to avoid the rain showers, try to stay away from being highlighted against a cloud, and still look for trucks on the Trail and direct air strikes against them.

Often, the gunners on the ground, who we called "Gomers," would shoot at us through clouds at the sound of our engines. Seeing glowing AAA tracers leaping out of the top of the clouds directly below us was an especially heart-stopping vision. There was no time to turn to evade. There was no time to react or do anything helpful to avoid those rounds. There wasn't even any time to think much about anything except we were going to die. We had to sit where we were, all 10 of us, watch those glowing rounds arc up toward us and hope they would miss. We had no other choice.

I was learning early on about dealing with stress while performing my co-pilot duties. I couldn't imagine what it was like to be an Aircraft Commander and be in charge of every little part of every mission, including dancing around AAA coming our way or while AAA zipped past the aircraft or burst all around in white-hot, smoky flashes. Even the smoke was visible at night from the flak bursts. We smelled the burnt explosive when we flew through the airbursts. Sometimes the rounds would explode close enough to the airplane that the shrapnel would ping around on the outside skin of the plane like monster hail. It wasn't unusual for the shrapnel to penetrate the thin aluminum of the C-123 and rattle around inside the cargo compartment until the energy of each piece was finally extinguished. I was learning that FAC missions weren't always fun.

One night, as we were flying near the southern part of our assigned area, I saw another C-123 turn on all of its lights—red and green wingtip navigation lights, top and bottom fuselage red beacon lights, landing lights on the forward edge of the wing, and even the cargo-compartment lights glowing through the open doors and windows. The crazy person flying the plane then started to descend at a fairly steep angle. The aircraft leveled off several thousand feet below our usual mission altitude, within a thousand feet or so of the ground. Normally, we flew high and dark at about 3 or 4 thousand feet above the ground to be nominally above small arms fire (but not outside of the range of the AAA that was becoming more prevalent every night). I couldn't believe my eyes. What the hell was he doing over there?

I asked my aircraft commander: "Who's that crazy person flying with all his lights on?" He informed me that the nut was the executive officer of the squadron, a bored old guy who was just trolling for gunfire, so he could call in the fighter aircraft circling over a safer part of the country and waiting for us to find enemy targets. He said the guy hated to have fighter planes in orbit and on call, and then let them go home without dropping their bombs on something—hence, the trolling. I told the commander that I would never do anything as stupid as trolling for gunfire during my tour. That idiot is totally crazy. Probably suffering from "combat fatigue." Probably too old to care if he got shot down and died in the jungle. What an idiot, I thought.

Later in my year's tour, after I had been upgraded and had been flying as an aircraft commander for several months, it was the beginning of the monsoon season again. On one very boring mission, with few trucks moving on the Trail and no one shooting at us, I found myself turning on all of the lights inside and outside of the airplane, descending as fast as I could, flying as low and slow as possible, hoping to get someone to shoot at me so I could call in all the fighters circling at altitude several miles away.

There I was, trolling for gunfire, because it made me mad to have all those aircraft orbiting nearby with bombs and not having anything to use them on. Now I knew how my old executive officer felt. OK, now I was the idiot, but it didn't seem to matter to me much. Killing trucks was now the name of my game.

THE LETTER

⭐

About a week after Arnold's (that is, Mr. Fuhrken's) second call, I got a call from the Air Force to come to the nearest Air Force base to take a flight physical, just to see if I measured up to their standards of height, weight, and physical condition. I drove as fast as I could to the examination site on Bolling Air Force Base near D.C.

A week or so after my flight physical, I got a letter in the mail from the Air Force. I had been selected for pilot training. I was to report to Officer Training School at Lackland Air Force Base in San Antonio, Texas on February 19, 1968. There were lots of other instructions with that magic letter, but all I could read were the words "YOU ARE SAVED!" Now I had the chance to become a jet-pilot hero, just like John Wayne in all those old war movies I had watched as a youngster. Now I could fly—just like my Dad during WWII.

Shortly after I received THE letter, I got another call from Arnold (now he was "Arnold" again). He asked me how things were going. I told him how great things were and that I had received a letter from the Air Force inviting me to become a hero.

"That's fine," he said. "Can you make me a copy and send it to me right away? As soon as I receive confirmation of your enlistment into the Air Force, I can destroy this letter on my desk with greetings from the President, inviting you to join the Army as a draftee."

I told him I'd get the copy of the letter in the mail "first thing tomorrow"—which I did.

Life was looking up again—literally.

I learned that for every one pilot training slot available at that time, there were over 200 applicants. I also learned that the reason I had been notified so quickly. The Air Force and the rest of the military were building up their manpower for new, major involvements in Vietnam.

NIGHTMARES

On nights I flew, I would return to my trailer so pooped *(and sometimes a little tipsy)* *I couldn't do anything except strip off my flight suit, throw it in a corner for the maid to pick up the next day, and hit the sack.*

On the nights I didn't fly, I tried to stay up as long as I could, so I wouldn't change my sleep patterns. But on those nights, after falling asleep about 4 a.m., I would generally have a nightmare. I always dreamed about getting popped by anti-aircraft artillery fire, and working to keep the airplane airborne while rapidly trying to diagnose the systems that were shot away or damaged. In my dreams, I would always forget what to do in the emergency of the night. I couldn't remember which systems could be fixed, even if I knew what was wrong. I couldn't remember the emergency procedures given in the aircraft operator's manual (called the Dash—One), which I memorized and re-memorized every day. Usually in those dreams, I sat helpless and panic-stricken. I would always crash and kill all ten of us on board. I would wake up, in a cold sweat and shaking, as the plane crashed.

I could never get back to sleep after a "crash" nightmare, so I always grabbed my C-123K Dash-1 and started re-learning the airplane systems and emergency procedures. These dreams recurred so often that I was probably the best systems analyst and emergency-procedures pilot in the squadron within the first few months.

Sometime near the end of my tour, the crashing nightmares ended and I started dreaming I was both invisible and invincible. In those dreams, I personally whacked every truck I came across on the Trail. I completed even the most complex airstrikes, with lots of truck kills, loud acclamation from my crew, medals from a grateful commander, and no sweat. I was Super Pilot! And then I would wake up in a cold sweat and shaking. It was just another kind of nightmare.

I worried more about those dreams, because it obviously reflected my growing confidence in my abilities as a pilot and airstrike commander, and I began to worry that I would become too confident and start doing something stupid and dangerous. Being a FAC over Laos was hard enough without becoming someone who would unnecessarily endanger the lives of the other 9 crewmembers on every Candlestick mission. I continued to study my Dash-1, but I made new efforts to become acquainted with the people who were assigned to fly with me each night, hoping that by knowing these other 9 men, I wouldn't do anything seriously stupid that would get us all killed in the bottom of a large smoking hole in the Laotian jungle.

OFFICER TRAINING SCHOOL

Officer Training School wasn't really that hard. I found myself submerged into the routine. It was a kind of comfort. Some of the rules and games were silly, but I had the feeling I was accomplishing something more important than writing memorandum briefs for a bow-tied law school professor.

I knew pilot training was waiting at the end of this brief period, so I wasn't as uptight as before. I felt a lot better physically and mentally and I prided myself on doing everything there "by the book."

Church every Sunday was a special treat for me, for reasons I still don't understand. I didn't miss a single Sunday, except when Vicki came to visit. It gave me a great deal of comfort to sit in a church packed with strong, young, burr-haircut guys like me, all in the same uniform and all singing together as if we each knew what we were doing. After church, I was content to return to my room, turn on the radio, shine my shoes, roll my underwear "just so," or get ahead on my lessons. The 90 days of OTS went pretty fast.

At graduation, after we marched past the stands in parade, showing off all of our new marching skills, parents and loved ones were invited onto the parade ground to pin the new second lieutenant's bars on each graduate. Mom pinned one bar on my shoulder and Vicki pinned the other. I was now a commissioned officer and gentleman (by Act of Congress), and on my way to Laredo Air Force Base in Texas for flight training.

LAREDO: THE T-41

The first phase of pilot training was flying a Cessna 172, which is a civilian airplane known as a T-41 in the Air Force. Our lessons were given at the civilian airport at Laredo by contract flight instructors—mine was a good ol' home boy from Texas, slightly overweight, and somehow out of the draft (by "war-related" critical employment, I think).

Since I had taken civilian flight lessons from the age of 16, and had flown several different kinds of airplanes, the Cessna wasn't too hard for me. Once my instructor found out I could already fly, we spent a lot of our "training" time buzzing locals and doing aerobatics like barrel rolls, loops, and aileron rolls. We did our training syllabus maneuvers as well, including emergency procedures, stalls, slow flight, turns about a point, navigation, and radio procedures. Part of the time, we were just flying over south Texas, watching the countryside glide by underneath, talking about airplanes and flying, generally just shooting the bull. I enjoyed my flight instructor and we seemed to get along pretty well. I had fun, didn't learn much new, never got sick in the airplane, passed with "flying" colors, and moved on to the T-37 phase.

LAREDO: THE T-37

⭐

The T-37, also manufactured by Cessna, was a twin-jet, small, fighter-jet-like aircraft. The pilot and instructor pilot sat side-by-side and each had identical controls and instruments. Even though the jet engines were small, they were extremely loud, which earned the plane the nicknames "Tweety Bird" and the "9,000-pound dog whistle."

It was a true jet, meaning you had to think ahead of the aircraft because things inside and out happened pretty fast. It felt to me to be more like pointing and hoping, rather than flying.

I just couldn't get the "feel" of the airplane. I was doing great in the books, but I was trying to "think" my way mechanically through some of the tougher maneuvers—like landings and aerobatics. I could recite how to do a maneuver, I could fly the maneuver with my hands or with a model airplane in the squadron training room at my instructor's desk, but I had trouble adjusting things in flight to accomplish those maneuvers to the standards required for passing each item on the training syllabus.

At the end of each critical part of the training, there would be a flight check ride called a "phase check," given by one of the designated check pilots or the squadron commander. I choked on every phase check. I was getting along in the progression, but every instructor who flew with me told me I was flying with my head and not my hands. I was too mechanical—I didn't *feel* the plane, or become one with it while I was strapped inside. It just didn't feel like I was flying. It was different than the civilian light planes that I had learned on before. I was trying really hard, but not successful with either getting ahead of the aircraft or flying it like I had the T-41.

I began to doubt myself. I became afraid of check rides. I always seemed to choke in pressure maneuvers. I was not having fun. It was work. I dreaded each day. I wanted to learn to fly that bird more than I wanted anything else in the world. I had breezed through the application process for Air Force pilot training and here I was choking on simple flying stuff. The fact that I had to pass the check ride or flunk out and become a navigator, weatherman, or some other non-flying ground-pounder made me tense up and want to puke.

The last phase check in the T-37 was the biggie. I studied my hind-end off in the books. I stuck a plumber's friend on the kitchen floor, so I could have a "joy stick," sat on a chair there, stated the book description of each maneuver, and visualized in my mind the maneuvers I had to perform with perfection for my check pilot on this final T-37 check ride. I had to pass. I didn't want to become a weather forecaster in Fairbanks, Alaska. I didn't want to let my parents, especially my WWII pilot/father, down. I didn't want the embarrassment of being a failure. I was in trouble.

But alas, it happened again —a bust! Since this was the ride that had to be completed in order to progress further in flight training and into the T-38, it was the most important. My re-check was scheduled with my squadron commander. If I failed this check, I would be kicked out of pilot training and sent to another base to start training as a ground-pounder—a total failure in my book.

My commander was a major, somewhat short and a little overweight too, just like my T-41 instructor. But Major Heanue knew his T-37. The instructor pilots in the unit all respected him for his capability as a solid instructor, a good leader, and a "fighter jock."

I learned he had been in the Air Force long enough to have moved five times to different air force bases in different towns. He built the same house, with the same floor plan, at every new location. He was a nice guy, partied with "his boys" whenever he could, and participated with the class as much as his "commander" duties allowed. Now he was to be my final chance to stay in the pilot training program. Right then, he was God.

The check ride started out pretty normal, but when the flight maneuvers and aerobatics started, that old choking feeling reappeared and I felt the flight going south very quickly. At one point, near the end of the flight period, the major took the controls and told me to relax a minute while he showed me some ways to "feel" the airplane fly. He then gave me the controls and asked me to re-do the maneuver, using his "feel" technique. I was concentrating so hard on using his suggestions I didn't even notice I was flying the required acrobatic maneuver perfectly.

When I completed it, he just said: "Quit flying with your head, Hyland, and get the feel of the airplane. You know the maneuvers and I can see that you can do them, but you need to relax more. When I got you to think about something other than the 'perfect' maneuver, you did OK. You pass!"

With that said, he took back the controls, and told me to just sit there while he had a little fun. There were white, puffy clouds in the maneuver area that day, large and towering over the Texas outback. It was a beautiful day, clear blue sky in between towering cumulus. He started to skim the outside of one really pretty one, then climbed on the outside of it to the top. Then, without warning, while I was still in my head about passing the final phase check, he rolled that bird upside down and started to descend on the back side of the cloud inverted, with the cockpit canopy just sliding a few inches away from the cotton candy side, straight down. I was so relieved that I had passed my final phase check in the T-37 I promptly threw up inside my oxygen mask—right in the middle of the Major's perfect loop. The mask provided oxygen under positive pressure and fit very tightly around my face for correct use. When I puked into that stream of pressurized oxygen coming into the mask, the effect was to blow bits and chunks around the outside of the mask and all over me, the instrument panel, and some onto my squadron commander's lap. Major Heanue merely looked over at me, looked around at the chunks of gunk and stuff all over the cockpit, and calmly stated "I guess we'd better get this Tweety Bird back."

On the way back to base, he flew. He also told me "Hyland, you either have to clean up this cockpit yourself or pay the ground crew member who takes care of this plane to do it for you. If you don't do it, you'd better pay the ground guy something for his trouble, because this was your puke." Enough said. After we landed, I went to the guy who had guided us into a parking slot, asked him if he was this aircraft's keeper, and promptly paid him five bucks to clean it up for me. I figured that I had a big enough problem on my hands trying to clean out the oxygen mask to the satisfaction of the airman in charge of our survival gear and masks. Major Heanue told me to come to his debriefing after I had completed all of my barf duties. After several tries, I finally got my oxygen mask cleaned and working again. I was a little woozy by that time, so when I reported to Major Heanue, he merely signed my flight check grade sheet, looked at my hand carefully before he shook it, and wished me good luck in T-38s. I was still in the program and moving on up to the last phase of flight training, the supersonic trainer, the White Rocket, the T-38.

That was the first and the last time I ever puked in any aircraft in flight, but it wasn't the last time I would think of Major Heanue.

A-1 DOWN

It was late in my tour, in late summer of 1970, when I was assigned another trip over the Trail on what was supposed to be a routine mission in the southern half of Laos, in the operations area (AO) called Steel Tiger. This southern half of Laos was the area with the most AAA guns, which was the origin, I think, of steel in the name. It contained that section of the Ho Chi Minh Trail that separated into multiple side-roads leading east into South Vietnam. It was also believed to be the area in Laos where the North Vietnamese Army (NVA), Viet Cong (VC), and Pathet Lao (Laotian) enemy soldiers congregated and forayed into South Vietnam to fight American soldiers there.

Everything started out normally. It was the end of the dry season, with the wet season looming, so there were trucks running everywhere on the Trail. Every C-123 was busy finding trucks moving south and calling up strike aircraft to direct in air attacks against multiple targets. Most of the fighter aircraft available that night were A-1s from NKP, since they were based closest to my area in Steel Tiger. That proximity allowed them to drop or shoot all of their ordinance, return to their base for re-fueling and re-arming, then hot-foot it back to the mission areas to wait for another call to use their bombs and guns on a new target.

I had the late mission that night. I took off after midnight and would be back to NKP sometime around 4 a.m. We always returned before first light because of the dark colors of our airplane and the number of enemy gunners between our working areas and home base in Thailand. I found some trucks. We went to work marking the strike area with ground-burning flares, briefing the incoming strike aircraft, settling into a left-hand orbit above the targets, and directing the bombs from the strike aircraft one at a time until each truck below was destroyed. There was crazy noise—anti-aircraft artillery zipping skyward past us, bombs finding their targets beneath, crewmembers talking to each other, shouted directions from my crew to turn to avoid tracer rounds coming up from below, chatter from our strike aircraft on our frequency, and other aircraft on a different frequency we monitored from command and control aircraft above us.

Somewhere in the hubbub, we heard the most-dreaded sound on our radio. It was the automatic beeper from a crewmember's personal survival radio (the PRC-90). That personal radio turns on whenever a parachute was deployed by any U.S. airman. Someone's plane had been hit and the pilot or crew had bailed out. We all hated that sound.

Several pilots transmitted the usual response, "Beeper, beeper, come up voice." This was the radio call to any person in a parachute, informing them that their emergency radio had been heard. This call instructed the person in the parachute to turn off the beeper beacon and switch the emergency radio to the frequency that would allow that person to talk to aircraft. The survival radio was tuned to 121.5 and 243 khz, the emergency frequencies monitored at all times by every aircraft in Laos and Vietnam.

After a short wait, the beeper stopped and we heard a voice on the emergency frequency say: "This is Zorro XX. I'm OK. I've punched out somewhere in Steel Tiger near the border." That told me several things: the pilot was assigned to A-1s at NKP (his call sign being Zorro), he was not injured in the rocket-assisted extraction from his airplane, and he was coming down somewhere in my area, near the border between Laos and North Vietnam. It was very late by then, very dark and way too close to North Vietnam for either me or that poor slob drifting down toward the jungle in his all-white parachute.

I finished my strike as fast as I could, ordering the two aircraft under my control to drop everything on their next pass, so I could go help one of their buddies. It didn't take long before I was headed east, toward the border, trying to talk to the downed pilot on his emergency radio. He had landed somewhere near the border and had resumed talking to me on his handheld radio. I told him to switch to the alternate frequency on that small transmitter, so we wouldn't

Candlestick: Night FAC over Laos

be talking on everyone's emergency frequency. That would cut down on the chatter other aircraft would hear on that frequency and allow them to monitor it for any other aircraft in trouble. Also, by switching frequencies, we hoped that any gomer who had captured a U.S. aircrew radio wouldn't know how to change the frequency from the emergency one to the alternate, so he wouldn't be able to listen to me talk to the pilot on the ground.

Suddenly, there was silence. I couldn't talk to him on either frequency. Now I was worried.

As I flew toward the area where I thought the pilot had landed, I instructed the navigator to call Blind Bat—the control bird flying above us—and tell him we had a downed pilot, say where he was approximately, and ask him to start the search-and-rescue effort. My final communication with Blind Bat was to tell him that we were the closest aircraft to this pilot and that we would stay on site until the rescue helicopters (the HH-3's—call sign "Jolly Green Giants") and supporting fighter-bombers got to this area to extract him. The controller's last message to me was that he understood my message and would comply with my request to stay on site (i.e., he responded "Wilco").

Search and Rescue (SAR) was one of the great reasons aircrews were willing to fly over a totally dark country, filled with bad guys and good guns. SAR was our security blanket. Air Force policy stated that every effort would be made to find and rescue every aircrew member shot down in enemy territory. And so they did. Every day and night many U.S. Air Force aircraft were flying over enemy country. There were strike aircraft on alert, fully fueled, armed and ready to take off on a moment's notice to support rescue helicopters (the Jolly Greens) with suppressing bombs, bomblets, and bullets.

From NKP, the rescue aircraft were A-1s from any or all of the three squadrons stationed at the base. Rescue A-1s used the call sign "Sandy" instead of their usual squadron call sign of "Zorro" or "Spad" or "Hobo." There were rescue helicopters on alert also—the "Jolly Green Giants." It was their job to go to the downed crewman and drop a trained medic (called a "PJ," short for para-jumper) down to the airman on the end of a 200 foot steel cable on a jungle penetrator (called a "JP").

The JP was a bullet-shaped piece of equipment that was about 3 feet long, had a heavy point on the bottom, flat-bladed seats on 3 sides that folded up when lowered through jungle trees (the penetrator) and folded down so the PJ and a rescued airman had a secure place to sit on the ride back up to the helicopter. It also had straps attached above each seat, so the people being raised had a safety strap to put around their bodies and under their arms to keep them from falling off and to help the PJ assist wounded or injured crew. The PJ would ride with each downed crewmember back up to the helicopter on the rescue hoist. When all of the downed pilots or crewmen had been picked up, it was time for the Jolly Green to get the heck out of Dodge.

I wanted Blind Bat to call the rescue center in Saigon and get all of that SAR machinery started. The sooner you can get helicopters to the aviator on the ground, the better the chances are that everyone will get out alive. A quick response means less time for the bad guys to get their soldiers nearby, move their anti-aircraft artillery closer to shoot at rescue aircraft, or bring in their own planes or helicopters. Blind Bat called back and told us: "You are now the on-scene commander of the SAR effort as long as you can stay in the area. Keep Saigon (the search-and-rescue center, called "Crown") informed. Blind Bat out." So now I was in charge. Shit!

I tried again and again to raise the downed pilot on the alternate frequency. Finally, he responded that he was OK and trying to orient himself in the dark below triple canopy. He had taken a few scratches coming down through the trees, but he wasn't seriously injured. He informed me that he could move, if necessary. I told him to hunker down. I said we had called the SAR center to get that effort started and that I was going to start a grid search pattern toward the area where I thought he was located. I asked him to tell me when he heard my airplane directly overhead and from which direction he heard it coming toward his position.

Several miles west of the border, I started to fly a sweeping back-and-forth grid, flying pretty much north and south lanes. The navigator got right on it and started giving me directions on when to turn around and how to keep me on parallel tracks so I wouldn't have any gaps in my search pattern. I was flying legs about five miles long, about a half mile apart, moving my grid toward the east and closer and closer to the border of North Vietnam. Enemy gunners seemed to be everywhere along the border, on the North Vietnam side, shooting at the sound of our engines every once in a while as we crossed near their gun positions. We were getting closer to the border and Mu Gia Pass, an area where we were forbidden to fly because of all of the anti-aircraft guns permanently located there. Mu Gia Pass was one of the primary crossing points of the Ho Chi Minh Trail from North Vietnam into Laos. It was a very busy and well-protected area. This was not going to be fun.

Finally, as I came within a mile or so of the border, the pilot on the ground said: "You're flying to the west of me now. I'm straight east of you." Oh boy—closer to the border. So, I turned east, flew a new grid with shorter legs, trying to work my way toward him, with closer north-south legs now to close up my search pattern. Back and forth, north and south.

"You're getting closer," he said. "I'll tell you when you're over the top of me."

So I went on, telling everyone in the crew to keep their eyes open for bad guys and to look for any sign of the good guy on the ground. We hadn't gone very far when the pilot on the ground radioed: "You're going over me now." I told the navigator to mark the place on his chart and prepare the coordinates for the rescue aircraft coming our way. I turned the aircraft to fly east a very short distance, then turned around and told the downed pilot to tell me when I was over him again, as I flew to the west. He again called: "You're on top of me now." Now we had a very good idea where he was and the navigator had it marked on his map. We could tell the Search and Rescue folks his location. That was a good thing.

I told the downed pilot that I would stay overhead until the cavalry arrived, that I wouldn't leave him alone, and that I would try to help any way I could. He told me that he appreciated the company.

So I started flying grids again, so any enemy soldier watching or listening to me from below or on radar wouldn't be able to discern the location of the downed airman.

After flying over the top of the pilot several times within my "bogus" grid, he radioed. "Stop doing that," he said. "Every time you fly over me, I can't hear anything except you. I want to be able to listen for gomers and I don't want them to think you're flying over me." So I started flying grids nearby, hoping to throw any discerning enemy soldiers off the track. I told the pilot that I would fly overhead occasionally, so I could look for bad guys. He said that would be OK.

We hadn't been in the area very long before we started to hear a "wheep-wheep" sound on our FM radio. That sound told us a Russian-built and enemy-manned Fire Can radar was starting up and reaching out to find us. The "wheeping" we were hearing was interference on our FM radio caused by the powerful radar beams emanating from the enemy's radar system. Fire Can radars were usually attached to one or more anti-aircraft guns. Mr. Gomer wanted to shoot us down with 37 mm rounds, directed by his radar, and apparently seeing us from just across the border. We had been taking 37mm rounds during the time when we were doing the search grid, but only occasionally from guns located in Laos and from different parts of our grid. Nothing too serious yet. I made sure all of the crewmembers were stationed at different open windows or doors to look for gun flashes and tracer streams seeking us from the ground. All assured me that they had their eyes peeled. We had to "break" away from oncoming tracers a couple of times, but nothing that we hadn't seen before and were pretty practiced at avoiding.

Because the downed pilot was so close to the border, we couldn't get too far away from him, for fear we might lose him, or not see bad guys coming to find him. So we were always within range of that Fire Can radar. Then, shortly after we first heard the radar, we started getting 37mm rounds from across the border from North Vietnam. These guns seemed to be directed by the radar sweeps.

That gomer radar guy was smart. When we were flying toward the border, he wouldn't shoot. But when we were turning away from the border, going in any direction, he would sweep us with his radar then shoot when he thought we wouldn't be able to see the tracers reaching out from his gun positions toward us. If we couldn't see the origin of the tracers, we wouldn't be able to anticipate and avoid those basketball-sized balls of flame coming at us seven rounds at a time. Sometimes in multiples of 7, as if the gunner was reloading very quickly or there were more than just the one 37 shooting at us. Every time we turned, we heard the "wheep-wheep" sound on the radio, and then he shot—every time! He was getting better and better the longer we were near the border. I kept thinking "practice makes perfect." In this case, perfect meant that all 10 of us in the Candlestick were going to be sitting beside the downed A-1 pilot pretty soon if the Sandys didn't show up. Flying north and south, like plowing a field. Sometimes I made a little loop around or change of direction or sudden turn east or west, just to keep the gomers on their toes.

Nevertheless, a wheep-wheep coming from our FM would announce that 7 or 14 AAA rounds would explode below us out of North Vietnam and head our way. Sometimes closer and sometimes further way. But we knew he was painting us on radar and just having trouble coordinating his guns with the picture he was seeing on his radar screen. I had the feeling that this little encounter was not going to end well.

Since Mu Gia Pass was near, we knew it was only a matter of time before an enemy commander in North Vietnam started to send in foot soldiers to try to find the pilot on the ground. We were sure they had heard the pilot's emergency beeper go off when he punched out, so they knew there was fresh American meat nearby. Just the fact that we were staying in the area—even though we were flying over a fairly large chunk of jungle to confuse the guy on the radar—was pretty strong evidence that a serious effort was underway that was keeping us near enough the border to get shot at every few minutes.

I continued to talk to the downed pilot every five minutes or so, just to keep his spirits up. I didn't want him to use up his battery so he couldn't talk to the helicopters I thought were on the way. We all knew time was running out. And it was running out faster than I thought.

Scope—the Navigator using the large Starlight scope suspended from the ceiling of the cargo compartment and pointed down from the aircraft through the open escape hatch—suddenly called me on intercom and shouted: "Gomers are on the way toward the pilot's position. I see four or five trucks coming down the Trail toward him. They just came through Mu Gia Pass! They have their lights on and they're driving as fast as the Trail will allow."

I told the Zorro on the ground about the trucks.

"I hear them," he said. They were getting closer. I asked the navigator manning the maps on the chart table just behind the pilot seats to take a good look at his map and asked the Scope to check out the lay of the land below, so we could find a better place for the pilot to hide. They both spoke at once and told me about higher ground to the northwest of the pilot's position that might give him a better chance of hearing the gomers approaching him. It was also a place that would be easier for the helicopter drivers to find when they got into the area. The high ground was about a kilometer (a "klick") or so away.

I told the downed pilot about the better place, not going into detail about what it looked like, for fear that I was being listened to by the bad guys. I told the pilot to take a hike to the "state of Washington" from his position in "Texas." He understood my simple code to go northwest. I told him it was a "klick or so."

He knew he was in for a rough trip —it was dark, he couldn't use his flashlight, he was under triple canopy jungle, and the bad guys were within hearing distance. I told him to call me when he got to the "Rocky Mountains," meaning high ground where we wanted him.

He said he would and signed off: "Wilco. Zorro XX out." That told me he understood my instructions and he was off the radio until he got to the new location. I didn't know if he was going to run or crawl to the northwest, but it was going to take him away from the gomer trucks and hopefully give him an edge.

I called Blind Bat and asked how the launch effort was going for the Search and Rescue birds, meaning both strike aircraft and Jolly Greens. He told me he would check. A few minutes later, he called back to tell me that the SAR would launch aircraft at first light. By that time, it was less than an hour until dawn. There was already a little light coming from the east and slowly making the jungle below less dark. I told Blind Bat to start the SAR launch right away and to tell Saigon they should have a replacement for me on site while I was still in the area, so I could brief that new on-site commander before I returned to base (RTB). I also told Blind Bat that I was starting to run a little low on fuel. I had the navigator calculate approximately how long it would take aircraft (FAC, fighter-bombers, and rescue helicopters) to get from NKP or Vietnam to the downed pilot. He told me almost an hour. I had a little over an hour of fuel remaining before I hit bingo with any reserve ("bingo fuel" was just enough gas to get back to a US base with a little reserve "just in case"). The SAR had to launch now to get another FAC in the area for me to brief and for him to get acquainted with the gomers and gunners and for me to leave then and get back to base with the fuel reserves required. I told Blind Bat so. He radioed me to "wait one" while he talked to Saigon. I hoped for good news.

Blind Bat called back shortly to tell me that the SAR commander in Saigon wouldn't launch aircraft before first light because there was late-night fog forecast for the area. He wanted to wait until first light to make sure that there was no fog where the rescue helicopters and A-1's would be flying.

I asked Blind Bat to relay this message to Crown in Saigon: "There is no fog in this area, there are no conditions present that should produce late-night fog, and that even if fog does form at or shortly after dawn, rescue aircraft could hold at altitude until the fog burns off (usually a very short time). That would have the rescue aircraft as close as possible to the downed pilot to get him out fast."

Blind Bat said he would relay that message. I didn't have long to wait. Blind Bat came back and said: "Negatory on the early launch (that means "NO"). The general doesn't want to risk his rescue aircraft based on your report that there's no fog in the area. Blind Bat out."

We continued to fly nearby and get shot at every few minutes. My navigator was counting the rounds reported by the other crew members aboard, but I wasn't paying any attention to the numbers, only the calls from the back that told me to "break right" or break left" when strings of tracers appeared to be converging on us. Each minute seemed like hours.

The fuel gauges, however, seemed to be running on fast time. Each tank was getting very low and we still had about an hour's flight to get back to base. So I told the flight engineers to lean out the engines as much as they could, giving me a throttle setting that would keep us in the air as long as possible, and let me know when I was at the point where there was just enough fuel left to get home with a little reserve. The flight engineer gave me those throttle settings and I pulled the power back as far as we thought we could, to stay in the air and use a minimum of 115/145 aviation gas. We continued to fly.

Finally, the downed pilot called and said he was "hiding in the Rockies." I talked to him off and on after that. We didn't talk much, but it was enough for me to know that he was in a bad place and really scared. I was too.

The scope continued to give me reports on the location of the enemy trucks. They too had started a search grid on the ground, trying to locate the pilot, his parachute, parts of the wrecked plane, or anything that would indicate where the pilot might be hiding. I didn't think it could get any worse for either the pilot on the ground or for us in the air.

Boy, was I wrong.

The scope suddenly shouted, "The gomers are headed toward the high ground. All of the trucks have turned that way. There are trucks all around that hill the pilot is hiding on."

We continued to fly on. The scope told me to fly over the trucks, and gave me heading and distance. As we flew over, he said the trucks had all stopped at the base of the little hill and he could see soldiers getting out—the manhunt was on.

I called the downed pilot and told him to hunker down, because gomers were on the ground all around him and headed his way.

I flew away from his area so the enemy soldiers below couldn't see me in the growing light. After all, I was flying a big, ugly airplane painted varied-green camouflage on top and midnight black on the bottom —a very undesirable paint scheme for daylight camouflage with people on the ground looking up into a lightening sky and shooting at you.

I got on the high-frequency radio (HF) and called the Saigon SAR center directly, asking for the general commanding Crown. Soon he was on the horn. I told him as briefly and as succinctly as possible exactly what was going on. I told him I was running low on fuel and it was getting light. I told him that his fear of fog was unfounded, since I was there and I could see the ground with my naked eyeballs and THERE WASN'T ANY STUPID FOG! I suggested as strongly as I could that he launch the rescue aircraft RIGHT NOW, or we were going to lose one good pilot to gomers.

I was shouting into the radio. He started shouting back. He reminded me that he was a general and commander of the SAR center. I reminded him that I was on-scene commander and I knew a hellavalot more about what was going on right here and right below than he did. We were both shouting—this was not the way I wanted it to go.

Finally, he said he would launch another FAC pilot from South Vietnam to relieve me, since I was running low on gas. I said, "OK, but get his ass in gear." There was more shouting from Saigon. Then the general said: "I'll remember you, Lieutenant Hyland. Here's my operations officer, he'll tell you about the pilot inbound to your location. General XX out."

The ops officer told me that he would launch the new forward air controller as soon as possible. He estimated that the aircraft, a Cessna O-2 (call sign "Nail") would fly as fast as he could to my area to relieve me and would arrive in about 30-45 minutes.

My flight engineer told me we had about 30 minutes of fuel remaining before we hit "minimum bingo." I told him to throttle back a little more and pray. It was going to be close.

After 30 minutes more of flying time (an eternity on my personal clock) and getting slightly below the minimum fuel necessary to get back to the base with any fuel reserve at all, I heard the welcome call on my radio: "Candlestick, this is Nail ZZ, in your area. I should be in formation with you in about 10 minutes."

I told the Nail: "I can't wait that long. My navigator will give you the coordinates of the downed pilot while I start returning to base. Tell your general there's no fog here, and to launch the rescue aircraft." Nail told me that he was close enough to see there was no fog in the area, and he had already called SAR center to tell them to launch the rescue effort.

I told Nail: *"I'm outta here. You are now on-scene commander for Zorro. Don't let him down."* Nail responded, much as I had heard earlier in that long, long night: *"Wilco. Nail out."*

I turned toward home, hoping I didn't run out of gas three miles short of the runway at NKP. It was a long night and it was now very near dawn (in a place and at a time that no responsible Candlestick should ever find himself). We were on our way home.

"Cross your fingers, crew," I said on the intercom. *"We're going to need a little bit of luck."* And westward we flew.

I had my small Minolta camera on me, and since it was so light, I took a few pictures of the jungle and karst formations below as we flew at our best fuel-conserving airspeed (which seemed snail-like to me—were we getting even a little bit closer to home every minute?). Looking down to take the pictures, I realized how naked and exposed we were and how large the C-123 must look from the ground. We had a long way to go. I really didn't think we could make it all the way back, but there weren't any closer alternatives, except maybe a rice paddy somewhere just west of the Mekong River border in Thailand. That didn't look so good either—for lots of reasons. I flew on.

It was getting lighter. I started a slow descent to try to conserve a little gasoline. Slowly we approached the Thai border. Then we were over rice paddies in Thailand. We could see the air base in the distance. I called the tower and told them I wanted a close-in pattern to land, since I was low on fuel. They granted my request. I told the crew to strap in tight and assume the crash position. If these engines didn't keep running to get me to the landing strip, we would be crash-landing in Thailand in either rice paddies or jungle below.

I made my approach a little higher and faster than normal, just in case both engines decided to quit on short final to the runway.

I didn't start the jets for fear that even that small amount of extra burning fuel might make the difference between landing in the rice paddy on the north end of the runway or actually touching down on U.S. concrete. I waited until the last possible second to lower my landing gear and add landing flaps.

Finally, we touched down and rolled out to the taxiway. I started to breathe again. The crew had been pretty quiet up to that point, but then everybody started talking and laughing and joking about how close we'd come to buggering up the airplane somewhere in Laos. I had enough fuel to taxi to parking and shut down both engines. The flight engineer asked if I wanted him to check the actual quantity of fuel remaining by dipping the tanks, just to check the accuracy of the fuel gauges. I told him not to—I really didn't need any more information about how close we'd come to running out of fuel in bad-guy country.

We all got out, did our usual after-mission chores robotically and headed back to our respective hooches. Everyone was really dragging. Just another day at Naked Fannie Air Force Base.

I knew I couldn't go to the club for a beer or to my trailer without checking up on our Zorro in the jungle. So I went over to the command center, where the search-and-rescue effort was being monitored locally. I looked for and found the highest-ranking officer in the room—a lieutenant colonel with a Zorro patch on the sleeve of his flight suit. I asked him about the SAR. He said the area was too hot for the Jolly Greens to get in. There were gomers all around the base of the hill where the Zorro was hiding. The Nail was calling in lots of airstrikes, trying to destroy the enemy soldiers on the ground. Since I had left the scene, the Nail had already put in several airstrikes and there were two or three more strike flights orbiting in the area, ready to drop their loads on the bad guys working their way up the hill.

I asked the Colonel who the pilot on the ground was, since I had a friend and pilot-training buddy flying A-1s out of NKP. My buddy was Tom Powers. The Colonel said the pilot was an older guy who had just joined the Zorro squadron from a pilot training slot in the States. He told me that he thought the guy had been a squadron commander in T-37s in Laredo.

I was shocked.

"I sure hope he gets out," I said. "My T-37 squadron commander at Laredo was a Major Heanue and he's the reason I'm here as a pilot. He passed me on my final T-37 phase check. If he had flunked me on that T-37 check ride, I'd be a ground-pounder somewhere in Alaska and not an on-scene commander for the last three hours for a downed Zorro pilot."

"If it is your Major Heanue, it's a small world," the LC said, then turned his back on me to talk to an airman who had come up behind him while we were talking.

I couldn't keep my eyes open long enough to even go to the club for an after-mission beer. I grabbed a crew bus back to my trailer and crashed on my bunk with my flight suit and boots still on.

The next day, shortly before dark, I got up, showered, changed into a clean flight suit and went back to check on "my Zorro." No one was in the command center, so I checked with the Intelligence folks at the other end of the Tactical Unit Operations Center (TUOC) building. They told me they had gotten the Zorro pilot out right at dusk of that first full day, after he had spent the entire day hiding on the top of a hill. His only injuries were caused by our own suppression bombs that had exploded too close to him, trying to keep the enemy soldiers away. Apparently it worked. He was out—and safe.

If it was my Major Heanue—my old squadron commander—it was a small world. I was glad it was me who had helped. I knew then that Major Heanue had had enough confidence in me to pass me on that final phase check ride in T-37s, in spite of my own doubts about my flying ability. I wondered if he had experienced some special feeling about me during that check ride that made him want to pass me, so I could later be right here, at this very place, to help another pilot—and maybe even him personally.

I regret several things about this flight.

One—I didn't take the time the next day to follow-up and learn whether or not the downed A-1 pilot was in fact "my Major Heanue." The night before, when I went into the command center to check on the rescue effort, I was just too tired and coming down hard from a significant adrenalin rush. I wasn't sure the LC in the center said "Heanue" or whether he said something about coming from a T-37 training slot in Laredo. I got the impression then that it was "my Major Heanue," but I wasn't sure and I didn't take the time or trouble to check on either the name or the rescued pilot.

The second regret is that I didn't take the time during my last few months at NKP to put each member of the aircrew in for a medal, like a Silver Star or Distinguished Flying Cross. Each had performed their respective duty in a professional and extremely proficient way. Each was 100% into the flight. No one questioned or discussed the actions we were taking while watching over the downed pilot and getting shot at every few minutes for the hours we flew near the North Vietnamese border. Each crewmember could hear the radar sweeps on his intercom box and each clearly knew the danger we were facing by staying near the A-1 pilot below. But again, I was just too tired of the missions, too close to going home, and a little jaded by the thought of medals others were getting for less serious or less dangerous missions, so I didn't write up the crew for their outstanding participation. I should have done both of these things, but didn't.

A HOSPITAL: A SOBERING EXPERIENCE

During my time at Laredo, I learned from my hometown weekly newspaper that one of the local boys who was in the Army had been wounded in Vietnam. The boy's name was Mike Hood. Mike was several years younger than me, but I knew him and his family in Washington, Kansas.

The newspaper reported that Mike had been hit badly in one leg and part of his side by mortar rounds. Vicki and I decided that since he was a local boy and in the Brooks Army Hospital in San Antonio we should go visit him. We found the hospital without much trouble and were given instructions on how to find Mike's ward. Brooks is a huge hospital and in the middle of the Vietnam War (1969) it was a very busy place. Most of the seriously injured soldiers from Vietnam were brought to Brooks, since they had the specialists needed to treat serious combat wounds.

It was a quest to find him in such a big hospital with all those wards and all those wounded. We finally found Mike's ward, just one of many wards in that part of the hospital. The hospital section that Mike was in was one large open room, perhaps 20 feet wide by 50 or 60 feet long, with beds placed with the heads against the walls on both sides of the room, an aisle down the middle, and maybe three feet or so between beds. There were a lot of beds, each with a wounded soldier, in all sorts of bandages, wrappings, casts, wires and pulley arrangements, tubes, and other medical stuff. The room had a distinct odor—the smell of rubbing alcohol, Pinesol, blood, sweat, and unwashed bodies.

There wasn't much noise, even though there were so many patients there—just people talking in low tones, some moans, a few snores, and occasionally a yell as someone suddenly awoke in the middle of a nightmare. We walked along the feet of the beds looking for Mike. Each patient just stared at us, without smiling—just watching. Finally, we found Mike.

He was surprised to see me. I introduced Vicki and she gave him the few small gifts we had brought with us. Mike was a little drugged up and didn't talk much about getting hit, but he told us the explosion had taken a piece of his leg bone and he was really worried about being able to walk when he got out of the hospital. Several other wounds were visible on his upper leg and lower stomach.

We could tell he was in pain and uncomfortable with us being there, so we left after a very short visit. As we walked out of the hospital, I knew Vicki and I were thinking the same thing—I was being trained to go to Vietnam to fight a war and someday I might wind up in Brooks Hospital, just like Mike. We didn't talk much on the trip back to Laredo. Brooks had been a very sobering experience—a little too much reality for both of us.

LAREDO: THE T-38

★

Mike and I weren't the only military personnel serving from the little town of Washington, Kansas, population 1,800. On the day my class reported to the T-38 training squadron, we all met our respective instructor pilots. One of the part-time instructors was a young major who had grown up in Washington—Donny Knedlik. Donny was Chief of Academic Training in my student squadron at Laredo. His dad was my barber in Washington from the time I was big enough to sit on the plank on the arms of the barber chair until the day I left for college. The Major was "Donny" at home, but it was "Major Knedlik" to me at my new training squadron. Major Knedlik opted to become my flight instructor in T-38s.

Things started out really well with Don. He learned from my training folder that I was near the top of the academic rankings for the class, but near the bottom of the class in piloting skills having to do with critical maneuvers like acrobatics and landings. He started me out from the beginning talking and showing me a great deal about getting the "feel" of the T-38 and listening to the sounds of flight. He went back to basics. We discussed each training requirement in the syllabus and talked through each maneuver that he was going to teach me in the T-38.

The T-38 Talon is a supersonic trainer, a true fighter jet—thin swept-back wings, a Coke-bottle shaped fuselage, and as sharp as a dart in flight. It looked like it was going a thousand miles an hour just sitting on the ramp. This was the final phase of pilot training. This was the kind of plane that everyone wanted to fly after graduation from flight school—a fighter.

Don worked a lot to get me to stop "thinking" my way through the training syllabus, and relaxing when I performed the required maneuvers in the T-38. I started to catch on. I was feeling really great—things were looking up!

But not for long.

Don had to quit spending so much time on the flight line with me and more time at headquarters doing his primary job as a staff officer and not as an instructor pilot. He spoke to me about leaving my training to get back to headquarters. I was disappointed but understood. After all, he had volunteered for my training, knowing that he might have to move on at some later time. I was doing pretty well with his instruction, so I wasn't too worried about finishing my T-38 phase without him. I got a new instructor.

His name was Captain S. I called him Captain Jock. What a guy—or at least he thought so.

He had flown F-105s in Vietnam, through the famous "Thud Alley" near Hanoi. Captain S had flown 25 missions "up North" on "Route Pack 7" into and out of Hanoi, and had come home in one piece. Now he was a lowly instructor pilot (IP) in the middle of nowhere Texas. He was a "jock" in every sense of the word—arrogant, physically strong, aggressive, and never wrong. I recognized the Neanderthal in him that I had learned to hate from my high school football days. Instantly, we didn't like each other.

I went from one instructor who seemed to understand why I choked up on check rides, to a new one who thought all I had to do was grow up, be a man, listen to his ego-centric banter in the cockpit, and everything would be all right with the world. It was a freefall into hell for me.

Nothing I did was right or good enough. Every time he pushed me harder, I fell apart faster. Classroom academics and training flights became a blur of apprehension and aggression—my apprehension and his aggression. I don't remember much from those weeks, except that I continued to have that deep, gut-wrenching feeling that I was going to fail at this final phase of pilot training. I started thinking about new excuses for my failure in the T-38 phase to explain things to my parents and to justify my new desire to be a really great weatherman in eastern Greenland.

I do remember my nighttime solo cross-country flight. I was so glad to be alone that I flew the two-hour mission without a hitch, making all my checkpoints on time, at correct altitude, and with all the correct radio calls. It was perfect, but no one saw it except me.

I also remember a two-ship formation training flight, when I was flying trail, tucked up so close to the lead bird I could see the rivets on the belly of his jet. The student who was flying the lead aircraft was another choker like me. With me tucked just a few feet under him, he saw he was going to overshoot his line of final approach to the runway, so he knew he had to slow down and pull the turn tighter to line up. He forgot I was tucked in just under him. He slammed out his speed brake, which is a small, two-foot square panel of aluminum on the underside of the aircraft meant to slow the plane down and help the aircraft descend.

Both of which he did—slow down and descend —with me right under him. When I saw the boards come out, I deployed my own, without thinking and still concentrating on flying the aircraft as close to his as I could. My canopy almost touched his belly before my aircraft had a chance to react to my own speed brake's effect. All my IP could do was sit in the back cockpit and watch himself get crushed to death on the underside of my flight leader's plane. But it didn't happen. And I kept it from happening with my reflexes and instincts. It was a miracle—a non-thinking miracle.

When we landed, Captain S went over to the other student to cuss him out, but he didn't say anything to me, good or bad, about the part of the flight where a heartbeat of my flying skill saved both of our lives. At least he was chewing on the other student pilot and not me. He was truly a jock—and a jerk.

Not everything went that well. I was shooting touch and go's with Captain S in the back seat and screwing up royally every time—too long, too hot, too far left, too far right, etc. After about a thousand tries, when both I and the Texas weather were beginning to boil over, I really screwed the pooch.

I landed short, missing the runway, and touching down in the soft asphalt just a few inches shy of the concrete. S immediately took the controls, cussing the whole time, climbed to safe altitude, and asked another instructor pilot nearby to fly under us to see if "my student" had done any damage to the landing gear. The other pilot said that the gear looked OK. S continued to fly, brought the plane around and put it down with barely a kiss, rolled it to a full stop, taxied to the ramp, and shut down the aircraft without having said a word to me the whole time. Then he let me have it —both barrels.

He suggested in about a million four-letter words that I really should consider an immediate transfer to the Navy or the Coast Guard or the Girl Scouts, or anyplace else where I didn't have to try to miss a concrete strip 200 feet wide and two miles long. I knew my flying career was toast.

To add insult to injury, the class yearbook was just then in the final stages of completion, and since I didn't have a cool nickname yet, I immediately become "Crash" Hyland—that's the way my picture appeared in the yearbook. It wasn't a cool name, and I threatened several classmates with bodily harm if they ever called me that, but the damage was done. My self-esteem and self-confidence had just hit rock bottom.

BULAT

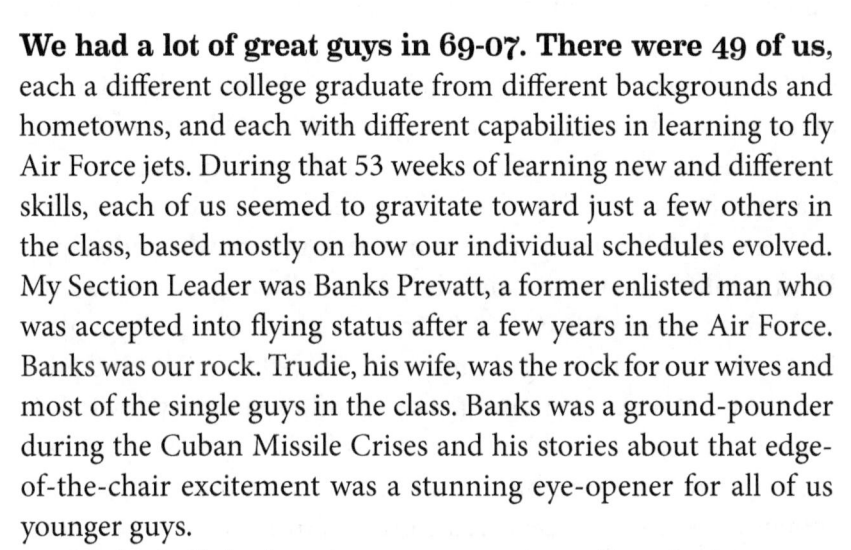

We had a lot of great guys in 69-07. There were 49 of us, each a different college graduate from different backgrounds and hometowns, and each with different capabilities in learning to fly Air Force jets. During that 53 weeks of learning new and different skills, each of us seemed to gravitate toward just a few others in the class, based mostly on how our individual schedules evolved. My Section Leader was Banks Prevatt, a former enlisted man who was accepted into flying status after a few years in the Air Force. Banks was our rock. Trudie, his wife, was the rock for our wives and most of the single guys in the class. Banks was a ground-pounder during the Cuban Missile Crises and his stories about that edge-of-the-chair excitement was a stunning eye-opener for all of us younger guys.

We had all the best in our two sections: Tore Aashiem was from Norway; Dick Alvarez was a Marine Corps aviator moving from the back seat of an Marine F-4 to the front seat as pilot after graduation (his wife Dale honored Dick and the Corps every morning at 4:30 to stand at attention and listen to the National Anthem and the Marine Corps Hymn, in preparation for Dick's day); Tom Power was a former AF enlisted man; and all the others. I tended to spend time with Pete Kelly and his wife Darlene, because Pete was so funny and I liked them.

And then there was Tony Bulat—we called him Bluto!

Tony had golden hands. Every pilot who flew with him said so. His instructor pilot (IP) in T-38s was a former F-4 driver who had shot down a North Vietnamese fighter jet during his tour in Vietnam. We all considered his IP hot shit. So did his IP. But Tony and his IP got along really well, primarily because Tony was such a hot shot in the air and a budding fighter pilot (with attitude) on the ground (known to party as hard as all the rest of us put together, hence the nickname Bluto).

One day in our section T-38 training room Tony announced that he had just purchased a new Corvette. He asked his IP if he wanted to ride in it after the flying session that afternoon. The IP said he would like that very much. After flying that day, they left together.

Since it was a Friday night and we had the weekend off, most of us eventually found ourselves together at the Officer's Club Stag Bar. It was a great place to be on Fridays. Happy Hour drinks. Free snacks, like baron of beef with biscuits, extra-hot nachos with cheese and chilis on top, peanut or snack mix bowls, and Happy Hour drinks (did I say that already?). Normally, only uniforms were authorized in the Officers' Club. The exception was Friday nights, in the Stag Bar, where flight suits were allowed for pilots and pilot wannabes. Women were not allowed, unless specially invited. It was too noisy, too ribald, too manly with all the hand flying and female anatomy descriptions, and sometimes too daring, with skimpily-clad local dancers prancing about to liven the atmosphere.

That night, Tony didn't appear at his usual time. It wasn't normal for Tony not to appear at the Stag Bar (or any bar) for Happy Hour.

Finally, Tony showed up. He was bedraggled and dirty, flight suit torn in several places, sheepish grin on his face and his IP in tow. He told us what happened.

When he and his IP were out driving his new Corvette, his IP said he would like to drive it. Tony said OK. The IP took the wheel and his fighter pilot personality took over. Tony said they were going more than 120 when the new car caught some air, got sideways to the highway, and started to flip over and over down the road and then into the ditch. Both got out of the wreck a little worse for wear, but after closer examination, without serious injury except the IP's red face. When they crawled out of the ditch, they were met by a Texas Highway Patrol Trooper. Tony said that the Trooper first asked if they were OK and then asked if they had been drinking. Tony said he told the guy that they were fine, but they hadn't been drinking yet, but intended to. The Trooper apparently believed them (probably standing toe-to-toe with each to check with his primary breathalyzer), since he loaded them both into his patrol car and brought them to the O' Club just then. Tony laughed the whole time he related this story of his wrecked, new Corvette and the piloting error by his IP, the MIG-killer.

Tony was true fighter pilot quality long before he graduated from pilot training with the rest of us.

ANOTHER SURPRISE

Sometime in the middle of flight training, when there was the barest chance that I would receive my wings and graduate as a pilot, but would probably rotate to Vietnam as a ground-pounder, Vicki wanted to discuss having a baby. She didn't mention Vietnam, but it was always lurking there, along with memories of Mike Hood in the Army hospital at San Antonio. There were always many pictures all over the newspapers and on-scene videos on TV about firefights, dangerous missions, and those wounded and killed in action overseas.

I said "NO, definitely not. Life is too uncertain now. Not until I get my wings. Let's wait until I get back from Vietnam."

We talked several times after that about a baby, but I thought it was a closed subject. I didn't have time to listen or talk more about it. It obviously didn't sink in about the "us" in this relationship. It was pretty much "me," and "me" was working really hard on everything else, especially getting through pilot training.

One day when I came home from the flight line, she informed me that she was pregnant and was going to have the baby sometime in mid-June, maybe even around my scheduled graduation date from Laredo. All I could say was "You gotta be shitting me!" It was precisely the wrong thing to say.

Things went downhill from there.

The last two or three months of pilot training in the T-38 were pure hell. I had moved out of the apartment off-base when Vicki decided to return to Hutchinson to have our baby there, near her parents, rather than at some point in the future when we didn't know where I'd be or what I'd be doing (weatherman, navigator, janitor, Girl Scout leader, etc.).

I moved into the Bachelor Officer Quarters (BOQ). I had

only my flight stuff, a few civilian clothes, a small TV, and lots of time after each flight to criticize my day's bad flying, my academic failures, my instructor's ragging, my loneliness, and my self-pity. I was a wreck.

Those last few weeks were very lonely and hard. During training flights, I kept trying harder and harder and failing more miserably each time. I couldn't get it right. No coordination on the controls, no feeling for the airplane, and no vision on how the heck I was going to get out of this training class either alive or with wings. Things at Laredo AFB looked really bleak.

SUPER SPOOKY AND THE GREEN GOBLIN

As the monsoon season approached Laos, enemy traffic *increased on the Trail. We saw more and more trucks moving south. Now we could also see small lights and occasional campfires in the jungle just beside the Trail that told us there was more foot traffic on the Trail as well. Missions up north in the Barrel Roll were seeing more and more materiel (military supplies) piled up on the North Vietnam side of the border, in plain sight, in preparation for the long haul to South Vietnam by truck, bicycle, and foot soldier. In our southern area of operations, Steel Tiger, things were happening nearer the South Vietnam border and our intelligence briefings in TUOC included more and more firefights happening just within South Vietnam near the DMZ.*

Our missions were busy—all of our target areas were full of Candlesticks every night, from just after dark to almost first light. We faced more guns and gunners who weren't afraid to use their ammunition, because before long, there wouldn't be any—the wet-season downpours would make jungle trails impassable. For the few trucks that would be moving south during the rainy season, supplies for the North Vietnamese soldiers and Viet Cong fighting in the south would take priority over anti-aircraft artillery ammunition. So the North Vietnamese gunners shot a lot, even firing saturation barrages (all guns in the area firing at once) through overcast skies at the sound of aircraft engines, with the hope of at least scaring us to death, and maybe hitting one or two of us in the bargain.

Monsoons in Thailand were something new to all of us. The days could be bright and sunny with just a few puffy, white cumulus clouds slowly drifting by. It was always humid, but now the days and nights were getting even more humid. There was a haze at dawn and dusk—almost like fog—but much thinner and a whole lot hotter. As the full monsoon season got closer, late afternoons would bring larger and larger cumulus clouds that would turn dark and ugly in no time. Then the rain would start. Not just a springtime shower or a summer afternoon drizzle—oh, no. This was a dam break. Drops as big as plums fell so fast and so close together it felt like you couldn't breathe for fear of inhaling more water than air. Huge bolts of lightning were followed almost immediately by rolls and rolls of ear-splitting thunder. The storm would go on and on throughout the afternoon and well into the evening, when finally it would move slowly east into Laos. Afterward, the humidity and heat would both be 95 or so and you could almost hear the palm and banana trees growing outside our squadron party hooch. I didn't much like monsoons.

But our work had to continue. It was my turn to take a mission into the Barrel Roll. Intelligence had learned there were convoys of trucks moving westward out of North Vietnam, along Route 7, and through the Plain of Jars. Our mission was to go there, find out what was going on, kill a few trucks, then boogie home before the serious and heavy monsoon demon got us. Monsoon storms were growing on the weather radar when we briefed, but the weather goon assured me they wouldn't move into Laos until well after the completion of the mission. I used to trust Air Force weathermen.

We took off as normal, crossed the Mekong River heading east, and flew our usual track northeast toward the Plain of Jars. Not long after we arrived in our assigned area, the scope spotted seven trucks moving from east to west on the southern side of the Plain. It was perfect shooting and bombing country —open plains below, with trucks moving along a fairly prominent dirt road, and us on top of them, thirsting for a reason to be there. We called the Airborne Communication and Command Center ("Alley Cat") and told him to send us some strike aircraft—we had trucks to kill.

We got this reply: "Candlestick, we don't have any fighters for you. Severe thunderstorms have closed up the nearby bases and the A-1s and A-26's on call can't get through all that rough stuff to help you."

"Thunderstorms?" I almost shouted. "I thought that weather guy said there wouldn't be any heavy weather until after we got back!"

"Well, Candle, I guess he was wrong. I'll see what we can do. Alley Cat out."

We discussed leaving the trucks alone, turning for home and hoping we'd get through the storms. So far, the Plain of Jars was clear and we could see only a few flashes of lightning to the south and southwest. The thunderstorm cells still looked a long way off.

Alley Cat called back after just a few minutes. "Candle," Alley called, "I've got something a little different for you if you want it." He said there was a "Super Spook" or "Shadow" in the area with a broken gunsight. This was a C-130 turboprop cargo aircraft, with rifle-bullet sized 7.62 Gatling guns and cannon-sized 20mm Gatling guns, both of which could really shoot. It was the newer version of the "Spooky" aircraft, the C-47 gunship that was still being used in South Vietnam. This C-130 had two 7.62 mm Gatling guns pointed out the side of the cargo compartment, through specially-cut openings, and 20 mm Gatling cannons also pointing out the left-hand side. Each of those guns could fire 4,000 rounds or so a minute. The legend was that the Super Spooky/Shadow planes could hit a pie plate-sized target from their orbit altitude of 3,000 to 5,000 feet above the ground and hold that small target until all of their bullets were used up. Sometimes the film shorts at the base movie theater would show both Spooky C-47s and Shadow C-130s firing, both day and night, and they were awesome in their firepower and capability to hit their targets.

We would be able to guide the Super Spooky to the target, using ground-burning flares and verbal instructions. We would guide his bullets to the target by verbal corrections, just as we did fighters dropping bombs. Piece of cake!

"Go ahead," I said, "I'm willing to try anything." None of us had ever put in a Shadow before. We were excited to have it come our way, so we could see how it worked. We didn't have long to wait.

"Candle, this is Shadow. You out there?"

"Shadow, this is Candle. Got you loud and clear. When will you get here?"

"Candle, I'm about 15 mikes (minutes) away."

"Spook, we've got seven trucks moving pretty fast below us, east to west. We'll mark ahead of them. Our navigator will brief you on all the important stuff while you get closer. What are you shooting tonight?"

"Candle, I've got two 7.62 mini-guns and two 20 mm mini-guns, and lots and lots of ammo to burn. Any gomer guns in the area?"

"Spook, this is Candle. You must be wearing your lucky underwear tonight. The trucks are moving fast to the west in open ground, so they've outrun their gun support. Usually, there are no serious fixed guns in this area and no one has shot at us yet. I don't expect much AAA here."

While the navigator was talking to the C-130, I had the scope direct us over the trucks, going in their direction, and drop three ground-burning flares (logs) just about where he thought the trucks would be when the gunship arrived. The Navigator finished his briefing, giving the C-130 pilots the current information about guns in the area, altitude we would be working at, altitude we wanted him to work (for tonight that would be almost the same altitude), direction to fly toward a safe area to bail out (parachute), direction and distance to NKP, known enemy units and unit capabilities in the area, barometer setting, and other important on-scene information. I instructed that pilot on how we worked in a circular pattern overhead, directly above the targets as they moved, in a left-hand orbit, and how we dropped ground-burning flares to use as aiming points or offset points for strike positions. He said he understood and that he would be in our areas shortly flying at "Angels 6"—meaning 6,000 feet above the nightly changed base altitude, which for that night was 2,000 feet mean sea level (MSL). So he was coming in above us, since we were at Angels 2 (4,000 feet above MS), or about 3,000 feet above the terrain below (AGL or above ground level), our usual working altitude.

When he called that he had arrived, we each flashed our lights on once so we could see each other.

"Candle," he called, I've got a visual on you in your orbit." I instructed him to descend to Angels 3, or about a thousand feet above us. I also asked him to enter his orbit around the logs in a left-hand turn, directly opposite from me. That way, we would both be "in the carousel," at nearly the same altitude to avoid running into each other, and in sight of each other if we needed Mark 1 eyeball confirmation of each other's position. This was no time for a mid-air collision with an aircraft twice as big as my little ol' Thunder Turkey.

"I'm opposite you above your altitude, and I've got the burning logs in sight on the ground. Let's get started," the Shadow reported.

So we started our carousel —he on one side of the circle and me on the other. The scope told me where to have him shoot so we could make corrections onto the westbound trucks.

Talking on the radio we always said the other aircraft's call sign first, then ours. Scope called to "Shadow-Candle. These are shooting instructions. From the eastern-most of the three ground-burning logs, which is a red burner, shoot northeast about 75 meters. The lead truck is approaching that position now. You are cleared hot."

"Roger, Candle. Correct my fire."

I could just barely see the shape of the C-130 orbiting opposite me, about a mile or so away. He was blacked out, but I could see him blank out the stars and distant lightning directly out my left cockpit window. Soon, a stream of light started from his position—and a very eerie hum, like an old refrigerator kicking on during the hot summer.

The stream of light was the tracers of his 7.62 caliber bullets. It was a continuous line of fire that looked like it was about the size of a garden hose, only sparkly, and it descended fairly slowly toward the ground. The lighted hose arced downward. The stream of fire seemed to dance, caused both by the light turbulence in the air and the small corrections the pilot made as he visually aimed the stream toward the ground at the point where I had directed him. The line of fire wiggled and snaked in a small looping pattern that started at a black spot in the sky to a point on the ground that never changed.

When the stream contacted the ground, it looked like a string on fire between the ground and the aircraft above. It weaved and arced and danced. The top of the stream went around in a circle as the Shadow orbited overhead, but the end of the stream was hitting the ground in approximately the spot that I had called.

The scope called corrections to me, so I called: "Spook-Candle, move about 20 meters to the east and you'll be on the lead truck." The trucks were still traveling along the road at a pretty good clip for the rough terrain below. They could obviously see the stream of fire coming down toward the road in front of them. Maybe they were chained or handcuffed to the steering wheel like the intelligence officers maintained. Why would they keep on driving after seeing that dance of death coming at them?

The stream started to move along the ground as the C-130 pilot adjusted his aiming point. Again, the stream bent and weaved and shimmied downward. Seemingly in slow motion, the point on the ground where the bullets were hitting moved east. It wasn't very long before I started seeing tracers bouncing off of something hard. Ricochets were going everywhere now —up and out in every direction.

"Pilot-Scope. He's on the lead truck. Have him fire for effect."

"Spook-Candle. You're on the lead truck. Hit him hard!" (I couldn't help but call him Spooky because it was.)

The top of the hose-sized stream stopped. The rest of the stream continued down to the point on the ground where the bullets were bouncing around and ricocheting off the metal of the truck below, but the top of the stream was dark.

Then a larger stream started—a fire hose compared to a garden hose. This larger line of fire continued downward on the same path as the smaller stream, with the same weaves and bends and arcs and sways as the other, but it was much, much larger. And the hum coming from across the orbit got louder —now it was clearly discernible, a steady HUMMMMMM. Super Shadow had stopped using his 7.62 guns for sighting in and was now using his 20 mm guns to eat up those trucks. As soon as the larger stream hit the ground, more ricochets bounced everywhere—and then they stopped too —but the fire hose continued.

"Stop!" shouted scope. "The lead truck is gone. Move the fire 25 meters to the east and resume firing."

I passed that along to the Spook, and the larger stream stopped at the top, while the smaller stream started again at the top of the arc, and slowly followed the larger stream to the ground, but the smaller stream moved away from where it was hitting the ground before. Now, it was moving to the east very slowly.

"Pilot-Scope. Move the fire 10 meters to the north from your present aim point to hit the second truck."

I told Spook. The arcing and bobbing and weaving of the smaller stream moved again until the point on the ground where the bullets were hitting again changed to the new location given. Then ricochets and sparks started again

"Fire for effect!" the scope yelled, all excited by the action.

"Spook-Candle, you've got number two. Sic' em!"

The fire hose began again—following the wake of the preceding bullets as faithfully as a blind man following his dog. The hum was clear again, not coming and going like it did when the 7.62s were in the air. This time, the Spook pilot used a little rudder to make the bullets hitting the ground go around in a small circle, kicking up ricochets everywhere, as well as a little cloud of dust that even I could see through the side window. When the ricocheting stopped, the Spook pilot stopped shooting. He knew the truck was toast.

And so we moved on. Five more trucks. Five more kills. Now I knew what the expression "shooting fish in a barrel" really meant. I told the Shadow pilot to cease fire so we could see what damage he had done. The snake streams stopped and everything turned dark again.

Since we had to make a battle damage assessment (BDA) in our action report, we turned back west and flew over the remains of the seven trucks. There were still small fires at several places where we had put in the gun strike, caused either by the tracers from the gunship hitting the grass or by the small secondary explosions of the ammunition or fuel one of the trucks must have been carrying. I asked our scope what he could see of the trucks we had targeted.

"Well, pilot," he said, "the biggest thing I see of all seven trucks is the double rear axle of that second one we killed. All the others have been ground down to metal chips by the Shadow. Man, that's some awesome firepower." That said it all.

"Candle-Spook. What else do you have for me?"

"Nothing, Spook. The gomers are all gone here. We'll take a little look-see back over to the east, just to see if any more trucks are trying to come this way."

"OK, Candle. My navigator just talked to NKP radar and it's looking pretty Delta Sierra (DS = dog "shit," which means pretty ugly) back there. I think I'll start heading home. Call me if you find anything else. I have bullets to burn."

OK, that was a rude awakening for us. We'd been so wrapped up in chasing the trucks we had forgotten all about the monsoon thunderstorms creeping up on us. I turned to see what I could see —and immediately wished I hadn't. There were towering cumulus thunderstorms everywhere we looked to the south. The lightning was almost constant. It wasn't near us yet, but the ugly, black thunderheads we could see in the flashes of lightning covered the entire horizon. It wasn't looking good.

I called the base radar for an update—he said it was Delta Sierra. He also said the thunder boomers were in a line from the coasts of North and South Vietnam back to the west, well into central Thailand. The cells were growing above 40,000 feet, and there were two or three lines of storms following each other. When I asked if he could see the thunderstorms in my area, to help me fly around the biggest and baddest ones, he told me his radar couldn't see past the nearest cells because they were so thick with rain.

I decided to start for home. I still had plenty of gas, but not enough to fly around these lines of storms, either east or west, and obviously my old Thunder Buzzard wasn't going to climb over the top at 40,000 feet. So I had no choice but to try to keep the green side up and the black side down inside the storm cells and hope that we'd be spit out the back side over the base, all in one piece.

"Cross your fingers," I told the crew. "This is going to be a wet and wild ride. Strap everything down, then sit down and strap yourselves in, and say a little prayer to the rain gods." We started flying south.

As we got closer and closer to the nearest storms, things really looked bad. Lightning flashed everywhere. We could hear the thunder and see a sheet of dark rain illuminated by the lightning just ahead of us. It looked like a vertical swimming pool right in front of us. As we flew into the first squall line, I noticed my copilot holding his breath—as if he didn't want to drown in all that water.

As soon as we hit the wall of rain, the turbulence started—heavy, wing-bending, people-throwing turbulence—up, down, sideways, corkscrewing and flapping every which way. I had slowed the aircraft to the best penetrating speed, but it still felt like we were inside an unlighted washing machine. Water started coming into the cockpit and through the open doors and hatches —it was everywhere, inside and out.

I was flying as I was taught —hold a level-flight altitude by concentrating on the artificial horizon on the instrument panel; don't change power settings unless absolutely necessary; don't fight the ups and downs, just let the turbulence take you where it will, because fighting it will put a huge strain on the airplane structure and wings. Every lightning flash helped me turn slightly to avoid the darkest parts of this first line of storms, but I wasn't missing all of them. It felt like I was hitting every one of the damn things. And this was only the first one—we had at least one and probably two more to penetrate before we were over friendly Thai territory.

We popped out the south side of that first line of storms—a brief reprieve, because the next line was just ahead. Waiting for us were walls of water, lightning, thunder—everything we had just flown through and maybe more.

I tried calling NKP radar again. "Radar, Candlestick. Are you seeing any of these storms getting smaller or going away?" I asked.

"No way, Candle. They're still there and moving east. NKP is starting to clear up, but we've had seven or more inches of rain in the past hour."

"Can you help us find the holes in the storms now, so we don't have to guess where they are?" I asked.

"Nope, still no can do, Candle. The rain in these puppies is just too thick to see through. Call when you cross the river and we'll get you home as quick as possible. Radar out."

No help and more lines to penetrate. I told everyone to strap in as tight as possible, because we were about to hit the second wall.

"Candle-Shadow. You still up radar frequency?" I heard.

"Hey Spooky, yep we're monitoring this frequency in case we go down in this crap. What are you doing up this frequency?" I asked. Boy, he sure sounded calm.

"I heard you call radar. I'm just a little way ahead of you and heading back to my house. I'm a little higher than you and my radar on board works well enough to see those storm cells you told NKP about. Can I help you get through them?"

"Can you see me too?" I asked.

"Sometimes I see your echo, Candle, but I know about where you are and the airspeed you're flying. I think I can direct you away from the real killers out there. Want to try?"

"You bet, Spook. I'm already wet and scared enough. I think it's time for you to help me a little —you've got the eyes I need now."

Super Spooky started giving me directions to miss the strongest portions of the storm cells. It was still wet and like riding a bucking bronco every second. Lightning zapped nearby and thunder boomed too loud for even our headsets to muffle. Up and down and around and around—it wasn't fun and it wasn't easy, but at least we had some help now, and we all felt we were avoiding the worst of it. Things were looking up.

Then my copilot came on the intercom and said, "Pilot, what's that green stuff on the right wing tip?"

"Green stuff, what green stuff?"

I looked out his window and saw a greenish glow all over the right wing tip. I looked left and saw it on my left wing too. I told the flight engineers to carefully unstrap and go to each side of the airplane to see if they could identify the green stuff. Neither of us knew what it was. It was glowing brightly and seemed to wash off the back of the wing when the rain got really heavy. Weird.

Then it started to crawl along the leading edges of both wings toward the engine housings, the nacelles. It wasn't moving in one piece, it was growing. The wing tips were still glowing, but now the glow was spreading toward the engines—and us. Slowly, but steadily, it streamed toward the engines. It crawled over the bottoms of the nacelles, not far from our cockpit windows, and oozed into the front of the engines and out onto the propellers. It actually crawled out along the leading edge of the three propeller blades of each radial engine toward the tips as the propellers were whirling through the air. The prop blur made the greenish glow look like a round fan of green light. When we flew through a heavy area of rain, the green stuff on the propellers was slung away from the prop arc in large globs. It looked like glowing Jello being thrown out and away from the prop tips. What was this junk? Whatever it was, I sure hoped it didn't make the engines quit.

And then that greenish glow started moving again along the front edge of our wings, headed right for our cockpit windows. The wings and engine nacelles were almost totally covered by the glow and the props were still slinging globs of it out into space.

It crawled over the top of the cockpit. Now we could see it up close through our overhead windows. It was not only glowing, but dancing and moving, getting brighter, then weaker. The top of the glow looked like the green flame tips from a fire and it was still growing.

The cockpit was almost totally dark, since I'd turned down my instrument lights so I could retain as much of my night vision as possible. When the copilot looked over at me as the green stuff started to cover the overhead windows, I could clearly see the whites of his eyes—and they looked like extra-white golf balls with threads of red running through them. He was frightened—me, too. No one in the crew spoke, as the airplane started to glow inside and out in that greenish hue.

Slowly, the stuff oozed through the side cockpit windows, which were both open just a crack to keep the inside of the windshield from fogging over. It crawled along the window frame and jumped onto the instrument glare shield in front of us. It covered the entire top of the instrument panel, glowing and dancing right in front of us, like green fire.

The smell of ozone filled the cockpit. The hairs on my arms and on the back of my neck were standing straight up—whether it was from this glowing-green stuff or my horror and fear, I couldn't tell. It started to blanket the instruments on the panel in front of us. I wanted to take my hands off the control yoke, to keep it from touching me. I looked back and could see the same greenish glob dancing over many of the surfaces of the inside of the cargo compartment behind me. It was very quiet, even in the midst of violent turbulence.

"St. Elmo's fire," the navigator whispered. "It's like lightning, but looks different." I began to worry about it burning out our instruments, since the odor in the cockpit was starting to smell like an electrical fire.

Suddenly, a bolt of lightning flashed past outside the cockpit window on the copilot's side, just missing the wing. The thunder was instantaneous, loud enough to make the airplane shake and vibrate even more. And then the green stuff was gone—like it had never existed. But the slight smell of ozone was still in the air, like the ghost of the glowing green. And it was very, very quiet.

"Candlestick, Candlestick, you still there?" I heard from the Spooky.

"Yep," I replied. "Still here and kicking. How we doing?"

"You're doing great. Just mosey to the south a bit and you should be clear of the worst of it. I lost you there for a while. Decide to take a break from the fun?"

"Nope," I said. "We had a little St. Elmo's fire on the plane and in the cockpit with us. It must have affected the radios. But it was discharged by a bolt of lightning and I think we're OK."

"Cool," the Spook said. "That sounds like fun. You're almost out of it, so I'm heading on south. It was good working with you. Have a large beer for me. Spook out." And he was gone.

We flew on for a short time. The rain lessened considerably and there were breaks visible between the clouds lit up by lightning.

And then we were out—the Mekong was just ahead. We were almost home. We had met the Super Spooky and the Green Goblin, and now we were back to good old Naked Fanny.

Just another night on the Trail for a Candlestick FAC.

THE THUNDERSTORM RIDE

I was out again in the T-38 practice area near the Mexican border, flying solo, and practicing for my final acrobatic phase check. Things weren't going too badly for me when I was alone, but I was still doing things very mechanically. I couldn't seem to get the proverbial "feel" of the airplane when an instructor pilot or check pilot few with me. I couldn't stop feeling that I was merely an incompetent "aimer" sitting astride two powerful jet engines like a monkey riding a rocket ship, hoping my aim was good enough to get me through a training mission alive. I just knew that someday that jet was going to get the best of me and leave me in a multitude of separate small parts at the bottom of a large smoking hole. But I continued to practice—failure was not an option. I still wanted to be a jet pilot more than anything else, worse than any humiliating language or physical torture any instructor pilot could dream up. I kept doing the acrobatic maneuvers over and over again, trying to get the feel of the airplane.

Near the end of that solo flight, at the furthest distance from the air base, the area controller called me to tell me a thunderstorm was approaching Laredo and conditions would be very dangerous for the next hour or so. He wanted to know my fuel state. I told him "Only 30 minutes of fuel remaining." Texas thunder-boomers are notoriously bad and the wind shear that goes with them can sometimes be as bad as the lightning, hail, and up-drafts. I had to get back.

I requested departure from my training area and headed back to base as fast as I could go. The storm arrived ahead of me. When I arrived in the Laredo landing pattern, the controller in the tower told me to divert to another field. But I didn't have the fuel to go any place but here. He also said the wind was crossways to the runway and strong enough to be out of the limits the aircraft could handle. There was no way I could land that rocket ship, no matter what I did. If I touched down, the wind would blow me off the runway and I'd crash in the desert nearby.

The tower controller asked me if I wanted to punch out—jettison my canopy and pull my ejection-seat firing handles, to ride a parachute down instead of that jet. But I'd already felt the cactus needles in my butt when we were pulled up 200 feet on a long rope behind a racing pickup truck, with the parachute as a glider. When I released the rope tow, I was forced to fall 200 feet to the desert below. These two paragliding trips during pilot training were to let us practice "parachute landing falls." Landing, obviously, must occur if a pilot has to bail out or eject from a plane in flight. I didn't like that practice or the "boom-bucket rides," where we were strapped in an ejection seat fastened to a rail running about 50 feet into the air, then ordered to pull the ejection handles to fire the blank mortar shell under our seats. Being slammed to the top of a 50-foot rail in a heartbeat, twice, to prepare us for ejections from an airplane, weren't any fun either.

I didn't even want to think about doing both of those things while coming out of a fighter jet doing 150 mph over the desert in the middle of a thunderstorm. I decided to land, wind or no wind. And I did, with just the sweetest kiss of tires on the concrete and just the right amount of control touch to keep the airplane from either rolling off the side of the runway into the desert nearby or rolling wing-over-wing down the runway in a jet-fuelled ball of fire.

I stopped in the middle of the runway, as instructed by the tower controller, and shut down the engines right there. A tug would come and pull me and the jet back to the ramp, since taxiing was still unsafe with the thunderstorm roaring overhead, the wind blowing like a Texas banshee, and the rain coming down in buckets. But I was safe and the airplane was safe and I had done it alone, by myself, by feel—it was a miracle. My walk back to the squadron training room from the aircraft, carrying my G-suit, helmet, and other gear, was a sole-celebrated victory march. It didn't seem like the long way that it was. When I got back to the training room, my IP had already left, trying to get back to his living quarters before the storm. Again, I had proved to myself that I could fly that damn thing if I just let my mind think about the flight and my body to accomplish the flying part. And again, my IP had neither seen my latest miracle nor did he ever comment on it later. Jerk!

My T-38 training finished shortly after that thunderstorm ride. Even my instructor was surprised. The miracle of the wind had given me enough pride and confidence to complete my final phase check without incident. I graduated second or third in academics and smack dab at the bottom of the flight scores. But I did graduate.

My mother pinned on my wings at a ceremony on the parade ground of Laredo Air Force Base Texas, in the summer of 1969, since Vicki had gone home to Kansas to have our baby. I had met and barely whipped pilot training and graduated in the class of 69-07. Our motto was "The Magnificent Seven!" I felt like "The Magnificent One," and I know each of the others in 69-07 felt the same way. We were all walking on air and excited about getting sent to new aircraft and new assignments.

GETTING AN AIRPLANE ASSIGNMENT

Next was the hard part—waiting for our new aircraft assignments. We were told that there would not be many instructor-pilot slots for our graduating class, or many fighter-pilot choices to other bases. We were told that most of us would get cargo planes to Vietnam and a few would get stateside missions in B-52 bombers or KC-135 tankers in Nebraska or Guam (pretty much the same place as far as I was concerned).

Several of my classmates got instructor-pilot slots, two to T-38s and one to a T-37. Several others got fighter slots. My Section Leader, Banks Prevatt, was initially assigned to C-7s, but was re-assigned to C-130s. My friend Jake Jacobs (who drove his 1965 Corvette roadster to Laredo with his guitar-picking, beautiful wife Wendy) got an F-100 along with Tony Bulat. John Dickinson and John Labouliere got F-4s, and Tom Powers (one of the older, married students) got a prop-fighter slot in the A-1 and was later assigned to NKP during my tour there.

The rest of us got what was left. I was assigned to a C-123K and given orders to report to Hurlburt Field for combat crew training, just outside of Eglin Air Force Base, near Fort Walton Beach, Florida. The next phase of my flight training would be in a Korean War-era cargo aircraft with two radial engines pulling big-bladed props and two jet engines in pods under the wings. I was going to Hurlburt to learn to become a trash-hauler in Vietnam.

But first, I had to make it through Air Force Survival School at Fairchild Air Force Base near Spokane, Washington.

FIVE DAYS WITHOUT FOOD

Survival school at Fairchild Air Force Base near Spokane wasn't too bad for the first week or so. Most of that time was spent in the classroom studying edible flora and fauna, learning about staying alive in the wilderness, emergency medical techniques, and surviving captivity. One of our instructors was a man with a Russian or Eastern European accent, who gave us his name (now forgotten) and who informed us that he had walked out of captivity in Eastern Siberia to Western Europe during World War II. It was a trek of thousands of miles. He taught us how he survived that long walk and what he learned about himself and his will to survive during the many months it took him, though several winters, to reach safety in the West. He was very interesting and helped me understand the importance of positive thinking and planning in survival situations. This phase of training lasted a little over a week, with daily classroom studies.

The second phase of our survival training was to take place out in the mountains near Spokane. The school issued us a rucksack (a small pack), a sleeping bag, a shelter half (half of a tent), an entrenching tool (small shovel), an onion, a potato, a small can of pemmican (dried chicken lips, pig ears and other miscellaneous animal parts), and a small bag of salt and pepper. We were given instructions to take as few clothes as possible and go forth into the mountains to live off the land for five days.

We were split into small teams, each with about ten students, and an Air Force survival specialist. We hiked about 10 to 15 miles per day, mostly uphill, both ways, and always against the wind. We all soon discovered that natural, lost-in-the-wild food was scarce.

By the second day, everyone had eaten all of the rations given to us by the school. After that, we were eating fingerling trout, fern tips, dandelion leaves, cattail roots, and other miscellaneous twigs and critters. One day the instructor brought a rabbit to skin, cook, and eat. We all had a small bite each. It made great stew with the dandelion leaves and the fern berries. But one little bunny does not make a big meal for 10 hungry Air Force campers. As hungry as we were, when the instructor offered the eyeballs to us "as good protein," no one took him up on the offer, so he had to macho them down himself. Yuk!

One of our team members was an Air Force major who was the bane of our existence. He was probably 40 years old, but acted 80. He bitched all the time about everything that happened. Most of the time we had to carry his pack the last two or three miles of each daily trek. We talked about tying him to a tree and leaving him for the bears, but our instructor said that probably wouldn't work.

His daily whining just served to make it harder for all of the rest of us. It made me ashamed of being a pilot, because he kept saying that pilots shouldn't have to do all that work, since there were enlisted airmen to help him do stuff, and carry stuff, and wash stuff, and fix meals, and stuff. What a pig.

By about the fourth day, everyone was pretty well beat. We had been sleeping on the hard ground, hiking up and down the mountains, pulling the complaining Major along, and thinking about our stomachs chewing on our back bones. We were all tired. Toward the end of that afternoon, we were climbing steadily and trying to get beyond a high mountain on our left. We had walked in heavy timber most days and all of that day and it was fairly warm. We were all hungry and everyone was just about done. Just when we thought we would stop for the night, we walked out of the trees into a high meadow.

There were wild flowers and knee-high grasses swaying in the slight breeze. The air was softer and kinder out from under the tree branches and much lighter with the sun shining out from between the cotton ball clouds racing over the mountaintop.

Someone shouted, and then someone else shouted, and everyone ran to where the shouters were standing, looking at the ground and laughing. I realized with the others that we were all standing in the middle of a wild strawberry patch, at least an acre in size, with a million marble-sized strawberries stretching out toward the edge of the meadow.

Everyone got down on their hands and knees and began to graze strawberries like a pack of hungry grizzly bears. We all had strawberry juice from knee to nose. Even our instructor was amazed by these wild, wonderful berries. Everyone smiled a lot after that. We walked just a little bit further and made camp. I think we all felt like we could finish the week then —with or without any more real food. It was an amazing day.

We eventually finished the trekking part of the training and even the whiny Major survived (just barely). We loaded onto buses on the last day and went immediately to the mess hall, where the chow line had hot food and was clearly ready for a pack of hungry survivors. Hot showers were next —long ones. And for me, even before the shower, there was the telephone call to Hutchinson to see if I was a father yet, even though the "official" due date wasn't for another couple of days. But, no luck, no baby—but Vicki was doing fine. I told her I was doing OK too and that I had had strawberries at a picnic in the mountains.

After the shower, everyone went to bed early. Even the military beds in the dorms felt pretty good after all of the previous nights on hard and rocky ground.

For the next day or two we spent more time in classes on base. This time, there was more emphasis on surviving in a prison camp as prisoners of war. I called home every evening to see whether or not I had become a daddy, but not yet. The doctor assured Vicki that it would happen within two days, or so.

PRISONER OF WAR TRAINING

At the end of this round of classes, in the late afternoon, we were taken out into the forest again and told to find a POW camp in the area, somewhere downhill from our release point. We were instructed to try to sneak into the camp without being caught. That didn't sound like it was going to be too hard. There were about 40 of us in the class and there was only one little, bitty ol' camp, with just a few lazy, good-for-nothing guards. How hard could this be? We were each told to cut or break a short stick, about 18 inches long, to use to try to detect trip wires, so we didn't set off any flares that would allow the guards to see us. Armed with the sticks and our new POW training still burning in our brains, we set off as a group to sneak into this mysterious camp.

We arrived above an open prairie valley just before full dark. There was enough light left for us to see the camp directly below, in the middle of a broad meadow, surrounded by a hundred yards or so of open grass. The grass was about knee high. A high wire fence surrounded the camp, with higher guard towers at each of the four corners of the enclosed area. The fence was attached to a large metal building to one side. Lights were on inside and all around the perimeter of the camp. Outside of the camp wire was an open area with wire stretched about waist high all around the camp in rings. There were mounds of dirt spaced around the inside of the rings of wire. There were no light poles or towers in this open area.

Just outside the camp in the area nearby, the grass was mowed short. There were at least 5 rows of barbed wire on which cans were hanging, about a foot or 2 off the ground and spaced at close intervals within the concentric rings. They were too high, too uneven, and too close together to walk or run over, since that would be so awkward and slow that the few guards patrolling the interior rings of the wire would surely see us. The guards were carrying weapons and flashlights. Now we could see searchlights on the top of the guard towers just lighting up, and reaching out toward the tree line.

The 40 or so of us lying in the grass wondered how our 18-inch sticks were going to get us through all of that. But we had our orders, so we had to try.

Some tried running around the outside of the outermost ring of barbed wire, nearer the tree line, to get behind the camp, thinking it might be easier to get in there. Some decided to start early, before the guards were alerted, thinking they could sneak between those guards who were easily visible. I decided to get into the middle of the pack, just to see what happened to those going ahead of me. There were enough others around me, I thought, that I couldn't or probably wouldn't be singled out for extra attention if I got caught.

So I started crawling toward the camp, holding my stick out in front of me like a dowsing rod, hoping to find anything on the ground before it found me. I went under a couple of strands of barbed wire without anything happening. And then it started.

One of the first adventurers crawling toward the camp hit a trip flare. The guards turned on all the lights—lots more than we had seen when we first spotted the camp from the trees. They started shooting at anything that moved (blanks, thank goodness). Sirens went off and people started to scream. Explosions started near the walls of the camp in boxed pits near the guards' stations that had appeared to us earlier as mounds of dirt. It was bedlam. It was confusing. It was scary.

There was noise and gunshots and screaming and dirt and dust everywhere. The guards started running through, over, and under the wire, awkwardly and slowly, but a heck of a lot faster toward us than we could run away from them. It was almost as if they had done this before—which, of course, they had—and they were catching us by twos and threes all around the camp perimeter.

Two were headed directly for me. I was caught. They took my

stick. One laughed. Then they pushed me over each ring of wire toward the open gate of the camp and marched me with others into a holding pen.

It seemed like I was cooped up in that very small pen with a very large number of dirty, sweaty, pissed-off stick bearers for a very long time. Eventually, the noise quieted down and the guard at the holding-pen gate eventually opened the door for the last of the survivors, as if they knew exactly how many of us there were trying to sneak in—which, of course, they did.

They took us out of the pen one at a time. We were each taken to an interrogation office and grilled loudly, but not violently, by a soldier wearing what looked like the uniform of the Soviet Army. He was an officer type. He tried all the usual interrogation techniques—offering cigarettes, offering cool water, offering more if we would become a spy in the camp, threatening us with beatings and worse if we did not agree to betray our brothers, threatening us with the worst kind of torture if we didn't obey every camp command, and on and on and on.

I think everyone practiced the routine we were taught in the classroom—name, rank, and serial number and told the interrogator if we had any injuries or needed medical treatment. No more, no less. However, there may have been some swearing going on, between interrogator and prisoner, but that wasn't verified.

The interrogation room was hot. By then, it was the middle of the night. I stank, I was thirsty, I didn't smoke, and some guy with garlic on his breath was trying to entice me to become a rat for a cigarette. Boy, was I smarter than this guy.

They physically threw me into a cell with solid steel walls that was exactly five feet square by six feet tall (I paced it very carefully over the next day or so, about a million times). There was a peep hole in the door and an opening at the bottom of the door that was about two inches high and about eight inches wide. The floor was concrete; the walls were dirty. There was an empty one-pound coffee can in the corner and the place smelled like the inside of a very dirty outhouse.

It was my home for an indeterminate time. No one had told us how long this phase of the training would last. No one had assured us that this was just a game. No one had told us whether or not the guards were allowed to use physical violence on us, since they all looked like retards in their Soviet Army uniforms. This was not a good home to be in.

The guards told us that if we sat down or laid down at any time, day or night, a guard would come into our cells and beat us to death with his billy club—all in a Slavic accent and in a very convincing manner. Anyway, I was totally convinced. The guy who took me to my cell slammed the steel door shut with a loud clang that vibrated around all four walls and left me there alone in the semi-darkness, feeling sorry for myself, and wondering what would happen next. As the sounds of steel doors slamming shut finally ended, about the time I estimated to be dawn, I remembered what this new day was—the day my baby was due to be born. There was no way to call home, for however long they meant to keep me locked up in that small, smelly steel box.

I'm not sure how long they kept us in the cell. Judging by the indirect light coming into the steel building housing our cells, it was probably 36 hours or so. During that time the guards continued to prowl the area, banging on doors with their clubs, peeking in the peepholes to make sure we weren't sitting or lying down, and generally harassing us all the time. I have no way of knowing how many cells there were in that large, open warehouse, but my guess would be 40 or so. The guards took turns going into every cell to take us out one at a time to "question" us.

When they were coming to get us, two or three guards would march down the row of cells, clicking their boots on the concrete floor, so everyone could hear them come. When they were on the way down the hallway of cells, I would get up from trying to get some secret sleep and stand at the back of my cell (I later learned everyone else did too).

If the guards passed, I would sigh and relax a little, and sit down for a short time, thinking that all the guards were busy. That didn't always work. Sometimes another guard would sneak up on a cell, peek in the door, and catch someone on the floor. That person would be dragged out of the cell and taken away into the inquisition room. I got the pleasure of going into that room several times during my stay in the POW Hotel.

The interrogation room itself was just an office in the steel building/warehouse. Nothing special, just a desk and a few chairs, and usually two or three goon guards standing around the room trying to look mean. The questions were always given by a person who was dressed like an officer and who acted like one, ordering the guards around, yelling at them if they were rough with us (to get us on his side), pacing around the room smoking and drinking soda (he usually offered us something when we came into the room).

But when the questions started, he was no longer Mr. Nice Guy. No matter what the questions or answers were, they always punished us in some way. Several times, I was merely yelled at. Some of the others related later that they were slapped, or made to stand at an angle to the wall and hold themselves away from it with just their fingertips, or made to "duck walk" around the room until they fell over, and similar stunts. No one was seriously hurt during these sessions. But everyone did get "the box."

When it happened to me, three guards grabbed me by the arms and legs and threw me to the floor. They then pulled out a box from the corner and placed it right in front of me. The box was an open-ended wooden box with reinforcement boards on all four sides. The opening was about 18 inches square and it looked to be about two feet deep. The guards ordered me to crawl into the box. I had to get in by duck walking into the opening. Then the guards pushed me from behind, tipping my head and shoulders slightly forward, until all of my body was inside. My head was almost touching my stomach. My knees were touching the top of the inside of the box and my butt was crammed tightly against the door that had been closed and locked behind me. My body filled every inch of that box. I could barely breathe.

In our training, our instructors had told us to count to ourselves if we ever got into a painful or scary situation. The counting would help divert our attention away from the painful circumstance. So I started counting. "One Mississippi, two Mississippi, three Mississippi…" At about 120, my legs fell asleep and my shoulders began burning so badly I thought the guards were trying to set me on fire. At about 200, I was panting pretty hard, everything was asleep except my brain, which was frantically trying to figure out a way out of that box. I lost count. I was just touching the fringes of panic—that evil, uncontrollable need to run or fight or cry. Parts of me were shutting down. I could no longer concentrate on counting. I was done.

I began thinking about screaming, or yelling, or offering to tell the interrogator anything he wanted to know. But I couldn't work up enough courage to yell. It wasn't conscious thought, just Hyland stubbornness. And then the front part of the box opened, the guards tipped the box up at the butt end, the back door was opened, and those same goons that pushed me into the box then pushed me out of the box—head first onto the floor.

I was a mess. Nothing worked. I couldn't stand up. I was sweating and shaking. I wondered if I really had started yelling or whether they were just tired of seeing me crammed into that box. Whatever the reason, I was out of the box and I could breathe again. At least that was over. They dragged me back to my cell, propped me up vertically in the corner with a stern warning not to sit or lie down, and then slammed the door behind them. I sat down anyway. I was pooped. And I still didn't know if I had become a father yet.

Finally, after what seemed like months, the guards came to let us out of our cells. We were all led into a pen, just outside the walls of the warehouse. The area had once been a bomb-storage area, because there were six or seven concrete bunkers, covered with several feet of earth, within the confines of the pen. The pen itself was about 60 feet by 100 feet. The pen had 12 foot high barbed wire fences around all four sides, with guard towers at every corner. The entire fence was topped with coils of razor-sharp concertina wire. There was a small wooden building inside the wire, which we learned was where the officers gave lectures every day on the benefits and advantages of Soviet Communism.

As soon as we were released from the cells and herded into the pen, we were fed a cup of thin soup and given a slice of bread. After that, we were divided into small groups. Each group was assigned a bunker for quarters. The guards tried to find out who the highest-ranking person was in each group. Some groups gave that information and that person was immediately taken out of the pen and disappeared. It was a lesson about how POWs are stripped of leaders.

As the first day in the bunkers wore on, we were led by groups into the classroom in the wooden building to hear droning lectures for several hours. Every instructor had a heavy Slavic accent. The classroom itself was adorned with posters in Russian: some were communist slogans; some were theater sheets; and some were event posters (ballet, lectures, travel, etc.). I spent most of my time in the classroom trying to stay awake in the hot and crowded room and trying to translate the posters. Most of the lectures were drivel, but sometimes questions were asked and if a "prisoner" didn't answer correctly or respectfully, that person was dragged outside and put into a coffin in a trench in the ground and covered with dirt. Some were forced to stand with their fingertips pressed against the wall at the front of the room, with their legs spread out and away from the wall far enough to cause all of their weight to rest on their fingertips—a very tiring and painful position.

At the end of that first day in the pen, after a day (or two or three?) in the steel cages, everyone was tired, hungry and a little bit cold. We had another meal of gruel and bread at dark, then everyone was ordered to go into their respective bunkers to try to get some sleep on the cold and hard concrete floor. There were no cots, no bunks, no blankets, no pillows or pads. Everyone crushed together on the floor to share body warmth. Thankfully, there weren't many taking trips to the outhouse during the night, because everyone was dehydrated and too tired to get up. I didn't sleep and I'm sure no one else did either.

The next morning, we were told by our leaders that we had to make an escape attempt. The plan was to select six or eight guys still in good shape to try to sneak under the wire at different points of the pen. While they were on their way to their jump-off points, the rest of us were ordered to storm the front gate of the pen to try to distract the guards and focus their attention on us, rather than the great escapers.

Everyone gathered together in front of the centermost bunker. Then we all started toward the front gate, shouting, picking up clods of dirt, shaking our fists, and making as much noise as we could. I thought that was such a great idea that I hurried to the front of the pack just as we all approached the front gate. There, behind the wire, was a soldier dressed as an officer and carrying a Russian submachine gun. He pointed the gun at us and walked up to his side of the wire. Other guards came to stand beside him. But none of them said anything—they just stood there with their Russian-made weapons pointing at us.

Most of the time in the POW camp, I could mentally understand that this whole thing was training—a game—and wasn't really meant to hurt us or incarcerate us indefinitely. But this time, probably because of my hunger, discomfort, and worry about my baby being born, my mind made the jump to that place that told me this was real.

Suddenly, I became a part of this real mob charging the front gate of our prison toward that officer on the other side. As I got up to the wire gate, I started shouting at the officer with the submachine gun—in Russian. I called him a dog and an idiot and a peasant and everything else I could think of. I really thought I had him, that American soldier, in a Russian uniform, carrying a Russian machine gun.

And then he pointed his weapon through the wire, directly at my chest and said, in Russian, "Step back or I'll shoot your ass off." I was stunned. I was immediately transformed from a smirking smart-ass American to a totally cowed prisoner of war. All of a sudden, it had become real to me. And I wasn't sure how much more I could take of the discomfort and misery and hunger and cold and droning lectures—it seemed like it would go on forever.

More guards reinforced the few at the gate. When the full mob approached the wire on the gate, we all realized that there was nothing we could do. If we tried to go through the wire, the guards would congregate at that point and hit us on any part of our bodies that came through the wire. Then the siren went off, signaling that an escape was going on, and more guards came into the pen and started shoving all of us back into the bunkers.

We were all locked inside our concrete man-made caves, in the cold and dark, and no one knew what was going on outside. It wasn't long before the guy who was selected from our group to try the escape was thrown back in with us. He told us that he had been caught just outside the wire, brought back inside the pen, and buried underground in the coffin for a while —he didn't know for how long. Eventually he was dug out of the ground and brought back to our current underground concrete home.

Everyone was discouraged and tired. Most were ready for the nightmare to stop, but we didn't know when this portion of our training was scheduled to end. Everyone was at the point that they believed that it could go on and on forever.

At nightfall, we were released from the bunkers. Buses pulled up to the front gate and the officer who had the machine gun during the riot announced in pure American English that the training was over and the buses would take us first to the mess hall at Fairchild, and then to our barracks. The guards opened the gate and shook hands with each of us as we filed out of the pen.

As soon as I arrived at the mess hall, I ran to the telephone and called Hutchinson to see if I was a daddy yet. But no, I wasn't. Not yet. The doctor had told Vicki that it would probably be in about two more days.

After dinner, everyone went to their barracks, took a long hot shower and went to bed. The next day was a day of rest. Most of us spent the day in the mess hall, just sitting there, drinking coffee, eating what snacks were available, and talking about the training up to that point. We knew there was only one more exercise and then we were done with survival school.

WE'LL BE RUNNING DOWN THE MOUNTAIN WHEN WE COME

The second day after finishing POW training, after a big breakfast, we were instructed to pack our things and be ready to get out of the training site as soon as we finished the final exercise. We were told that everyone would be finished by dark. Just before noon, the buses pulled up to the main building and picked us up. While the driver took us up the winding mountain road, one of the camp instructors told us the rules of this final exercise.

The set-up was that we were escapees from a prisoner of war camp. We would be taken to the top of a ridgeline and released. It was then our job to evade re-capture and make our way to the bottom of the slope where buses would be waiting to take us back to camp. There would be guards in the timber below our release point, pretending to be hunters contracted to capture escaped prisoners. All of them would be armed with firearms (with blanks). None of us had anything but the clothes on our back. If we were caught by any of the guards, we would be taken back to the top of the mountain and released, to try again. It sounded like it was going to be a long day.

Sitting in the bus, I realized that this day was the new due date for Vicki to have our baby. And here I was, lumbering up a steep gravel road in a beaten up old bus, to some drop-off point in the mountains. I didn't know what would happen next or if I would be caught, taken back to the top of the mountain and released, just to be caught again. I didn't want that to happen. I had to get to a telephone as fast as I could. I wanted to be the first one on the bus at the bottom of the mountain so I could call home and get to the airport as fast as humanly possible. I had a baby on the way!

I enlisted the help of a friend, Steve Pomajzl, who I'd first met at pilot training in Laredo. Steve was in 69-07 with me, but was in Section II while I was in Section I. He'd also been assigned to a C-123K and would be going to Combat Crew Training at Hurlburt Field the same time as me. Steve was from Wilbur, a little town in the south central part of the Nebraska, just north and a little east of my home town in Kansas. Steve was a good guy, a little shorter than me, and rip strong. We got along famously.

I told Steve about my baby being due that day and my need to call home as soon as possible to see if I was a daddy yet. We decided to stick together during our trek down the mountain, so we could help each other hear or see the trackers and avoid them and getting caught.

Finally, the buses stopped near the top of a wooded mountain. Everyone got a final drink of water, a final explanation of the rules, and a map. The location of the waiting buses at the bottom of the mountain was clearly marked. There was nothing on the map between us and the buses except rocks, trees, and the downhill slope.

Steve and I talked as we looked at the map together. Everything was downhill. The straight line between the let-off point and the buses was about four miles. It seemed like the entire distance would be in timber—fir, pine and some aspen, by the looks of it at the top of the slope. We discussed various plans. Steve said: "Let's go the straight line down, as fast as we can, and just outrun anyone in our way!" It sounded good to me.

So, we started running downhill. We quickly ran past other students carefully picking their way downhill. We ran as fast as our legs would carry us—sometimes too fast. On more than one occasion we couldn't keep up with our legs and found ourselves flying downhill to come to a sudden stop against a tree or a rock. But up we got and down we ran.

On several occasions, we heard gunshots nearby and people

shouting. We figured those were the bad guys, so we sped up—faster and faster—ever downward. About two-thirds of the way down, a guy with a rifle stepped out from behind a tree and shouted at us, "Stop, or I'll shoot." We ignored him and ran right past him as fast as we could, almost flying again. By the time he overcame being startled and ignored, we were well past him and picking up speed. Apparently he decided to pick on slower game, because he didn't give chase.

And so we continued. Near the bottom of the slope we encountered a small stream. It was too wide to jump and looked too deep to wade. Steve and I decided to split up to look for an easy way across the water. Steve went left. I went right. I found a tree lying across the streambed and decided to try out my high-wire act and cross on that slippery tree. It worked. I ran back toward where I left Steve to find him standing in the road near the buses soaking wet. He told me that he had also found a tree to cross the stream, but had slipped off trying to cross and fell into the water. He was OK, he said, just wet. We both laughed with relief and headed toward the first bus in line. Steve was a rock, resourceful and strong. I thought we worked well together. His strengths were important to me in my shaky circumstances and uncertainties.

We weren't the first students at the bus, but we were in the first group. The buses had water jugs and soft seats. We were pretty bushed by then, but happy to be through the final day. Steve and I each picked a seat, laid down, and tried to get some sleep.

When our bus filled, it took us back to base. I called Vicki again and was told that the baby was still not there yet. With training over, I felt like I had to hurry to get to Kansas before the baby came. I hoped that I had enough days of travel ahead of me to get there before that would happen.

I got a shower and a last meal at the mess hall then got on a bus going to Spokane to catch any plane to Wichita. After several days of travel and a few stand-by rides on military aircraft, I finally arrived in Wichita. Vicki's dad picked me up at McConnell Air Force Base and took me to Hutchinson. Vicki was still there, as pregnant as ever, and the doctor said that the following day was to be THE day. I had made it in time.

Vicki went into labor early the next day, and after about 15 hours, she gave birth to our first child. We named her Kelli (out of the air because it sounded good to us) and Jo, after Vicki's sister. Kelli was a beautiful baby. One I would soon be leaving.

It was June 20, 1969. I was due in Florida in four days for combat crew training in the C-123K. After that, I'd be on my way to Vietnam.

TRYING TO KILL THE BEETLE

The beginning and end of the monsoon season in Laos *were always slow mission nights. When the first rains started, they were full and heavy rainfall events. The beginning of the season just meant these heavy showers weren't occurring every day and night—just every other day or night or so. Traffic on the unpaved Ho Chi Minh Trail became very sparse during these heavy showers. Sometimes we would spot a small convoy moving south on the Trail. We usually considered these trucks to be low priority, because Air Force intelligence indicated there were few secondary explosions from attacks on these trucks from other strike aircraft. We assumed they carried men. We attacked them anyway. Enemy soldiers moving from North Vietnam south on the Trail was not a good thing, especially for our military brothers in South Vietnam.*

One night, after a brief but heavy rain shower in our assigned area, we spotted a single, small car driving north on the Trail. All other traffic I had ever seen anywhere on the Trail had always been moving south, away from North Vietnam and toward South Vietnam and Cambodia. When our Navigator/Scope first spotted this vehicle through his Starlight scope, he said it looked like a small car or jeep. So, being curious, we tried to spot it again, which we did as it passed through an open meadow near the Trail. We began to follow it as we called for strike aircraft. The scope eventually got a good look at the vehicle. He said that it looked like a Volkswagen Beetle with the top taken off. We assumed that it was a small Soviet-built command car that looked like an old World War II German command car or what was then driving around in the U.S. as a Volkswagen "Thing." The Soviets called that type of command car a "Frog." We just called it "the Beetle."

Since traffic numbers were down all over the Trail, there were lots of fighters of all kinds and varieties available to us. All pairs of fighters were loitering in different orbits around Laos or northern South Vietnam. We called our highest Airborne Communications and Command Center (ACCC, called "A triple C") aircraft, call sign "Alley Cat," and asked for every fighter-bomber flight we could get. There were at least six flights of slow- and fast-mover fighters nearby available, with all kinds of ordinance aboard. We told Blind Bat, our next-higher ACC Center that we had a "command car" moving north on the Trail and we wanted to kill it. The Blind Bat controller started routing fighters toward us without asking any additional questions. Each set of two fighters were assigned an altitude a thousand feet above each other, so these six pairs were orbiting above us at a 1,000 feet intervals.

We dropped at least eight different groups of ground-burning flares along and across the Trail and directed all six sets of strike aircraft. The Beetle was moving the whole time, so we had to adjust our aim points based on the expected location of the vehicle at the exact time a fighter was at the ordinance-release point. As one pair of fighters dropped bombs or bomblet clusters or napalm or "funny bombs," and informed us that they were "Winchester" (out of ordinance), we would send them home and have the next pair orbiting overhead at a higher altitude descend to strike altitude and direct their ordinance at that fleeing mini-jeep.

Sometimes the Beetle ran under heavy canopy and didn't come out the other side. So we bombed the trees. Sometimes there were stretches of jungle where we sent the fighters into every part where we expected the Beetle to be. Sometimes the bombs, napalm, canister bomblets and bullets came close, but no cigar. We directed, and fighters dropped every piece of ordinance and shot every bullet available to us that night trying to crush that bug. Our Scope even watched as it drove through a small stream in the middle of a meadow and came splashing out the other side, almost tipping over. But it straightened out and continued going north, generally at a speed that was truly crazy, considering it was using only slit convoy lights for headlights and it was a very dark and cloudy night.

We must have directed in 15 tons of bombs and miscellaneous stuff trying to kill that silly little car. But when the last fighter went back to base and Blind Bat told us there were no more fighters or bombs available, we could still see that little car racing north. We knew we had lost. That was one for the Beetle and zero for the good guys.

COMBAT CREW TRAINING

Hurlburt Field, within Eglin Air Force Base, near Fort Walton Beach, Florida, was the home of the Air Commandos, the Special Operations people from WWII fame. It was also where Jimmy Doolittle and his unit trained to take off from aircraft carriers in B-25 twin-engine bombers for an early April, 1942 raid on Tokyo. When I was there, there were still stripes painted across one of the auxiliary fields that represented the exact length of the flight deck of the USS Hornet, the carrier Jimmy and his boys had used to bomb Japan. We could take off on that field in the length of the aircraft carrier flight deck, just like the Doolittle Raiders, but only with our jets on full power. Those Doolittle boys were real heroes and great pilots!

When I arrived in Laredo, to start pilot training there, I met and trained under a Washington, Kansas boy—Don Knedlik (Major Knedlik to me in public). When I arrived at Hurlburt Field, to start my combat crew training there, I was met at the arriving aircraft by another Washington native, Duncan Dodds. Somehow Duncan had found out that I had departed McConnell Air Force Base in Wichita, Kansas, to Eglin. I suspect that my Mother had something to do with that, since she and Clara Dodds were friends in Washington. Duncan was also an Air Force Major and based at Eglin as a Meteorology/Weather officer. Duncan invited me to have dinner with him and his family in Fort Walton Beach. His wife was from Washington also, and both were older than me by four or five years. They were both already out of high school when I started as a freshman. But I knew their families. When I was about 5, I had tagged along with my older brother Tom and his friend Jimmy Dodds (Duncan's youngest brother) to steal a pie from Jimmy's house where his mother had placed it on an open window ledge to cool. Duncan's other younger brother was Calvin, who was called "Toad." Toad was the hero of the Washington High School basketball team when I was in Grade School. I had grown up with all of the Dodds boys.

It was a great gesture to be welcomed to Hurlburt by Duncan and to spend a little time with his family before I started the final phase of my journey to Vietnam. After dinner, very late, Duncan drove me to the Officer's BOQ and helped me check into a room. That was the last time I saw him there. I was too busy trying to learn the C-123 in preparation for my rotation into the war overseas.

Combat crew training at Hurlburt was a blur. Too much input! All we talked about and trained for was Vietnam, except for the time we spent flying low over the beaches near Fort Walton Beach, trying to see the girls sunning topless on the beach, or the times we flew out over the water, where it was shallow, trying to spot sharks, dolphins and manta rays.

We also flew hours and hours of low-level, point-to-point navigation over the piney swamps of that part of Florida, seeing half-sunken timber barges in backwater canals, alligators sunning themselves on logs along creek banks, and miles and miles of flat nothingness making navigation almost impossible. We spent time dropping aerial parachute flares at night, to help the people training on the ground see what they were doing under million candlepower parachute flares.

We spent lots of hours shooting touch and go's, doing all kinds of take-offs and landings, including short-field takeoffs, soft-field takeoffs, assault landings, and extra-steep approaches simulating landing under gunfire. We were getting trained and ready for the C-123K's typical mission in Vietnam, which was carrying cargo and people from place to place (which we called "trash hauling").

We also practiced quick off-loading procedures, like parachute cargo extractions (where a parachute pulls a pallet of cargo out of the open rear door of the airplane while flying two feet above the ground), and hook extractions (where the pallet of cargo is pulled out of the plane by the Loadmaster throwing a hook over a wire stretched a foot off the ground while flying two feet above the wire and hoping the pallet won't get stuck in the door when it starts to go), and quick off-loading and quicker turnarounds for a hasty takeoff under simulated small arms fire. Any of these maneuvers could end in disaster if we had a serious malfunction. The parachute and hook extractions were the most dangerous, since any malfunction could result in our aircraft slamming down on the runway, which we were told usually resulted in a wrecked airplane and damaged pilots.

Somewhere in all that heat and noise and concentrated flying, all the time practicing the skills we were told we would need in Vietnam, I learned I could fly. One day, I was flying with my instructor pilot, chatting while I was doing some difficult assault landings. I discovered I was doing all the right things with the aircraft while thinking ahead to plan the landings and takeoffs and shooting the bull with my instructor. I could fly! It was an amazing self-revelation. My IP had said that I was doing "good," but it wasn't until that point in my training on the C-123 that I finally "felt" the aircraft and could fly that puppy any way I wanted to and any way I needed to for any mission, dangerous or not. I was a pilot! This was how it felt to become a real pilot, in control, in command, doing everything that needed to be done without choking or crashing. Now I knew that I could be a great pilot in Vietnam doing whatever needed to get done. It was my flying epiphany.

That day—the day I realized I had become a real pilot after all—I finished my final assault landing. I came to a complete stop so I could get in the back of the plane and let my fellow student (my stick buddy—Pete Walto) get his share of that day's training. For the first time in over a year, I discovered I could now relax, because I was, at last, a pilot. I sat back on the nylon passenger seats near the part of the cargo compartment where the wheel wells protrude into the compartment, clipped on my seat belt, put my head against the thin aluminum of the wheel well, and closed my eyes to rest for a minute. I fell asleep.

I was rudely awakened just a few minutes into my stick-buddy's flight when he pressed too hard on an assault landing, landed long, and slammed on the brakes too hard, causing both tires to blow out with a loud explosion just behind the skin of the wheel well where my head was leaning. I woke up thinking I was now a dead pilot.

But no real harm was done. Another instructor pilot flew in to pick us up and take us back to the squadron briefing room, where I continued to smile a lot and my stick buddy was forced to endure a very loud, face-to-face debriefing by his instructor and the squadron commander. It was a great day for me, but not a very good one for my stick buddy. But we both graduated. We both succeeded. We were now off to Vietnam. My orders read that I would report to Phan Rang Air Base, Republic of South Vietnam, to join a trash-hauling squadron there.

But first, I had to attend Jungle Survival School at Clark Air Base in the Philippines , which everyone at Hurlburt called "Snake School." The pace was picking up.

REALITY CHECK

In late July, after a hard and sweaty training day in the C-123, I heard on the car radio on my way back to my beachside rental house that Neil Armstrong had walked on the moon that day. I walked down to the end of our rental house property to the edge of the water to catch a breath of air and try to relax a moment. I sat down, looked out toward the bay, and wondered what I was doing learning to fly a Korean-war era airplane to be in Vietnam, with people there who would try to kill me. Somehow, the US had sent a man to the moon. I couldn't understand that night why the powers that be couldn't also find a way to end the war and allow me to stay home with my wife and new daughter. Surely that was possible with all of the power and ingenuity of the American government. Wasn't it? But I knew that the next day would be another grueling day in the cockpit of that old war bus and that pretty soon I'd be in Vietnam trying to stay alive.

In August, near the end of my combat training, Vicki and our new baby daughter, Kelli Jo, joined me in Florida. We had been apart since April, during the last and hardest part of my pilot training days in Laredo. I really had no clue about married life, fatherhood, or even Vicki in a lot of ways. Her sister came to Fort Walton Beach to help with the baby. The idea was that she would help take care of Kelli while Vicki and I had some time alone together. The way it worked out, however, was that the sisters had time together while I was working my ass off in hot, muggy Florida in daytime and nighttime flying exercises. On most days, or in the evenings when I got back to the rental from Hurlburt Field, everyone would be asleep. I would take my one beer out of the fridge, walk out to the beach, and sit there on the sand to finish my day and unwind.

From near the end of pilot training until the time Vicki and Kelli joined me in Florida in August, I had been alone all of that time. Even before joining the Air Force, our lives had been so separate and different that we had never discussed things like starting and raising a family, or religious beliefs, or who we each wanted to be, or me going off to war. During pilot training, before she left for Kansas to have the baby, Vicki and I had very few chances to be alone together and discuss the important issues of our lives. I was consumed by pilot training, afraid much of the time, and deeply concerned about my chance to graduate as a pilot and not get washed out to become a ground pounder somewhere.

We'd been married more than 2 years and we had never even started conversations about most of these important things. Each of those past 2 years had been so different. We had been doing things in such different places and involved in such different events that it seemed like we were merely trying to hold on to the merry-go-round. Much of those years had been in circumstances where we worked apart and came together briefly on some evenings before collapsing into bed. It seemed like there just hadn't been enough time to catch our respective breaths, think about the future, or talk about those things that were important to each of us.

I admit that I didn't consider her outlook very much or her daily problems while I was away flying training jets in Laredo. By the time Florida rolled around and Vietnam grew closer and closer, I realized that I had been alone with my worries and fears for almost two years and I still hadn't fully grasped my role as a loving and thoughtful husband and now new father.

After completion of my combat crew training, Vicki, Kelli, and I drove to Kansas to be with her parents and mine for a few days each. After those brief family reunions, we went on to Topeka to find a suitable apartment where Vicki and Kelli could live while I was away. We found a nice apartment, completely furnished. Again, the time flew by. I was soon on my way to the Topeka airport to catch a plane to Travis Air Force Base, near San Francisco, which was the major port of debarkation to Vietnam.

At Travis, I boarded the "Freedom Bird," which was taking my freedom away, and flew directly from California to the Philippines. And still the pace was picking up.

JUNGLE SURVIVAL SCHOOL

Stepping off the "Freedom Bird" at Clark Air Base was a new experience for me. The weather was hot and humid, the sky was blue with lots of towering cumulus clouds, and the air smelled like warm flowers.

I grabbed a bus to the survival school training headquarters. Standing in front of one of the two-man trailers when I arrived was none other than Steve Pomajzl. The Air Force seems to be a really small world. I was really glad to see Steve—now I had someone I knew I could rely on at Snake School.

Most of the classroom training was similar to the survival school curriculum I had just finished at Fairchild, but with an emphasis on jungle survival, flora and fauna of the jungle, native living methods, local customs, and similar topics. We all knew we were heading for the jungle as pilots, and that meant we could be walking home through a bad-guy jungle some day, so we all paid attention.

After several days of classroom instruction, we were put into small groups and lead into "virgin" jungle by an Air Force instructor and several Negrito natives. The Negritos were indigenous to that part of the Philippines. The adult males were no more than 4 ½ to 5 feet tall. They wore loincloths, and carried spears and bows and arrows made of bamboo. Every male wore a long jungle knife or machete ground down out of automobile leaf springs and sharpened. All were very dark-skinned. None spoke English, except the eldest guide of each group. They spoke a native tongue. They were very friendly to us and invited us into their village to see how they used bamboo for everything, from cooking utensils to clothes to building material. They were the ones who showed us the various plants and trees that were edible or useful in the jungle.

One of the trees was a "water tree." The Negritos showed us how to slice into the bark of the tree with a knife, place a small, hollow piece of bamboo into the slice and then drink from the "straw" in the tree. They said the tree could produce up to five gallons of fresh, potable water every 24 hours. It was like a well with leaves. We also learned about the healing effects of banana tree sap, the edible parts of the palm tree, and lots of similar edible plants. The Negritos also pointed out the snakes, bugs, birds, and other critters that we could eat.

JUNGLE BOY MARKSMAN

In a Negrito village that we were walking through with our instructors and Negrito guides, a small boy, no more than three feet high and probably about 12 or 13 years old, came over to our group and proudly showed us his bamboo bow. The bow was about as tall as he was. He brought along his bamboo arrows.

The string of the bow was a type of vine found in the jungle woven into string or rope. The arrows were about 2 ½ feet long. One end had feathers notched into slices to form the traditional feather end of the arrow. The other end had been sharpened then put into a fire until it was very hard. That pointed end had been split in two about four or five inches down from the tip. A small twig was placed between the split halves at the end to hold the halves away from each other, about an eighth of an inch apart. On the split end were sharpened notches, which looked much like the barb of a fishhook, inside each side of the split.

We tried to ask the boy about the split in the sharp end of the arrow, using lots of sign language, but we couldn't communicate. An elder guide came over and translated. As the elder translated, the boy turned his back to the group and pointed to a tree standing 30 or 40 feet away. The top of the 40-foot tree was probably 50 to 60 feet away, straight line, as the arrow flies. The boy then looked at us and smiled, but no one could see what he was pointing at.

He turned toward the tree again, notched an arrow, pulled back on the string, and let the arrow fly toward the top of that tree. As soon as the arrow passed through the very top leaves, the boy ran over to where it came down point-first in the jungle floor, picked it up and ran back to our group. Wedged in the split, pierced by one of the half-shafts of the point, and held between the splits by the barbs, was a small bird about the size of an English sparrow.

He pointed at the bird, smiled broadly at us, pretended to pick the feathers off the bird, then put it up to his mouth, and rubbed his stomach. This little guy had shot a bird to feed himself. Not only was the bamboo bow and arrow an amazing weapon, but that young boy had just demonstrated how effective it could be.

DEAD BODIES

On one of our treks through virgin jungle, we approached a large area of mature bamboo. The Negrito guide was explaining how the different sizes and lengths of bamboo could be used for different survival purposes. The larger, shorter, and greener sections should be cut in such a way as to be used as a cooking vessel over an open fire. Longer, slimmer sections could be used as spears, bows, arrows, walking sticks and other useful items. While he was talking, one of our group looked further into the grove and started pointing. He then walked over to an instructor and told him that there was something strange in that bamboo grove. We all went to look. The Negrito moved into the grove and started to push smaller stalks of the plants aside. As he did this, we could see the rear end of a strange looking vehicle stuck in the middle of the grove, with large, tall stalks of bamboo standing through the body of the vehicle.

We looked closer and could finally make out an open vehicle, with some canvas fabric sticking to parts of the edge of the open part, and there were bodies inside. The three bodies were mostly skeletons and were in parts of uniforms. The instructor went forward through the grove to stand beside that skewed and skewered vehicle. He came back to the group and told us all to stand away from the grove. He said that the bodies were those of Japanese soldiers, that there were large bullet holes piercing different parts of the body of the vehicle, and that there were still rifles and grenades scattered about inside what he described as a "command car."

The instructor sent our Negrito back to base camp to inform the Air Force to send explosive demolition people out to the bamboo to remove the still live ammunition and grenades and graves registration people to come remove the bodies. It was the summer of 1969.

Those Japanese soldiers had been killed sometime in World War II, more than 25 years before we stopped there. I wasn't sure that was a good lesson to learn about the jungle and its hidden secrets.

SLEEPING WITH JUNGLE RATS

At the end of our training, we were told the "final exam" for snake school was a game the Negritos loved to play. We would all be taken out into the jungle and let loose sometime just before dusk. We would have a head start to try to escape and evade the Negritos. We could either run, hide, or both. We had no limits or boundaries. We were to be released at about 4 p.m. and the Negritos would be released sometime later to find us.

For every one of us they "captured," the Air Force would reward the Negritos with a kilo of rice. We asked how many students usually got caught. The instructor told us the Negrito village had earned about 30 kilos of rice just from the last class. There would be about 20 Negritos out trying to catch about 40 students.

The instructor told us to select a teammate. Each team was given a smoke signal flare, a jungle flare (a small pencil-sized device that would shoot a red flare through the tree canopy up to about 100 feet), and a signal mirror. The only other items allowed were an Air Force survival knife (a sheath knife with a hard steel handle and a 5½-inch blade), a small flashlight, and a camouflaged military poncho.

The rules of the game were that a rescue helicopter would come from Clark Air Base at first light the next morning to find anyone not captured during the night. If any of us avoided capture, we were to signal the helicopter in any way we could. If we were not rescued by the helicopter by noon, we were to make our way back to our release point, to ride a bus back to the base. None of us wanted to be captured and held by the Negritos, but neither did any of us want to ride that bus back to base rather than get a "rescue" helicopter ride in an Air Force HH-3 Jolly Green.

I looked around the large group of students standing near the bus at the release point, and saw Steve Pomajzl looking my way. We smiled at each other, nodded our heads, and told the instructor we were a team ready to hit the jungle.

As soon as we were released, Steve and I hunkered down to discuss our plan, just like the instructors recommended. We couldn't come up with any brilliant ideas, so at last I said: "You know, just running like hell worked in the pine forest of Washington, why wouldn't it work here?" Steve said "OK, let's try that again." We started to run as straight as we could, through the jungle, in the direction that we thought was toward Clark Air Base. We thought that if we could be closest to the base at dawn, we had a good chance of getting picked up first by the helicopter. We also thought that getting as far away from the release point and the Negritos gathered there, as fast as possible, might help us survive the night without being captured.

We ran, rested, and ran some more. We ran in the rain. We ran through elephant-grass patches that had stems several feet higher than our heads. We ran until it got dark and we continued to run. Sometime after sundown, before total darkness fell, Steve ran smack dab into a tall, slender, brown-barked tree. Thud!!

We decided then that we had probably run long enough. We had no idea how far we had come from the release point. We had no real idea if we were still going in the general direction we thought was toward Clark Air Base. We wanted to be the first "escapees" picked up by the rescue chopper at first light, so we decided that since we couldn't safely run any longer, we needed to find a place to hide for the night. We needed a place where the Negritos couldn't scare us to death by jumping on us and dragging us to their camp to be exchanged the next morning for a bag of rice. We walked a little further through the jungle trees until we came to another patch of elephant grass.

Judging by the distance to the tree tops surrounding the field of grass, the patch was about three or four acres and looked approximately round—perhaps 25 yards in diameter. Being the well-trained escapees that we thought we were, we each cut a small length of bamboo from a nearby grove in such a way that no one could see the stub. We then got down on our hands and knees and crawled toward the edge of the grass. We crawled as we had been taught—slowly, moving the grass in front of us out of the way with the stick, then reaching behind us with the stick and moving the grass back and forth behind us to extinguish our trail. Steve led and I followed close behind.

We continued doing the same thing through the elephant grass, crawling until we thought we were approximately in the middle of the patch. We then crawled around and around to create a mat of grass we could use as a mattress to keep us off the damp jungle ground. Finally, we put our ponchos on the ground, stretched out in the hot, muggy, bug-infested grass, and tried to get some sleep. It was pitch BLACK!

Sometime shortly after we had fallen asleep, something began to crawl on me and push at my feet. At first it didn't bother me, because I was so exhausted from running through the darn jungle for so long and ricocheting off trees in the dark. But soon there were a lot of things crawling over and around me, heavy things, sniffing and nibbling at my clothes, and scrabbling around my body. Steve was shaking too, bumping my back (since we were sleeping back-to-back), trying to get those things off him as well. Finally, we both were fully awake. We had one flashlight with us, which we hadn't used before in fear of alerting the Negritos, so I turned it on while I held my hand over the lens and let just a little light ooze out between my fingers. What were those things?

Then we saw the burning red eyes, the prominent teeth, and the huge bodies of jungle rats! They were as big as large housecats—each at least 15 pounds —and there were lots of them. I turned off the flashlight. Seeing those eyes was too darn scary and we still didn't want a Negrito to find us in our hiding place.

Steve and I jumped up and starting kicking the critters away from us, but they kept coming back out of the grass around us. No matter how hard we tried to keep them away, they kept coming back. We stood for some time like that, kicking a rat away whenever one would brush our feet or legs or when one started to nibble or gnaw on our boots or pants leg. But we were both very tired and knew we couldn't keep up the kicking and thrashing all night without drawing attention to our hiding place. We hunkered down to begin a whispered plan to take care of these rats. We decided on our new course of action—we would crawl under our ponchos, lying down back-to-back again, as close as possible, holding down the ponchos with various body parts, as tightly as we could, and try to sleep.

But there was little sleeping going on while there were four or five heavy rats crawling over us all the time, trying to get under a poncho, nibbling at parts of us that had become exposed when we would shake off the rats. During that night, the louder sounds of the jungle started. There were roars and loud squeaks and bird calls that sounded like parrots or vampires. There was a lot of rustling in the grass around us. Sometimes the sounds of the jungle would stop all at once and we thought it might be because of Negritos nearby on the prowl for scared pilots and free rice. But then all of the noises would start up again. They always sounded closer and louder after a silent period.

It was hotter under the poncho. We both knew it was going to be a long night. I looked at my watch every five minutes or so from about 10 p.m. until we finally began to see as the sky began to lighten near dawn. Tired, sweaty, and just a little bit queasy about fighting the huge rats all night, we stood up and watched the jungle brighten around us. It was going to be a pretty jungle morning. Birds and other smaller jungle animals began to caw and crow and squeak and rattle, but we couldn't hear any Negritos coming after us in the elephant grass. So far, we were safe.

Then, when it was light enough to see beyond our ring of jungle grass and surrounding trees, we made out a valley to our east. It was higher than us. We were in a valley ourselves, at a lower elevation than the area we were seeing. We were looking up at the valley and smoke rising inside. About seven or eight miles away, we guessed, we could see a city and an airport nearby. It was Clark. All of our running the night before had, in fact, been in the correct direction. We were closer to the base than we had been when we were released from the buses. And there to the east, as the sun got brighter, rose a giant green helicopter slowly climbing out of the jumble of houses and buildings and it was coming straight toward us. We were going to be rescued—we hoped.

We found our various signaling devices. I took the signal mirror and tried to focus the sun's rays toward that ever-enlarging helicopter coming our way. Steve decided not to use the smoke signaling device in the way we were trained—pulling the pin to ignite the chemical inside the cylinder that makes the smoke, but it would be too hot to hold. Throwing the device to the ground a safe distance away didn't seem like a good idea because of the dry elephant grass all around us. So he decided to use the pen flare, which would send a red flare a hundred feet into the air, or so, much like a Roman candle. He pulled the pin on that device and held it away from his body, pointed up toward the oncoming helicopter. He shot several of those flares. I was still trying to shine the mirror into the cockpit of the helicopter. I was sure that cotton-picking helicopter was going to fly right past us, without seeing our desperate efforts or our puny signaling devices, and leave us stranded in the jungle. This could be another long day trying to find our way back to the release point and the buses that waited there for dummy pilots. We decided that we had better try the smoke-signaling device, since we didn't want to be missed. Steve pulled the safety ring on the cylinder and dropped it to the place in the grass where we had kicked a bare spot. Red smoke immediately started rising above the tall grass around us.

Finally, as it got within a mile or so of our position, the Jolly Green turned more directly toward us. As it flew over the top of us, it wagged its "wings" and did a full slowing turn around us to indicate to us that we had been spotted. We now had to get ready for our rescue pick-up.

As the helicopter approached, Steve stamped out the smoke

device and smashed it into the wet ground so it wouldn't catch anything on fire. We both picked up our ponchos, slightly the worse for wear around the edges (where lots of tiny little teeth had nibbled away the hems leaving stringy fringes). As the helicopter hovered above us, about 50 feet or so high, a crewman lowered a steel cable with a "horse collar" attached. The horse collar was merely a circle of padded material on the end of the cable, which we would place around our body and under our arms, to be lifted up into the chopper. The trick was not to let the collar slip out from under your armpits or you would be a very dangerous falling brick to anyone below.

Steve went first, holding his hands tightly in front of him so his arms didn't fly up when his weight was taken up by the collar. When he had been taken inside the cargo door of the helicopter, the crewman dropped the collar to me. I had that wonderful ride up to the waiting door of the Jolly Green Giant. Steve and I were the first students rescued, so we rode the helicopter for about 45 minutes while others were picked up. When all the seats in the cargo compartment were full, we flew back to Clark.

As tired as we were, Steve and I were still smiling about surviving the night without being caught, living through the attack of the jungle beasts, being first to be rescued, and getting a long ride over much of the jungle we had spent the last few days exploring from the ground. We shook hands and went to our trailers to clean up and get some breakfast. Being rescued was hard work. I'm not sure I could have completed both survival courses without Steve's help.

After that final phase of training, we were given a few days to catch up on rest and do laundry. On the last day of school, we got our travel orders to Vietnam. Steve and I were assigned to the same contract airliner, to be taken from California to Tan Son Nhut Airport in Saigon. From Saigon, we were both assigned to C-123 squadrons. I was to be stationed at Phan Rang Air Base and Steve was assigned to Danang, Republic of Vietnam. The day we landed in Saigon would be the first day of our 365-day tour in Vietnam. Now all we had to do was survive there.

NEW FISH

We flew from California to the Philippines to Saigon in a contract DC-9 airliner. The DC-9 was a long, skinny airplane, and without the first class area and the stewardess sections, it was all one long and narrow tube from the inside. I don't know how many people it seated, but it was full. Everybody was headed into the 'Nam. I don't remember much about that flight except noticing that whenever the aircraft turned, sitting in the back of the plane, I could see the front start to twist and then the part I was sitting in would twist to match the front, and the plane would turn. It looked very weird—like sitting in a long garden hose and watching it twist and turn from the inside. I did wonder if I would ever make it to Saigon, but since this aircraft had been used many times before to transport unlucky guys to Vietnam, my luck would hold and I'd get there safely (probably to get run over by a baggage cart right after landing —crippled and maimed, but not killed).

Upon arrival in Saigon, we walked out of the plane in single file down the roll up stairway. As soon as I hit the door, I was physically struck by the heat and the smell of the airport —a mixture of burning jet fuel and avgas, diesel fumes, and other normal smells of a busy airport in the heat, but also the smell of the jungle, and the paddies, and dirty bodies, and excrement. No one really wanted to get off the plane and walk breathing into that place.

An airman at the bottom of the stairs pointed us toward a building that apparently was the terminal. A sign on the roof said, "Welcome to Tan Son Nhut Airport." We were directed to form a single file and proceed toward that building. As we filed off the plane, a line of soldiers was forming near the terminal building. These were guys who had apparently finished their tour, had survived a year in the jungle, and were eager to climb onto the "Freedom Bird" to fly back home. Many were thin and dirty. Not all had clean or complete uniforms or fatigues. There were no shined shoes among them. Quite a few had red dirt embedded in their faces and backs of their hands.

Now there were two single-file lines moving in opposite directions about a foot or two from each other—a line of clean, fresh troops getting off the plane heading toward the terminal and a line of dirty, disheveled, mean-grinning soldiers shuffling toward freedom.

By the time I reached the bottom of the stairs, the catcalls had already started: "You're never gonna make it" and "If I were you, I'd shoot myself and get the pain over with," and "Look Ma, new fish."

Many of the guys getting on the plane were pretty well loaded with something, probably booze. But there were a few who weren't yelling at us. Those were the ones who scared me the most. They were mostly gaunt and wearing worn out, faded, and torn fatigues. None of them looked at me—except one. He had the scariest eyes I've ever seen. It was the stare —what I thought they meant by "the thousand-yard stare." He looked straight at me as we walked toward each other. As we got almost abreast of each other, he whispered: "You're gonna die here." Then he looked away, as if I didn't matter or didn't exist, and he continued walking toward the aircraft. That brief look and his quiet curse really shook me. I didn't think I was going to like it here.

GOODBYE TO STEVE

We were all herded into the Tan Son Nhut Airport terminal and divided into groups. My group was mostly recent graduates of the C-123 combat crew training class from Hurlburt —Steve included. We were loaded onto a bus and taken to a barracks that had a sign out front identifying the building as the quarters of the Ranch Hand squadron.

The Ranch Hand's squadron was the C-123 unit spraying the forests of Vietnam with defoliant, so the bad guys couldn't hide. When we went into the building, every bunk reeked of a chemical smell they called "Agent Orange," but it smelled like the DDT used on farms around home. Here, in this hot and closed-up building it was everywhere and stronger.

In the morning, we had a quick meal in the mess hall, then were taken back to the airport terminal. When a C-130 Hercules taxied up to the building at mid-morning, we were told that anyone with orders to Phan Rang Air Base should board that plane for the short ride there.

Steve had orders for Danang, so he stayed behind. I didn't know anyone who got on the Herkie Bird (C-130) with me, except Bill Hood, who had also graduated with me in 69-07, Section II. Bill was the only person I knew going to Phan Rang, even though we'd all gone through Hurlburt in C-123s at the same time. It looked like it was going to be a lonely ride to my new home.

"VOLUNTEERS" NEEDED

We landed at Phan Rang, where the sign over the metal building entrance said: "Welcome to Happy Valley." Once we went inside the operations building, we didn't have to wait very long for things to get started. A young Air Force captain gave us a very short "welcome" speech, then asked us to line up "according to height." We had done this several times before, so we knew the drill. Each person looked to see who had been on either side of them before and jumped back in line with the same lieutenant on either side. We did it in a second, compared to the five minutes or so it had taken us the few times before.

In line, a sergeant came to the front and started handing out orders to each of us. These new papers instructed us which squadron we would belong to for the next year. Other documents had to be filled out to make sure that we had performed all of our pre-departure papers in Florida, such as making sure that we each had a will, that our pay allotments were correct and would be sent to the correct person each month, and other routine stuff. When those papers were handed in, a young Airman approached us and went through our individual shot records. Some needed update or booster shots. When that was done, while still standing in our alphabetic line, the sergeant told us to drop trousers and bend over. The Airman then went to each of us and gave a gamma globulin (GG) shot in the bare hip—long needle, large hole. It seemed to go all the way to the bone and left a large lump of fluid deep inside the hip muscle. That seemed to be the final act of our Vietnam welcome. We each pulled up our tan 1505 uniform trousers, straightened our gig lines, and resumed our "at ease" position in line.

The captain then proceeded to read from a sheet of paper, which was to inform us that the Air Force needed five volunteers out of our group to transfer to another base for a different mission. "I can't tell you the name of the base or the mission," he said, "but I am instructed to tell you that the mission is difficult and dangerous and needs the very best pilots."

Several of our slower pilots asked: "Can you tell us where we will be?" and "What will we be doing?" Faced with the usual comprehension capabilities of brand-new second lieutenant pilots, the captain patiently re-read the same speech: "I cannot tell you the name of the base or the mission, but I am instructed to tell you that the mission is difficult and dangerous and needs the very best pilots."

"Well, that explains it," someone said, "the Air Force, in its infinite wisdom, is looking for pilots to command the kitchen police in the local mess hall." Some of us laughed.

Now the captain got serious. "So," he said, "I want five of you young pilots to take a step forward to volunteer for this great opportunity to contribute to the war effort."

No one moved. I wasn't the only guy looking around. We'd all seen the old war movie where the line of soldiers who had been asked to volunteer for a dangerous mission stepped back, leaving the slowest of the line still standing forward, in front of their smarter companions. In the movie, the officer says: "Thank you for volunteering" to those left standing out front. "I know your wives and mothers will be proud of you today." Everybody knew from that movie that none of the "volunteers" ever survived the "dangerous mission." So no one stepped forward and no one stepped back. It was a draw.

Now the captain got more serious.

He told us how important the war was.

Bullshit, I thought. They're rioting back home and throwing chicken blood and rotten eggs on soldiers getting off the Freedom planes from Vietnam. The guys getting on the plane in Saigon told us we'd be sorry.

He told us how much each man could contribute to our country by being assigned to a dangerous unit, and how every man wanted to be a hero to his loved ones back home, and other such nonsense.

He then instructed us again: "I want five of you to take a step forward to volunteer for transfer to a different unit." Again, every one of us looked around at the others, but no one moved. It was either a Mexican standoff or a stalemate, but whatever it was, nothing was happening here. I wasn't going to do that thing, whatever it was. I was just barely comfortable about knowing what unit I was going to be assigned to in Phan Rang—a nice trash-hauling unit, flying from place to place during the day, and spending every night in my own barracks, in my own bed, in a place that didn't look too bad from the runway. After all, it was called "Happy Valley."

Now the captain had a good idea—you could almost see the light bulb go off over his head. He told us to line up by alphabetical order. There was a lot of shuffling and nametag gawking, with some of the guys singing that little alphabet song very quietly to themselves. We finally managed to get into order, again in line.

The captain went to the head of the line and ordered, "Attention." We all snapped to our best military attention—eyes front, arms straight along our legs, fingers slightly curled and thumbs along our pant seams, heels together, toes pointed outward at a 45-degree angle, and waited. The captain then stood in front of the first man in line, Bill Hood. The captain ordered: "Lieutenant Hood, take one step forward!" That first guy was on the spot—if he took the step, he had just "volunteered." If he didn't take that step, he would be in violation of a direct order from a superior officer, and he could become the commander of a local jail cell. So he stepped forward.

The captain then side-stepped to his right, centered on the next man in line and ordered: "Lieutenant Hunter, take one step forward!" At that point, the jig was up. We all knew what was going to happen, and to whom. I looked to my right and counted lieutenants. Even after a second count, just to make sure, I knew I was doomed. I was third in line.

The captain came to stand in front of me. He repeated the order. I too stepped forward—a very unvolunteering volunteer. I was not a happy camper in Happy Valley, but at least I had four other "volunteers" to go with me on our dangerous and difficult mission. The captain moved again and again, and the fourth and fifth volunteer had appeared. Lieutenants Hood, Hunter, Hyland, Jessen, and Johnson had all volunteered. It was officer magic.

An administration sergeant told us to relax while he finished processing all the other newbies. He collected the set of orders that he had previously handed out to the five of us. He then told us we would catch a C-130 later that day back to Saigon, where they would cut new orders for us. We sat down outside the administration building in Happy Valley until the Herkie Bird arrived. We all walked onto that aircraft like zombies, or death-row prisoners walking to the gallows. No one talked or joked—all of us were suddenly scared. We were leaving Happy Valley to go to an unknown place, doing an unknown mission that was difficult and dangerous, and there were only five of us against the world. Hood. Hunter. Hyland. Jessen. Johnson. For some reason, the C-123 pilots who had been given orders to fly to Phan Rang together had been grouped by alphabet, starting with Bill Hood. I thought the U.S. Air Force was such a wonderful thing that they had us lining up and dying in alphabetic order. Maybe this USAF pilot thing wasn't such a good idea after all.

I remembered an old saying that my Dad had told me while I was attending Kansas University: "There we were—80 fighting against 2 —waiting for reinforcements. Well, we got those reinforcements and we killed those two." I felt like it should have been five instead of two. We were off to Saigon too quickly and to an uncertain fate. I had the feeling that the five of us were already outnumbered.

WAITING IN SAIGON

We arrived back at Tan Son Nhut, just as we had earlier. We ended up at the Ranch Hand barracks again and asked to stay a few nights until our orders came.

When we told some of the Ranch Hand pilots what had happened in Phan Rang, we started hearing stories about other pilots who had the same thing happen to them. All of them had just dropped out of sight, never to be heard from again. There were lots of rumors about our new "dangerous" assignment—so many, in fact, we soon learned to discount all of them. Obviously, no one knew for certain what was going to happen to us next.

The first day, we spiffed up in clean uniforms and headed off to the administration building on the airport where we had been told our orders would be prepared. The airman behind the desk told us it would take several days for the orders to get cut. "Come back tomorrow before 5," he said.

So the next day, eager to see where we were going, we went back around 10 a.m., but no orders.

On the next day, we went back again, around noon. No orders.

From the third day on, we just managed to get through the administration building door at 4:59 p.m., and each day, we received the same answer: "Nothing yet, check in tomorrow."

TAKEN FOR A RIDE

The days stretched into a week, so boys being boys, we passed the time by exploring the local area.

During one of my walkabouts, I came to a fenced-in Army compound that included hangars and a helipad. There were several UH-1 (Huey) helicopters parked around the hangars. A door to one of the hangars was open. I could see other helicopters inside being worked on.

I was in my Air Force summer uniform—a tan, short-sleeved shirt with my rank and wings and tan slacks that looked like chinos (called "1505s"), so I thought I could go anywhere on base. I walked around the outside of the hurricane fencing until I came to an opening with a sidewalk that led to a building marked "Operations." That sounded familiar, so I walked on in.

I found an older guy in a flight suit with strange Army rank insignia and asked about the helicopters. I explained that I was a pilot (he smiled), and wanted to see if I could take a helicopter ride someday. He said, "Sure. In fact, I'm getting ready to take one out for a little test hop now. Why don't you come along?" When I asked if I needed to put on a flight suit, or do anything else, he replied, "Nope," grabbed two flight helmets from a table, and out we went. What a nice guy!

I asked him how he got the job as test pilot for Army helicopters. He told me he had been in-country for two tours (two years) and after he had been shot down and crashed in combat for the ninth time, his commander decided his luck had run out in the boonies and made him a test pilot. I thought that was pretty cool —all except that nine times crashed thing. We strolled out to the helicopter. He walked around it quickly, touching something here and shaking something there. He looked it up and down and said "I've been working on this one, but I still need to do a preflight." That was a preflight? He handed me the helmet, I put it on, and he showed me how to tighten the chinstrap. We both got in. He told me that since I was a pilot, and he was a mere test pilot, I should sit in the left seat. In Air Force aircraft, the left seat is reserved for the pilot in command (PIC) or Aircraft Commander (AC). I thought this officer/pilot (of some kind) was giving me the throne, so to speak, with due regard to my pilot wings. Once strapped in, however, he told me that in helicopters, the PIC flies from the right seat. This helicopter stuff was new to me, so I didn't mind the minor misunderstanding that I knew he had caused.

He was still talking as he got the helicopter through the pre-flight routine of button pushing and switch pulling and the starting drill. In very short order, he had the engine running and the rotor blades turning. (Do these guys ever use a checklist like real pilots, I asked myself?) He showed me how to communicate on the intercom and told me not to touch the other button because it would transmit outside the helicopter. Then, without further comment, he pulled up on the stick-thing on the left side of his seat (the "collective" he called it), waved the stick between his legs a bit (the "cyclic" it was called), and took off to a hover about five or six feet above of the concrete helipad. He looked over at me, smiled, and asked: "See how easy that is."

All of a sudden, without warning, he lowered his left arm very quickly and the helicopter dropped all the way back down to the concrete and slammed into the pad at about 10 g's (i.e., 10 times my weight of 1 g, or so it seemed). Before I could comment, he added power to the rotor system by pulling up on the collective stick-thing, climbed five or six feet straight up, then slammed it back down onto the concrete again. I looked out the side window to make sure the skids of the helicopter hadn't spread or gotten twisted in some way. What was this maniac doing, I wondered.

After about the third time, when I finally caught my breath and got my heart rate back to almost normal, I asked him, "What the hell are you doing?"

"Autorotations," he said, as if that explained everything.

I had to ask. "What are autorotations?"

He told me he was making sure the rotor disengaged from the

transmission in case of an engine failure. If it disengaged properly, the helicopter could glide (glide?) to the ground even without the engine running (boy, that was good news). He added that if the rotor didn't disengage correctly, the helicopter would crash if it lost power. That was why he was giving it a test hop, at low altitude first. He went on to say that if the rotor didn't disengage at engine failure in flight, the helicopter would then become a bathtub and with the same characteristics of flight—i.e., NONE. (I wasn't sure what kind of news that was, but I sure knew that I wanted that disengage thingy to work.) Now he tells me, I thought, thinking that I was surely riding with a crazy person in an aircraft that could have the aerodynamics of a brick. This didn't seem like fun.

But before I could tell him I had changed my mind about riding along, he added a surge of power and off we flew. Now I felt better. The thing flew straight and level, pretty much like a real airplane—just noisier.

We flew out over the city of Saigon and into the rice paddy areas outside the city limits. He had me hold onto the stick (the cyclic) and the throttle thing on the left side of my seat (the collective), and he let me fly the helicopter straight and level for a time using the attitude indicator and altimeter on the instrument panel. These round dials looked just like the ones in the T-41 I had flown in the first phase of pilot training. Not so bad: Look at the airspeed indicator, watch the altitude indicator, make sure the tiny wings on the attitude indicator are level and the dot representing the nose of the aircraft are on the horizon line, keep the ball centered in the turn and ball race (his suggestion)—piece of cake. I don't know how long he had me mesmerized by the things going on inside the cockpit that I was doing, but when he finally took back the flight controls, we were way outside the city over nothing but rice paddies.

And then he said it: "Just hold on, I have to do more autorotations to the ground from a thousand feet or so." I looked down and saw nothing but rice paddies—water, floating grass, and mud.

Suddenly, we went straight down. It was like an elevator dropping—my blood going to my head, my butt floating off my seat cushion, and my stomach slamming into the bottom of my throat. We were headed for a crash in the water. He was out of control!

When the helicopter finally hit the rice paddy dike, it was really no harder than we had hit the concrete helipad not long before. We skidded a few feet then came to a halt. There was water, green plants, and mud all around us, just a few feet away on each side of the helicopter skids. We were sitting safely on a dirt dike not much wider than those skids on the bottom of the Huey. I just had time to catch my breath and wonder how the heck he managed to hit such a small strip of ground, when he announced, "Well, hang on, I've got to do that a couple more times, and then we can head back."

As we were climbing out of that first dive to the mud of the dike, I noticed a huge thunderstorm off in the distance, but I couldn't find Saigon. I looked around the inside of the helicopter to see if we had a machine gun, an M-16, a .38 pistol, a water gun, or any other weapon, just in case we couldn't get back to Tan Son Nhut, because this guy was banging the crap out of the Huey in the middle of nowhere.

Somewhere in the second, third, or terminal autorotation to that teeny dike, I also realized he was in a flight suit and combat boots, without any survival vest, while I was wearing chinos and low-cut, tie-on shoes. I noticed that neither of us had a weapon out here in bad-guy country. Between the elevator drops and the thought of having to walk back to Saigon after this Army guy broke his tenth helicopter, I wasn't feeling so great. I was beginning to understand the difference between an Army pilot and an Air Force one. Air Force pilots knew how to fly but didn't know how to hike their butts umpteen miles back to base after breaking their aircraft, but Army guys did. This guy told me during our many adventures together that he was a Warrant Officer, which I didn't know what that meant either. My knowledge and understanding about Army vs. Air Force pilots might have been learned the hard way, and maybe way way too late.

Finally, he declared the aircraft in pretty good shape and turned toward the rainstorm on the horizon. We flew into rain for just a few minutes then the city of Saigon came into view as we punched out the other side of a small rain shower. I felt saved, even though we were *still over rice paddies. There were at least a few roads running around the paddies nearer Saigon and a few small villages nearby. When we got back, I thanked that unknown aviator, turned my back on the helipad, and never, ever went near that place again.*

THE MYSTERIOUS MAJOR

While we waited for orders in Saigon, the days blurred. I didn't want to venture outside the base perimeter. It was just too much—too much noise, too much hubbub, too many strangers, too much fear of the unknown. So I stayed inside and did whatever I could to pass the time.

I didn't see much of the other four —they were out playing somewhere. We all congregated back at the Ranch Hand hooch every evening to eat dinner together somewhere and to have drinks. It was a chance for everyone (but me) to tell their tales of bravado, exploration, and conquest.

One night, after we'd been there about two weeks or so, we decided to go to the largest Officers' Club nearby for dinner and drinks (and to watch the round-eyed girls on the arms of the old guys, mostly generals, and the slant-eyed and skimpier dressed girls on the laps of the younger old guys, mostly colonels). After dinner, we couldn't think of anything exciting to do, so we continued to sit around this nice, big, round table near the stage, ordering drinks, ogling the girls, and telling stories of Saigon adventures and home. While we were sitting there, a major came up to the table and asked if he could join us for dinner, since the other tables were filled with brass (officers much higher ranked than second lieutenants and also higher than majors). He sat down, ordered dinner and a drink, and mostly sat and listened to us youngsters spout off.

After the major finished his meal, he asked if he could buy us all drinks. Well, that started the ball rolling, so each of us had to buy a round of drinks. Somewhere in the midst of the melee, the major asked us what unit we belonged to. Since he outranked us and wore wings, we decided our only recourse was to make stuff up. So we proceeded to tell him all about our secret assignment to a secret base in a secret place doing really dangerous things we couldn't talk about.

The Major finally asked us how we had gotten this rotten and dangerous assignment, so we decided to tell him the truth—we had each stepped forward and volunteered to join the unit when we were asked at Phan Rang Air Base, without hesitation, and before any of the other new C-123 pilots had a chance to volunteer ahead of us. He was duly impressed.

"Where are your orders being cut?" he asked. We told him where we had gone every afternoon for the past week or so.

"Where did they say you were going to be sent?" he then asked. We replied that it was "out of Vietnam," but we couldn't tell him more, because of the secret nature of the assignment. He acted more impressed. He told us how proud he was of us that we had stepped up to the plate and firmly grasped this opportunity to do the right thing with this dangerous unit. He told us he was proud to be in the company of such brave and steadfast men. He even bought another round of drinks for each of us. We were very impressed with ourselves as well.

Somewhere in the middle of all this, the Major excused himself and left the table. When he returned, he told us he was so impressed with the five of us that he'd called a personal contact in Saigon to help us get on our way to our new unit. He said he didn't ask any questions about the secret nature of our assignment, but merely told his friend that "five brave boys" needed some assistance getting orders. He said his friend had assured him our new orders would be cut as soon as possible, and that the five of us should report to the administration office around 1 p.m. the very next day. "Hopefully," he said, "your orders will be ready and you can get on your way." With that, he thanked us for the drinks and said his goodbyes.

We decided we'd better stagger back to the barracks and get some sleep, so we could pack our gear and drag it to the airport by 1:00. I didn't feel so good now that orders were on the way. It felt much safer to be rambling around Tan Son Nhut Air Base than flying off to some unknown destination in the middle of a dangerous war. We all thought that we should have kept our mouths shut. The optimists among us (not me) opined that we were in for better days—we could finally get on with our Air Force careers and fly the venerable C-123 in combat. I wasn't so sure.

Shortly after noon the next day, we dragged our bags and aching heads down to the administration building on the airport. We went together into the office, where the sergeant told us that orders had miraculously appeared just that morning, and that he was holding them.

When asked why, he said a friend of ours called our new unit and asked them to send a bird to pick us up. The sergeant was to give the orders to the pilot of that aircraft.

Well, no one knew what that meant. We were told to sit outside on the ramp and wait for our ride.

Late in the afternoon, after we had tried to get comfortable and snooze on the concrete flight line, the major showed up, all brimming with good humor and rosy cheeks. He asked us about our orders and how we were feeling about finally getting off to war, and lots of other cheery questions. As he did the night before, he continued to ask us questions about the orders and what we had learned about the new unit, and who was picking us up, and on and on and on. We had no answers. We were mystified. And now somewhat scared.

Soon, a C-123 taxied off the runway and onto the ramp in front of the building where we had stacked our stuff. It taxied right toward us and stopped not 50 feet away. We were impressed. That was real service. We asked the Major if that was our ride.

"I don't know," he said. "I'll go out and check for you." When the major came back, a taller man came out with him. As they drew nearer, we could see that the taller man was a Lieutenant Colonel. He was wearing a flight suit, a powder blue baseball cap, and a powder blue and white polka dot ascot around his neck. As they continued toward us, they would stop for a moment while the major said something, then they would bend over with laughter, straighten up and continue walking toward us again. When they finally got to us, we saluted the lieutenant colonel and the major introduced him.

"Gentlemen, this is Lieutenant Colonel Spearel. He's the executive officer of your new unit. He has personally come to pick you up and take you to your new assignment —the 606th Special Operations Squadron."

The lieutenant colonel smiled as he shook each of our hands, then pointed at the major and said, "I understand you already know my operations officer, Major Dixon. He's assured me that you young men are highly motivated and eager to join our special operations unit. He's also told me everything you said about your new assignment. We've been laughing about it ever since he called me last night and asked me to fly here to pick you up."

It seems you can't really trust even older pilots in Vietnam.

He told us to grab our gear, throw it in the airplane, get in, and strap ourselves down. He would cherish the honor, he said, of taking us to the 606th. Sheepishly, we did as he said. The engines started right away, and with the major at the flight controls in the aircraft commander's seat, we started our journey into the unknown.

I was thinking: *We should never have made up those stories about secret missions. We could have stayed out of sight in Saigon for our 365-day tour. Damn!*

LEAVING SAIGON

Even though the side windows in the cargo compartment of the C-123 aren't very big, the late afternoon sun and the number and kinds of vehicles moving nearby—both in the air and on the ground—made the first hour or so of the journey very interesting and enjoyable.

We flew over rice paddies, then atop forested areas with palms, banana trees, and grass-roofed huts. Next, we traveled along the coastline, seeing beautiful beaches, slow white-topped rollers coming in from the sea, high rocky cliffs where the beaches shingled out, and lots and lots of water to our east.

As it got dark, we turned inland again. We could see small villages dotted around the landscape, recognizable by their few lights and small wood fires. Occasionally there were larger towns, with real buildings. We also flew near some Army bases and an Air Force Base or two —no one knew which ones they were, and we didn't want to ask. The further inland we flew, the higher we climbed. A flight engineer came by and told us to cinch ourselves in, because we were headed for some monsoon thunderstorms and would soon be crossing into Laos—bad-guy country. Someone asked if they would shoot at us and the flight engineer just grinned and said: "Oh, yeah!"

Then we flew into the thunderstorm—lots of ups and downs. The cargo compartment got both cold and wet. Lightning was everywhere. Thunder boomed right outside the airplane. Somewhere in the middle of it, the major came down from the cockpit, asked how we were, then proceeded directly to the relief tube to take a leak. We were more impressed with his ability to relieve himself in that short, little black funnel during a thunderstorm than his ability to keep the shiny side of the aircraft up during all that tossing around in the storm.

As for us, we were all tired and shaken, cold and wet, and just a little bit green around the gills. Pilots are meant to fly airplanes, I thought, not ride in the damned things. It was a long ride.

Eventually, we came out of the storm and began a slow descent. The engine sound changed, the wheels thumped down, and flap motors started to spin just over our heads. We knew we were almost to our new home.

Once we landed, we were led to a building located right next to the hangars on the flight line—our new squadron building. We waited inside for about 15 minutes for the major to close down the aircraft log books and make arrangements for the other crew members to put the plane away. Finally he rounded us up, loaded us into a crew bus, and told us he was taking us to the Officers' Club for a drink.

"Welcome to Nakhon Phanom Royal Thai Air Force Base, Thailand," he said, "more affectionately known as "Naked Fanny.""

BOTTLE BUSTERS

The bus dropped us off at the front door of the Officers' Club, a low, single-storied, rambling affair reminiscent of the Officers' Club at Laredo. It was late and I expected it to be fairly quiet, so I wasn't surprised that the main dining room and bar were almost vacant.

"Come on," the Major said, "follow me. We're going to the late bar. Since this base goes on all night, we have different bar hours than most. We have the 5 o'clock happy hour for the strap-hangars and ground-pounders who work nine to five and want their little pick-me-up after work. Then we have the midnight happy hour for night flyers, which include pilots and navigators from our squadron as well as pilots from the different fighter-bomber units who have the early night shift. Then, mostly for us, there's the 4 a.m. happy hour. That's the one that's really wild." I checked my watch. It was just after midnight.

All the time he was telling us this, we were descending some dark stairs toward the sound of rock and roll music coming from somewhere below.

When we got to the bottom of the stairway, we found ourselves in a long dimly-lit, rock-walled basement. The bar was just in front of us to the left, maybe 30 feet of highly polished dark wood. A local man, a Thai, was tending bar and waiting on the five or so others in the room. Behind the stairs to the left were five or six small tables, with two or three men sitting around several of them.

On the far end of the bar, about 30 feet in front of us, were two guys in flight suits, throwing unopened beer bottles at a roughly drawn red bulls-eye on the rock wall about 20 feet away. Both were laughing and talking in a slurred way and getting bottle after bottle from the barman, then throwing the bottles against the wall.

I was amazed at the sound and sight of all that beer foaming and splashing on that far rock wall. I have no idea what rank those two guys had, or what unit they were from, or whether they were pilots or ditch diggers, but they were sure having fun. They were all wet and shouting and cussing. It was bizarre, like a scene from inside an insane asylum.

The Major didn't even pay attention to them. No one else seemed to be paying attention to them either. The barman stood behind the bar polishing glasses with a towel and looking tired and bored. Everyone there appeared to be just guys sitting around, as if nothing unusual was happening at the other end of the bar.

The Major herded us to the other end of the room, selected a couple of tables to pull together, and yelled at the barman to bring us each a beer. "Heineken night," he said, "Special price for happy hour—10 cents a bottle." At least now we knew why those guys were throwing beer. It was so darn cheap.

But why Heineken, I wondered. What a waste. And who were these crazy people? And, of course, I wondered whether or not I'd soon be crazy like the loonies throwing beer bottles at a wall in the basement of the Officers' Club. I hoped not. But at this point, every thing was new. I had just started my Air Force career on a strange base in Thailand. Welcome to Naked Fanny!

MAD MINUTES

★

I don't know who started it, but I do remember getting an *order from my aircraft commander while I was still a copilot that we were going to have a Mad Minute. We always flew the C-123 with all doors, windows, and hatches open or off. The airplane had an open side window on each side of the cockpit, an open escape hatch in the floor of the cargo compartment just aft of the cockpit, a crew entry door on the front left side of the airplane, a crew door on the aft portion of the cargo compartment (for parachutists), and a back ramp that opened the entire rear end of the cargo area.*

When the aircraft commander gave the order, all 10 crewmembers would shoot their .38 Special revolvers, loaded with tracer ammunition, out of the nearest opening. The commander told us not to shoot any part of the plane or propeller, but otherwise "give the gomers hell." Each one of us shot six rounds of tracer ammo every which way out of the aircraft. It wasn't much—peashooters against anti-aircraft cannon—but it was all we had and we felt a whole lot better afterward.

I thought it was a great idea. I ordered a Mad Minute every month or so when I became an aircraft commander with my own crews. It was a great way to let off steam and a chance to shoot back at the frightening blackness that held lots and lots of bigger guns shooting at us. We were always "alone, unarmed and afraid as hell," so this was our chance to give back a little.

GETTING STARTED

For a few weeks or so, all we did was fill out paperwork, get briefings about the mission of the 606th Special Operations Squadron, get shown where the various parts of the base were located, and other mundane chores of settling into our new home.

The most interesting briefings had to do with our new jobs as night forward air controllers over the Ho Chi Minh Trail in Laos. All of us had top secret clearances, but we had to sign and sign and sign that we wouldn't discuss our mission with anybody, ever, and that we would never, never, never talk to anyone about where we were flying. Since the government publicly maintained that the U.S. was not involved in Laos, we were all threatened—repeatedly—with court-martials and firing squads if we even breathed a word about our mission and where we worked.

These threats and briefings were conducted in the Tactical Units Operations Center (TUOC), a separate building near the flight line surrounded by 8-foot high hurricane fence and an armed guard posted at the front door. Even more ominous were two strange pieces of equipment standing near the gate, inside the wire. A single-barreled cannon on wheels (which we later learned was a captured Soviet 37mm anti-aircraft cannon, plentiful along the Ho Chi Minh Trail) and a red, 30-gallon barrel half-full of sand, with a sign taped to the outside that said: "Clear all weapons before entering building," whatever the hell that meant. Lots of questions came to mind about that big anti-aircraft cannon with Russian-language markings all over it and that little red barrel. I had a lot to learn.

Inside the operations center was a fairly large briefing room. It had radios along the side and back and a small platform holding lots of different maps at the front.

The most interesting feature of the larger room was the aerial photo map of the Trail, in large scale, showing lots of detail (rivers, open meadows, bomb craters, jungle, some small villages, and other topographical and noteworthy features, both natural and man-made). This, they told us, was where we were going to earn our money as brand-new first lieutenants and forward air controller pilots. The next map they showed us truly scared the bejesus out me—it was a smaller scale map that showed how far the Trail was from NKP and how much jungle, mountains, rivers, and rocks there were in between. It sure looked like we were going to be working a long way from home.

A string hanging on the map could be used to determine distance and direction from Nakhon Phanom. Having flown the C-123 long enough at Hurlburt Field, I guesstimated that the closest part of the Trail to this base was more than a hundred and fifty miles away—about an hour's flight time.

But the real scary parts of that map were the areas showing the northern and southern ends of the Trail that were in our area of operations. The northern end was directly west of North Vietnam, with roads and highways running directly west out of Hanoi into Laos. Another highway out of North Vietnam ran out of the southern end of that country into an area called the Plain of Jars. There was also a highway further north in Laos that ran through a village called Ban-Ban. That road was a long, long way from where I now stood. That entire area, in our new AO designated "Barrel Roll" was more than 200 miles away—an hour-and-a-half flight, or longer.

The southern area was called "Steel Tiger," and ran all the way down the eastern border of Laos to the Cambodian border, which was south and west of the Marine base in South Vietnam called Khe Sahn. It looked to be a little over an hour and a half's flight time away from our base in Thailand. Parts of the Trail in northern, northwestern, southern, and southeastern Laos were even further away. It wasn't the flight time to the Trail in those distant areas that scared me, it was the walking distance and the bad stuff in-between.

That map was a real thought-provoker.

TRUCK KILLERS

During that first week, the squadron operations officer and his assistant explained our mission. In specific, down-to-the-bone detail, they told us what we would be doing as pilots in the 606th Special Operations Squadron. He informed us that our call sign on the radios would be "Candlestick." The unit's unofficial motto was "Truck Killers." That was to be our job—authorizing and directing fighter-bomber airstrikes against North Vietnamese trucks, war materiel, and personnel on and along the Ho Chi Minh Trail in Laos.

As forward air controllers, we would be going out over the Trail at night, looking for enemy trucks, camps, storage sites, anti-aircraft gun positions, and other enemy areas, then call in and direct Air Force, Navy, and Marine aircraft to drop ordinance (bombs, napalm, cannon-fire, bomb clusters or bomblets, napalm, etc.) on those enemy sites.

We were to be the controllers of the airspace in our assigned portion of Laos. We would give each fighter-bomber a report of his performance, called a battle damage assessment (BDA) after each strike. We would report enemy troops killed and equipment and trucks destroyed.

We would provide light to any ground forces in Laos, i.e., Laotian Army fighters, by aerial flares to any friendly soldier who requested illumination. These flares burned at two million candlepower and would remain airborne for 3 to 5 minutes. We would act as on-scene commanders for any aircraft shot down and help pilots who had to bail out, in any way we could. We would report any intelligence information we heard or saw in our assigned areas.

It sounded like it was a lot to do, flying the huge, old C-123K cargo planes we affectionately called "Thunder Buzzards."

MY DOLLAR RIDE

My first night combat mission was called a "dollar ride." I was to be a passenger only, and not in the cockpit except to stand between the pilot and copilot and watch and listen to what they did during a combat mission. The day before our mission, we were given our instructions at squadron headquarters. We also got several unique and interesting items to place in our flight suits in addition to the usual things already stored in our survival vests. Our vests routinely carried a Smith & Wesson Model 10 .38 caliber revolver, ammunition, compass, KaBar knife, AF pilot's survival knife, a small survival radio (PRC-90, which had the emergency frequency and an alternate frequency built in), extra radio battery, rubber water container, first aid items, and other bits and pieces to be used in case of being shot down over the jungle. The ALSE (Aircrew Life Support Equipment) personnel offered me a round metal plate, about 1 inch in thickness, that some aircrew members used as bullet protection. I asked the instructor pilot on my first flight about that plate. He said few pilots used the plate, since both pilots sat in an armored seat with a back parachute on. He did, however, say that a few other crewmembers did take the plate to sit on, to protect their special body parts from bullets and AAA coming up through the bottom of the aircraft. I decided to skip the bulletproof plate, since I was already carrying so much gear. I hoped that wasn't going to be a big and messy body part mistake.

One special item in our survival vests was a normal-looking wooden pencil with a sharpened lead point. We learned that the lead point extended only about an inch inside the pencil. The rest of the pencil shaft was drilled out and a round, steel-cutting file was placed inside the wooden part. That file was accessed by pulling off the eraser and tipping it out of the pencil. It was to be used as a file to cut steel bars should we become prisoners of war in a North Vietnamese prison camp.

Another interesting item was a small "button" compass, about twice the size of a normal aspirin. We were told to swallow the compass if we were captured, then retrieve it from the latrine after a bowel movement, so we could use it to escape.

We were also given a short, flexible steel saw with a ring on each end and another small, flat, steel-cutting file about the length of a ballpoint pen and as thick as a penny, both of which could be used to cut through steel or steel bars to escape.

Another important item kept in the safe at the survival shack, to be placed in our survival vests before each mission, was a "blood chit" and several gold one-ounce Kruegerand coins. The blood chit was a rectangle of silk cloth with several paragraphs of different languages printed on it. The words on the chit generally stated that the person carrying the map was an American soldier or airman and that anyone finding this person and helping him to get to American lines or an American military base would be rewarded with payment in gold. The gold coins were to be used to pay our way back to any friendly camp or base if shot down.

The final item was a rubber map, about three feet square, showing the topography, rivers, towns, and other important information of Laos and surrounding countries. The map would be used to help us return to NKP if we were shot down and could also be used as a shelter, water carrier, and multiple other uses during a survival situation.

During the mission briefing, I met with my instructor pilot and his copilot. New pilots to the squadron were usually assigned an instructor pilot, who would teach them the ropes and help them get started toward upgrading from copilot to aircraft commander. Until that upgrade, I would be the copilot for several instructor pilots in the unit.

I learned before that first ride that these mentor/instructor pilots were special people. Most were older than me and my contemporaries. Many had been selected from active duty Air Force positions because they were either high-time and well-experienced pilots or they had previously been assigned and flown the C-123, or both. Several had Ph.D. degrees. There was at least one Aeronautical Engineer among them who had come from an engineering division back into the cockpit. All were very experienced senior command pilots. I was lucky enough to be assigned to Major Glen McNutt and Major Al Vivona. Both were exceptional pilots and both were very qualified instructors, dedicated to helping me and my friends learn the art and science of forward air controlling and surviving the dangerous environment of free-fire zone Laos.

My dollar ride was an early one—we were scheduled to take off about 10 p.m. That night, we met at the airplane and started our pre-flight inspections. Since there were 10 crewmembers and each had a different flying schedule, most crews were different for each night's mission. The aircraft commander (AC)—who was the pilot in charge of the rest of the crew (regardless of rank)—discussed the mission, each person's responsibilities, and emergency procedures for all crewmembers. The aircraft commander's job was to try to forge each crew into an efficient working team, each night, to be able to accomplish the assigned mission and get home in one piece.

Each person made himself ready for a sweaty and dangerous night over the Trail. After the pilots' preflight of the aircraft and the mission brief by the AC, I was surprised to learn about the squadron's usual practice of having the flare kickers bring food. The flare kickers were not rated aircrew members. Each was an Airman who had another primary job on base, but volunteered to help our Loadmasters with the deployment of parachute flares. Their job was to load flares into the holding box in the middle of the cargo compartment before flight, move that box to the rear of the aircraft during flight, position it near the upward opening rear cargo door, load flares into the flare chutes before a "Candle" mission, and push flares out of the aircraft when light was needed below. Additionally, these brave young men stood near an open door or window during each flight to call out AAA rounds coming toward the aircraft from enemy gun positions along the Trail. Since these volunteers were selected from a larger list of volunteers, it seemed like the Squadron Commander seemed to prefer cooks as flare kickers, since they were the ones who could bring treats from the enlisted men's mess hall each night.

Before each flight, we all went to the back of the aircraft where goodies and drinks (usually Kool-Aid, iced tea, and coffee) were placed for everyone to snack on. These were the treats provided by the flare kickers. When the AC decided to start the flight, he indicated that it was "time to saddle up." Everyone climbed into the aircraft and started their respective checklist. Engines were started, the pilots taxied the aircraft to the end of the runway and performed power checks on the engines. When all of the checklists of each crewmember had been completed, the pilot radioed: "NKP Tower, Candle 454 ready for takeoff," on tower frequency. "Candle, NKP tower, cleared for takeoff." The pilot started the jet engines, made sure both were running at 100%, ran the radials up to full power calculated for that night, held the brakes until all four engines stabilized and the pilot confirmed that everyone was ready for takeoff. With that confirmation, the pilot released the brakes and started the takeoff roll. Shortly, the plane was airborne. There was little takeoff roll, because the airplane was light, having only 10 people on board (tonight there were 11 with me as the extra dead weight) and a pallet of parachute flares. The plane weighed well below the maximum takeoff gross weight. As the pilot ordered the gear to be raised ("gear up") and the flaps raised ("flaps up), the airplane started to climb into that hot and muggy Thailand night. My first mission had begun. I would complete 164 more of them, first as copilot, and later as a fully trained and qualified aircraft commander. Tonight was going to be interesting.

THE AIRCRAFT

In 1969, our C-123s were old. The aircraft stationed at NKP had already been in theater for about two years when I arrived. Most had a lot of flying time. Despite that, they were strong and handled well. Most pilots became very fond of them, because they helped us find the enemy along the Trail, protected us from anti-aircraft artillery fire during airstrike missions, and brought us home every night.

The C-123K was a twin radial-engine cargo plane with two additional jet engines attached to the lower side of the wing in pods, outside of the radials. The old-fashioned radial engines were Pratt & Whitney R-2800-99 engines with 18 cylinders in two rows of nine centered around the crankshaft. The propeller was attached directly to the crankshaft. The engines in rows encircled the crankshaft and fired in a sequence that resulted in a circular motion and which powered the propeller around. Most of the aircraft were built in the mid-1950's. It was a high-wing, high-tailed aircraft with an opening in the back of the main fuselage to load cargo or troops. It had the capacity to carry about 25,000 pounds of cargo, 60 passengers, or 40 fully loaded combat soldiers or paratroopers. Made during the Korean War from a design for a large cargo glider, C-123s still had a ring in the very front of the aircraft on the tip of the nose, covered by a round aluminum plate, where the towing line was to be attached for the airframe as a glider. These aircraft had been built by Fairchild Aircraft Company and designated the "Provider."

The aircraft statistics were: Length, 76' 3"; Wingspan, 110'; Empty Weight, 35,360#; Max Takeoff Weight, 60,000#; Max speed, 228 mph; Cruise speed, 173 mph; and range at normal cruise, 1,035 miles. It normally carried a crew of 4 for pre-Candlestick missions.

The two jet engines, which were J85-GE-17 turbojets used

115/145 aviation gas. These engines were auxiliaries used for heavy weight operations, takeoffs, or in case one of the radials failed in flight. These small jet engines were the same models that I had become familiar with earlier, since they were also used to power the T-38. However, in the C-123, these engines burned aviation gas, rather than JP-4. As a result, the exhaust edge at the very back of each jet engine was coated with lead from the burning of the av gas. We were warned not to touch these parts, because any wound caused by the sharp edge could result in fatal lead poisoning very quickly.

The Provider earned the "buzzard" nickname because they were so loud on take-off with all four engines running. They looked sort of funny in flight, kind of awkward and ungainly with their fat bodies and high tails. Each aircraft was painted varied green and black camouflage on the top, and black along the entire bottom. Only Candlestick C-123's had the black bottom. All other C-123's in the Thailand or Vietnam theater had white bottoms, because they flew during the day and that paint scheme would help reduce their visibility by enemy soldiers on the ground looking up toward the sky. Ours were black, to help hide us in the dark nighttime sky over Laos.

MY FIRST COURT MARTIAL

It was Air Force procedure to check each aircraft thoroughly before every flight. *Part of that "pre-flight" included the computation of engine output from the aircraft operator's manual (the "Dash-One"), based upon temperature and pressure altitude of that day compared to a graphed "perfect" engine operation parameters shown in the manual. The final check of the aircraft just before takeoff required that the pilot (AC) run up the engine on the taxiway just prior to taking the active runway for takeoff, hold the brakes, and compare the actual engine readings on the instrument panel to the pre-flight output calculated from the Dash-One. The actual engine output was shown inside the aircraft cockpit by an instrument called a "torque gauge." This instrument displayed the actual amount of torque, or output, being generated by each of the two radial engines (one gauge for each engine).*

Air Force policy dictated that if the actual torque of the engine, displayed just prior to takeoff, did not fall within 10% of the pre-flight, calculated figure from the manual, the AC was required to abort the takeoff, take the airplane back to the parking area (the "ramp"), shut off the engines, write up the deficiency in the aircraft logbook, and walk away, leaving the aircraft for the mechanics to fix.

It was also Air Force policy that the Aircraft Commander is the absolute "captain of his ship." He is the only person who can decide how an aircraft can be operated during each flight.

All flights technically begin when the aircraft taxies under its own power from the parking ramp. AC status is independent of rank, i.e., a 2nd Lieutenant AC can order a Colonel or a General, that is, anyone who is acting as co-pilot (CP), navigator, or any other person in a flight position (crew member), to do whatever the AC wants and directs during the flight. This procedure is inviolate in the Air Force, just as it is in the Navy regarding commanders of naval vessels.

I was upgraded from being a co-pilot to AC after I had been in country about five months. This occurred primarily because I volunteered to fly more missions than my contemporaries (who liked to do other things, including spending time in the local town of NKP). As a result, I usually flew with the other guys who I came to NKP with, who were still co-pilots but only a few hours behind me. In that way, pilots would fly together that had about equal flying time in-country (combat time), as opposed to having a new AC fly with a low combat-time co-pilot. Recently advanced ACs flying with a higher-time AC acting as co-pilot could sometimes cause problems with egos, in spite of AF tradition and policy.

All of our aircraft at NKP were so old that they never performed within the calculated, pre-flight torque parameters required by the Air Force. Even though we took off at night, which was the coolest portion of each day in the tropics, it was generally warm enough to degrade the output of the old radial engines. We all knew that. We checked every aircraft every night and flew even though the torque gauges displayed engine output usually below the pre-flight calculations. Many checked out below the 90% required. Although the regulations required that engine performance meet the calculated standard, each pilot knew that no aircraft could do that except on very unusually cool nights.

One night, I was assigned a flight engineer who seemed to always have mechanical problems with the aircraft that prevented the takeoff for a combat mission. Or, after takeoff, the aircraft would return to NKP with mechanical problems, observed by that engineer. There always seemed to be something wrong or some problem with an engine that prevented this particular flight engineer from going on combat missions. Additionally, he had another job on the base that required him to be assigned to only a few combat missions a month. Other flight engineers told me that many of this particular engineer's combat flights mysteriously never made it out of the local airport area or to the area of combat operations. So, he wasn't assigned to many flights, but of those few, many were aborted on takeoff or shortly after. Anyway, that was the scuttlebutt among the pilots and flight engineers in the 606th.

Each night before every flight, after the aircraft had been examined and pre-flighted, both inside and out, the entire crew would meet at the back of the aircraft to sit on the lowered ramp, chit-chat, eat food brought out to the plane by the flare kickers, and prepare for the AC to brief the crew about each night's mission. So that night, in my briefing as AC, I specifically instructed this particular engineer to tell me of any and all mechanical problems he found with the aircraft before flight or after takeoff. He didn't report any pre-flight problems to me. It was the flight engineer's job during the takeoff roll to monitor the engine instruments and inform the AC of any problems. It was also his duty to announce any problem to the AC that might be dangerous if the takeoff was continued and shout "Abort!" during that critical phase of flight. Those were the usual and stated duties of the Flight Engineer, by Air Force regulations and squadron policies. However, that night, I instructed the flight engineer to first tell me about any problems that he saw with aircraft performance, so I could look at and consider the threat posed by any such difficulty, and then I, as AC, would inform the crewmembers whether we would abort the mission or continue—not the Flight Engineer.

The usual briefings instructed the flight engineer to call the words: "abort, abort, abort," and the pilot flying the aircraft would then abort the takeoff and evaluate the circumstances that caused the flight engineer to shout that warning. I informed the crew that if that occurred, I would evaluate the perceived problem during the takeoff roll, while continuing the takeoff, and then I would decide whether to abort or continue. If I decided the aircraft was unsafe in any way, I would state "abort, abort, abort" over the intercom, stop the aircraft from taking off, and taxi back to the ramp.

Just prior to takeoff, per AF procedures, I ran the engines to takeoff power and stated aloud on the crew intercom that the engines were not up to the pre-flight calculations. I then stated that I would continue the takeoff in spite of the low readings on the torque gauges. Sure enough, a few seconds into the takeoff roll, the wussy flight engineer cried: "abort, abort, abort." I asked him "what is the problem" (while continuing the takeoff roll). He stated that the torque gauges were too low and out of limits. I said "Bullshit," or words to that effect, and stated that I would continue the takeoff roll and the mission in spite of the low torque readings.

I continued the takeoff, flew to our area of operations, flew our normal 4 hour mission putting in air strikes and dodging anti-aircraft fire (AAA), and returned to base (RTB) about 3:00 a.m., one of our normal landing times. All during the mission, I noted that the flight engineer was very nervous. He suggested several times that he was worried about our "bad" engines and also suggested that we RTB early. After several such suggestions, I told the flight engineer to "quit whining and do your job."

At about 9:00 a.m. the morning after that memorable mission, I received a summons by one of the squadron administrative staff to report to the squadron commander. During my year's tour in Thailand, I had three different squadron commanders. This one was relatively new to the unit, but had already earned his reputation with the pilots as a "paper eater," i.e., a pilot who would rather work on paperwork in an office than fly a combat mission (as opposed to a commander who liked to fly combat missions—a "tiger" or "killer" in our vernacular—of which I had several).

I reported to the squadron commander's office as requested and found the flight engineer from the previous night's mission also waiting outside the commander's door. We were both summoned into the presence of the commander together. The commander proceeded to inquire of me, in stern and accusatory tones, why I had not obeyed the instructions of the flight engineer the previous night. He stated that AF regulations required any dangerous flight to be terminated or aborted by the flight engineer if he determined any condition that would be dangerous to continued flight. I tried to explain to the Squadron Commander that I had given specific instructions in my AC's briefing about what the flight engineer was directed to do in case of any difficulties he might see. I acknowledged that my briefing had not been the "usual" one, but that it was my decision and prerogative to brief whatever I wanted, because I was the Aircraft Commander.

Although he acknowledged that I had the right to run my crew however I wanted, he nonetheless proceeded to chew my ass for about 15 minutes. His primary theme was that he was a former MAC (Military Airlift Command) pilot before he was assigned to the 606th. He said that the flight engineer had also been a MAC flight engineer prior to his assignment to this squadron. Because of the flight engineer's previous experience level, the flight engineer's previous training in MAC, and my young age as Aircraft Commander, I should have aborted the takeoff that night solely on the flight engineer's call. He also stated that I had violated Air Force regulations by continuing to fly an aircraft that was not performing to AF standards, as required by the pre-flight calculations of engine output (torque). Because of that violation, I had needlessly endangered the lives of all ten crewmembers aboard that aircraft, including myself. The fact that I had successfully completed the mission was outweighed by my careless disregard for the requirement that C-123's should not takeoff if the "run-up" torque just before takeoff was not within the stated requirements of the pre-flight calculations.

Of course the squadron commander's ass chewing made me a little angry. I asked the Commander if I could speak to him frankly without the presence of the Flight Engineer. He excused the FE and told me to speak my piece. I told him that the reason I had briefed my crew as I had was based upon my 6 or 7 months' experience at NKP, with these particular aircraft, of which none would perform to the Air Force's required standards based on the pre-flight calculations. The squadron commander was appalled by my accusation that these old aircraft could not perform according to their designed specifications. He said that he should write a letter of reprimand and put it into my personnel file, stating that I was unfit to remain an Aircraft Commander.

Getting a little hotter myself, and racing my mouth before engaging my brain, I asked the squadron commander to select any number of the squadron's C-123's, calculate the expected engine output from the aircraft manuals just as we do as part of all pre-flight checks, then take those aircraft out to the takeoff point and do the run-up check as "procedures" dictated. I told him that if any aircraft that he would select could pass the AF requirements for actual engine output compared to pre-flight calculations, I would accept the letter of reprimand he wanted to place in my personnel record.

He said, that because I'm such a hot-shot, First Lieutenant smart mouth, if any aircraft did pass the run-up test, he would not write a letter of reprimand, but personally ask that I be court-martialed for my reckless endangerment of my crew. He said that he would personally check 3 or 4 aircraft, selected at random, that very evening, to test for actual engine output. He also stated that if my stupid statement was true, which of course he knew that it wasn't, he would have to ground all of the squadron aircraft, and we wouldn't be able to fly or perform our missions until any and all deficient aircraft were repaired (a really bad idea for a Commander, who has to report all squadron deficiencies, including aircraft groundings, to higher headquarters).

That evening, after the earlier missions had already taken off, the Commander went out to the flight line, with an experienced Flight Engineer he trusted, to prove me wrong. He selected 3 or 4 aircraft. He calculated their expected engine output as provided in the Dash-One. He then taxied each aircraft to the takeoff end of the runway and performed a run-up test to compare calculated torque output to actual output shown on the torque gauges. None of those first few engines passed the test. He tried several more. No aircraft he selected passed the run-up test.

The squadron commander did not call me back into his office to tell me the results of his survey, but his Executive Officer (XO—the second in command of the squadron) did inform me the next day that all engines on all aircraft tested had failed. He also told me that I would not be given a letter of reprimand. The XO went on to inform me that I would never be given that same flight engineer ever again.

The XO informed me of what had happened. It seems that the squadron commander discussed the problem of our old aircraft with his commander, who was the Wing Commander of NKP. He found out that if he grounded all of the C123's in the unit and was unable *to perform the mission he was assigned, he would lose his job, receive a letter of reprimand in his own personnel file, and be sent back to the US to a MAC squadron where he would be "just another pilot" (a disgrace to any squadron commander).*

I didn't really know if every aircraft performed under the calculated pre-flight torque, but since I suspected that was true after flying most of the C-123's in the unit, I let my mouth run off on it's own. I had been lucky.

I, and all of the rest of the pilots in the unit, continued to fly full missions in the C-123 with their aircraft technically violating the requirements of Air Force policy with regard to the torque output of their engines at the run-up test.

Since it was a small squadron, I kept some track of the flight engineer and learned that he had given up flying and was devoting his full time to his other office tasks as a "ground-pounder" or "desk jockey." I also learned that the squadron commander continued to consider me a "smart-ass" and that he continued to monitor me to make sure that I did not endanger my crew needlessly again. We didn't see each other often, because he worked during the day shuffling his important papers and I flew at night. But when we occasionally saw each other, I was always uncomfortable. It was almost like he was watching me, trying to catch me in something that he could really hang me out to dry. And it wasn't long in coming.

Steve Pomajzl at Snake School

Me at Snake School

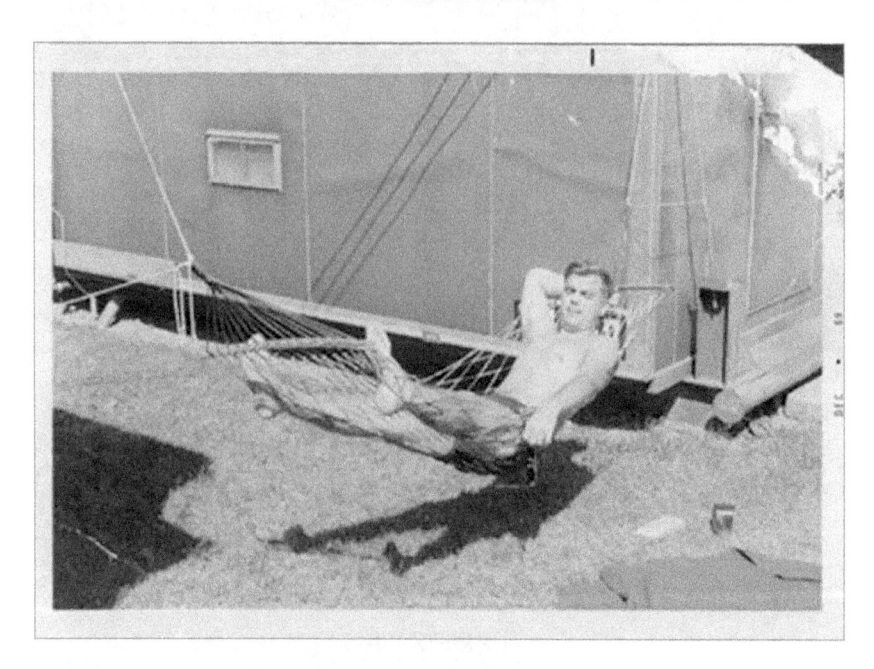

Me catching a nap outside my trailer

My party suit

Lt. Colonel Firebaugh, on left, and me.

Half a flight Crew on a crew bus

DEPARTMENT OF THE AIR FORCE
HEADQUARTERS 3640th PILOT TRAINING WING (ATC)
LAREDO AIR FORCE BASE, TEXAS 78040

AERONAUTICAL ORDER   14 May 1969
50

The following 2D LTs (unless otherwise indicated), 3641 Stu Sq, having successfully completed Crs 111103, UPT, Class 69-07, graduating 23 May 69, are awarded the aero rating of Plt, eff 23 May 69, per para 1-14c(1), AFM 35-13, and are rqr to participate freq and reg in aerial flts in such rating per Sec 102, EO 11157, 22 Jun 64, and para 2-5a, AFM 35-13. FSC changed from 7Y to 1Y. Off will comply with para 2-10, AFM 35-13. Auth: Para 1-7b(1), AFM 35-13.

NAME	AFSN	SSAN
PAUL JOSEPH GRIGNOT JR (CAPT)		
BANKS GOODALE PREVATT (CAPT)		
DONALD BIRCH MORROW (1ST LT)		
THOMAS MANFRED POWER (1ST LT)		
BERNARD JOSEPH PRAIRIE (1ST LT)		
GLENN DORRELL BERGDORF		
TIMOTHY JOE BOLLINGER		
JOHN DAVID BRYANT		
ANTONE STEPHEN BULAT		
RONALD JOHN CHADEK		
DOHRMAN GRAY CRAWFORD JR		
JOHN GEORGE CROSSEN		
ROBERT JOHN DICKINSON		
JOHN DALE GREEN		
HARLAND SCOTT HANSON		
THOMAS EDWARD HAUBER		
JAY DOUGLAS HAYDEN JR		
WILLIAM RANDOLPH HOOD		
CLARENCE ARNEL HUSTRULID JR		
JAMES PATRICK HYLAND		
DENNIS PETER JACOBS		
HORACE EARL JOHNSON		
RICHARD LEE JONES		
PETER WATSON KELLY		
JAMES HAROLD KLING		
COLIN DAVID KOWALSKI		
DENNIS LAURENCE KRUG		
JOHN OTIS LABOULIERE		
JAMES GROVER McMAINS		
KEVIN MICHAEL MAHAN		

AO-50

Class 69-07 at pilot training

AO-50, HQ 3640 PLT TNG WG (ATC), LAREDO AFB TX 78040, 14 May 69.

NAME	AFSN	SSAN
RICHARD RAY MARTIN		
DONALD ARTHUR MESSIER		
JAMES LESTER MOLSTAD		
ROBERT THOMAS MONTGOMERY		
THOMAS MICHAEL MULLEN		
ROBERT WILLIAM OGREN JR		
JOHN LOUIS PEEKE		
STEPHEN LEE POMAJZL		
JOSEPH RUSSELL PRESTON		
MARION GRAHAM PRITCHARD JR		
ROBERT THOMAS SHANNON III		
ROBERT BRUCE SKANCHY		
JAMES LYNN SMITH		
ROBERT THOMAS SNELLGROVE		
PETER ALAN WALTO		
LARRY DAVID WITTE		

FOR THE COMMANDER

SAN..........., 2d Lt, USAF
Chief of Administration

DISTRIBUTION
A Plus
46 DCO-S
46 SG-AM
46 CBPO-SA
1 MCS-EM
1 Hq ATC (ATPPR-CF)
1 USAFMPC (AFPMAJD), Randolph AFB TX 78148
1 USAFMPC (AFPMDRO), Randolph AFB TX 78148

RECEIPT ACKNOWLEDGED _____ IAW para 2-10, AFM 35-13.
(time & date)

2

Class 69-07 at pilot training

```
DEPARTMENT OF THE AIR FORCE
606TH SPECIAL OPERATIONS SQUADRON (PACAF)
APO SAN FRANCISCO CALIF 96310

SPECIAL ORDER                                              1 November 1969
74

1. Special Order 64, paragraph 2, 1 October 1969, is hereby rescinded.

2. The following named personnel assigned/attached to the 606th Special
Operations Squadron for flying are hereby designated aircrew members in
C-123K type aircraft, aircrew positions and specialties/additional quali-
fications as indicated. Authority: PACAF Sup 1/AFM 60-1 and PACAFR 60-5.
```

GRADE, NAME, SSAN	A/C	E/C/PCP	P	IP	SEFE	FCF	THR QUAL
LTCOL SPEAREL, DONALD W.,	X	X			X	X	X
LTCOL WALLACE, JOHN W.,	X	X			X	X	X
MAJ DIXON, DAVID L. JR.,	X	X			X	X	X
MAJ EDDINGTON, ROBERT R.,	X	X					X
MAJ MAXEY, WILLIAM F.,	X	X				X	X
MAJ MCNUTT, GLEN L.,	X	X	X			X	X
MAJ ROBERTSON, GEORGE S.,	X	X	X				X
MAJ ROGERS, HARRY K. JR.,	X	X			X	X	X
MAJ VIVONA, ALEXANDER A.,	X	X			X	X	X
CAPT BURNELL, LAWRENCE D.,	X	X	X			X	X
CAPT CALDWELL, QUINTON M.,	X	X					X
CAPT LABENNE, RAYMOND J.,			X				X
CAPT PURCELL, WILLIAM A.,	X	X				X	X
CAPT SOUTHERLAND, GROVER R.,	X	X	X			X	X
CAPT WIDEMAN, HAMPTON E.,	X	X					X
1STLT COLVIN, EDWARD M.,			X				X
1STLT EYE, DONALD K.,	X	X					X
1STLT JARDINE, EDWIN P.,			X				X
1STLT KELLY, FREDERICK T.,			X				X
1STLT SNOW, JERRY P.,	X	X					X
1STLT WHITE, JAMES H. JR.,	X	X					X
1STLT WHITE, JOEL E.,			X				X
1STLT WHITTAKER, LOREN R.,	X	X					X
MAJ PITKUS, EDWARD D.	X	X					X
1STLT LENIHAN, DENNIS M.,			X				
1STLT HOOD, WILLIAM R.,			X				X
1STLT JOHNSON, JAMES A.,			X				X
1STLT HUNTER, JIMMY L.,			X				X
1STLT HYLAND, JAMES P.,			X				X
CAPT CONN, JOHN C.,	X	X					

MAX M. AXELSEN, Lt Col, USAF
Commander

DISTRIBUTION
1 - Each Individual
1 - 56 SOW (DCMMQ)
6 - 606 SpOpSq (C-123)
1 - Each AF Form 846

SO - 74

606th SOS Orders, November 1, 1969

THE CREW

Each C-123 in our squadron flew with 10 aircrew members: two pilots, two navigators, two flight engineers, two loadmasters, and two "flare kickers."

We carried two navigators because a minor navigation mistake could put us over North Vietnam, which would be against our orders and our rules of engagement (ROE). It would also be a very dangerous mistake. One navigator would sit behind the co-pilot near the cockpit of the plane, at a small desk, and track our flight on a map with grease pencil. We called that navigator just "Nav."

The other navigator stretched out atop a mattress pad laid on top of a 3 foot by 7 foot sheet of one-inch thick steel plate, looking through a 5-inch, 4-power Starlight Scope suspended above an open escape hatch in the floor of the cargo compartment. This navigator, while manning the Starlight Scope, was called "Scope." The navigator used the Starlight Scope to visually determine our location (with the Nav helping by using a high-detail map as a guide), locate and identify enemy positions or trucks for airstrikes. Once enemy positions or trucks were spotted by the Scope, his job was to help the aircraft commander direct the fighter/bomber aircraft being used to put bombs and other ordinance onto the targets. The navigators changed places every hour or so to give the one on the Starlight Scope a little eyeball rest.

The Starlight Scope was a recent invention that amplified ambient light from the moon, stars, ground lights, and other light sources, in such a way that it allowed the Scope to "see" at night. Although the visual acuity was a varied-shades-of-green picture, the instrument allowed the operator to see vehicles driving at night with minimal lights or even enemy soldiers smoking cigarettes on the ground.

With just a little moonlight or a few stars, a practiced scope operator could distinguish darkened vehicles, unlighted anti-aircraft weapons, dark storage sites, and other enemy targets even through a thin cloud layer or on extra-dark nights. Our navigators were generally very experienced with a high number of flight hours in other makes and models of aircraft. These officers, every single one, were dedicated to helping the Aircraft Commander conduct each fighter-bomber strike as effectively and efficiently as possible. Each gave unquestioned support of the pilots during every mission, provided advice in difficult circumstances, and helped meld each new crew into a great working team. The good pilots asked for their help many times, and as a result, these few navigators gave their respect and assistance whenever they could. They were all exemplary Air Force officers, without exception.

Our flight engineers helped the pilots make decisions about the operation of the aircraft. One flight engineer sat at a panel of engine and systems instruments in the cockpit near the pilots. That engineer's job was to help the pilots by maintaining a watch on the engine and systems, monitor and track fuel usage, and provide aircraft knowledge should any inflight emergency or damage occur to the plane or engines. The other flight engineer helped watch for anti-aircraft artillery fire from one of the side windows or open doors in the cargo compartment, provided a second pair of eyes to the engineer's panel, and provided the pilots and other crewmembers with ideas, suggestions, and information at every opportunity. They exchanged places and positions every hour or so to help relieve the stress of our four hour missions.

The two loadmasters took care of the flare pallet that was loaded in the back of the cargo compartment near the rear door. This part of the airplane could be opened by a hydraulic system that raised the top half of the opening and lowered the cargo floor to a level position. This pallet of MK-24 parachute flares was loaded in a holder and attached to the cargo floor. Whenever we needed to provide flares for any friendly soldier on the ground, the loadmasters and flare kickers took flares out of the holder and put them into a home-made aluminum chute affair. This chute held 15 or 20 flares in individual grooves that were tilted down toward the back end. When we needed to drop flares, the loadmasters would open the rear cargo door, unlatch the chute pallet from the floor, and push it to the rear to hang with the back end of the chute pallet pointed down at the very end of the cargo opening. The upper door would then be lowered to touch the top of the chute apparatus to help hold it steady and in place. Upon command from the pilot, the loadmasters confirmed that the arming ring of each flare was attached to the chute pallet, then push the flare down the groove and out of the plane. When the flare reached the end of the arming cable, which was attached inside the plane, it pulled a pin out of the flare, which deployed the 15-foot parachute and ignited the magnesium (and other chemicals) inside the flare's aluminum cylinder. The 2 million candlepower light provided by these illumination flares was very helpful to our allies on the ground fighting the North Vietnam Army (NVA) and Viet Cong (VC) enemy in Laos at night.

The loadmasters were assisted by two "flare-kickers," whose job it was to help the loadmasters get the pallet of flares ready in the cargo compartment, to keep the chute pallet full of flares, to attach the arming cable to the pallet, and to push or "kick" the flares out of the launching chute when we were dropping them to help friendly soldiers on the ground. Each parachute flare generated light for about 3 to 5 minutes, depending on our drop altitude.

The flare kickers also helped man the windows of the airplane whenever we were being shot at and to call over the intercom to "break right" or "break left" whenever it looked like a string of AAA rounds was headed toward us. The flare kickers were not trained as aircrew members. They were enlisted men who wanted to fly with us and help us during their spare time at NKP, sometimes three or four nights each week. They all had day jobs—they would work the normal eight hours in their trained specialty during the day, then fly with us for half the night. Many were cooks, but there were also mechanics, truck drivers, security personnel, and others who volunteered for this hazardous work without any pay benefit.

We were indebted to these guys and the services they provided us. They were all good guys and wanted to help.

During the squadron commander's interview of those people wanting to work for us as flare kickers, he usually made sure we had a good percentage of cooks flying with us. Part of his interview questions included something like this: "If you were chosen to fly with the 606th Special Operations Squadron would it be possible for you to bring some type of food or drink to the aircraft before each of your missions?"

We always hoped for something special to eat before each mission, like cookies, or brownies, or cake. Occasionally, a cook/flare kicker for that night's flight would bring biscuits and gravy, or fresh rolls and sliced turkey, ham or beef. Most crew members brought cookies and snacks sent to them from home. After the pilot would give the mission briefing, telling the crewmembers where we were going and what we expected to see, we always had a little picnic on the lowered ramp at the back of the airplane each night just before takeoff. This was the time to get to know each of the crew assigned for that night's mission.

When it was time to get into the plane, most crew stepped to the side of the aircraft and took a leak on the landing gear. It became a good-luck routine for many, including me—a weird superstition, like always putting on your left boot first or touching your dog tags before starting the engines (which I also did before each mission). When the full crewmembers were all strapped into their various positions, the pilot would call for the Before Starting Engines checklist, which was read by the co-pilot and performed by the pilot-in-command. The night's mission had begun.

FLARE OR "CANDLE" MISSIONS

To provide light for our friendly troops, we carried a large number of flares. Each flare was encased in an aluminum tube about four inches in diameter and about three feet long. One end of the tube was capped, and the other had a pin protruding through a cap on that end, through which a steel ring was threaded. This was the safety pin, very much like the arming pin on a hand-grenade. It was the flare-kicker's job to put a flare into the sloping chute at the back of the plane, attach the pin, and "kick" the flare down the chute and out of the plane. As the flare fell, the fuse would ignite the magnesium compound inside the tube, which would jettison the cap on the bottom end and push the parachute out of the top end. The ignited flare would burn for about 5 minutes and give off a very bright light below the parachute.

Every ground troop who called for Candlestick light was a friendly Lao soldier. Sometimes it was hard to understand their instructions, but we always understood when we heard the words "OK" or "You number one" to describe how we were doing. Although there were few "candle" missions, the ones we flew were very important, because they supported soldiers who were under attack by enemy troops. Those ground troops needed our help with the overhead light we provided that would let them see and defend against the enemy attacks. Of my 165 night missions as a Candlestick, I had fewer than 10 or 12 "flare" missions. All the rest were FAC missions.

FIGHTER-BOMBER MISSIONS

Most of our missions involved directing and controlling all kinds of fighter-bomber aircraft delivering ordnance onto enemy positions and trucks. Our nightly missions were 2 to 4 hours long. When we spotted trucks or military materiel, we would fly directly over those areas for hours, directing slow-moving propeller aircraft or fast-moving jets dropping their bombs, napalm, bomblet clusters, and other weapons onto those targets. Missions were complex, complicated orchestrations of flying the plane, managing flight crew, controlling multiple nearby strike aircraft, and avoiding ever-changing enemy gunfire. AAA was everywhere along the Trail. Many nights, we would be shot at by all sizes of anti-aircraft artillery for the entire time we were flying in orbit overhead. Every mission, for everyone on board my C-123K, was a ride into hell, knowing that any of the many rounds coming up from the ground could make all ten of us ride a blazing junkyard into the jungle below.

Each night, every Candlestick was assigned a different area of operations within Laos, either in the northern portion of the country, called "Barrel Roll," or the southern portion, called "Steel Tiger." We were given general intelligence about what activity had been going on in our assigned area just before each mission. After takeoff, within a few minutes, we would fly over the Mekong River (the border between Thailand and Laos), turn off all our outside navigation lights (blackout), and fly directly to our area assigned for that night. We would patrol over all of it in an attempt to locate moving trucks, parked trucks and vehicles, supply-storage points, anti-aircraft gun positions, grouped enemy soldiers, or anything unusual on the ground.

The "Scope" navigator usually located a truck or convoy by seeing their headlights (taped or covered except for a small slit), or convoy lights (specially installed small lights also generally taped to allow only a very small slit of light to shine on the Trail or the vehicle directly in front). He would tell the pilot he had a target in sight and identify it for us, then give the other navigator the location of the target by identifying a distance and direction from a known point on the Trail.

For instance, in a specific location, the Trail followed the west side of a large river and formed what most navigators called the "Whale's Back." So, if the target was located near that landmark, the scope would tell the navigator that the target was three klicks southeast of the Whale's Back. Most navigators, after a very few missions, could locate specific areas of the Trail by sight and identify them by their common names used. The navigator would then plot the target on the map. In the meantime, the aircraft commander would call the Airborne Communication and Command Center—usually a C-130 orbiting at higher altitude over central Laos (call sign Blind Bat)—and request a flight (two) or more of fighter-bombers to come to our location to orbit until we could direct them to the target.

Each military service had slightly different procedures and techniques for putting their ordnance on target. For example, the Air Force fast-movers always came in high, came down the bombing run (the "chute") at high speed, dropped as much ordnance as we would let them at each pass, then got the heck out of Dodge as fast as possible. We would sing a little Candlestick ditty whenever we learned that we had Air Force fast-movers coming our way. It went: "F-4, F-4 going so fast; can't see shit, can't hit your ass ..." and several more ribald verses. This was not always the case, but it happened enough times that many of the aircraft commanders, when requesting aircraft to come to us for air strikes, would request "Air Force slow movers (i.e., A-1 or A-26 propeller-driven aircraft) rather than "Air Force fast movers (F-4s mostly, but sometimes F-105s).

On the other hand, there were Marine pilots also flying fast-movers. These boys had big brass cajones. They would request that we let them drop one bomb at a time, so they could hit what we were aiming for. Each pass down the chute was as slow as they could go and their pull-out at the bottom of the run (when they released their ordnance), was lower than any other pilots. They called themselves "mud Marines," even though they were flying the best jet aircraft available. They wanted to hurt the bad guys, because those enemy soldiers and supplies on the ground were all ending up in South Vietnam and used against Marines fighting from foxholes i.e., in the mud, in South Vietnam. The Marine pilots were the best—bar none—and a pleasure to work with. It was not unusual to report to departing Marine pilots that they had destroyed the target and all of their bombs and ordnance had gone within a 50-meter circle of the designated target.

Most Navy pilots were somewhere in between Air Force and Marines, but there were a few who were as good as the best Marines. Both Navy and Marine pilots flew off of aircraft carriers stationed offshore, in or near the Tonkin Gulf. These pilots seemed to be more aggressive and better pilots than Air Force, probably because they had to land each night after a mission on a pitching and rolling carrier deck and not on a 2 mile long, 200 foot-wide strip of concrete, like the Air Force types.

All fighters followed the same procedure in being called by the Airborne Command aircraft—they were either orbiting in the general area waiting for a call or they were on alert at an air base or on an aircraft carrier. When incoming pilots were within a few minutes of us, they would call. The navigator gave them our position, directions, told them what targets we had spotted, current weather, altimeter setting, and let them know where the nearest "safe" area was in case they were shot down and needed to bail out. Nav would also instruct the fighters to approach our area at a specific altitude above us. The incoming fighters would then inform the navigator their type of aircraft, how many aircraft were in that flight, what ordnance they were carrying, how they could drop each item or all of the ordnance, and anything else that we needed to know. When these fighters called again to tell us that they were nearby (on station), I would instruct them to enter an orbit at their instructed inbound altitude, near the designated target area, and wait for us to set up the target markers.

When the first pair of fighter-bombers approached and had been told to enter orbit above us, the Scope would instruct the flare kickers to three drop ground-burning flares at about two-second intervals, so that the three flares would burn on the ground in a line approximately 50 meters apart. Each of these ground-burning flares, called "logs," burned a different color, generally red or green. The logs would burn very brightly for about 15 minutes. We dropped 3 logs, in case some were hidden by foliage, in ravines, or behind rock formations (generally limestone "karst" in Laos near the Trail). The Scope would find the burning logs and inform the pilot where to fly to enter a left-hand orbit over the logs. The pilot could generally see at least one of the logs with the naked eye or with the smaller rifle-sized Starlight Scope (AN/PVS-2) stored in the cockpit. Candlesticks flew most strike missions at 2,000 to 4,000 feet above the ground (AGL). This altitude was generally above the effective range of small arms (e.g. AK-47s used by the enemy ground fighters), but not above anti-aircraft artillery (AAA) range.

With the fighters in the target area and the Candlestick flying above the target in a left-hand orbit, the aircraft commander would tell the fighters where the C-123 was located and ask them to report to him when they had Candlestick in sight. Sometimes it was necessary for the Candlestick pilot to turn on the upper-fuselage rotating red beacon to help the fighters find the C-123. When the fighters could see the Candlestick in orbit, the pilot would instruct the fighters to also get into a left-hand orbit, at the altitude above Candlestick as instructed, and space their flight on the opposite side of the orbit circle from the Candle. In this way, the fighters and Candle would be the farthest from each other to avoid mid-air collision, they could more easily see each other if needed by flashing on their navigation lights or rotating beacons, and the fighters' descent down through the Candlestick's altitude in the bomb-delivery "chute" would be as far away from Candle as possible.

Once the fighters could see both the C-123 and the ground-burning logs, the Scope would tell the aircraft commander where the strike point was located from the logs. For example, the Scope might tell the pilot to "have the strike birds hit 50 meters northwest of the center red log of the three logs." The pilot would then give those instructions to the fighter taking the first try at hitting the ground target.

When the lead fighter acknowledged he had the target area identified, the pilot would clear the first fighter for delivery of a specified number or type of ordinance. For example, if the first fighter was carrying six hard bombs (usually 500 pounders), the aircraft commander might instruct him to drop ("pickle") one bomb at a time until a bomb came very close to the target, then tell him to drop all the rest ("pickle all") at the point where the last bomb detonated. On each attacking pass, the Candle pilot would clear the fighter in "hot," which meant that the fighter was cleared to release bombs in the Candlestick's AO on the target designated by the Candle.

After each bomb was dropped, the pilot and Scope would discuss the correction to be made for the next drop, usually by the second fighter. The fighters would take turns dropping bombs or other ordnance (napalm, funny bombs, bomblet clusters, etc.). The first fighter, then the second, then the first again, and so on. Every Candlestick aircraft commander had absolute authority to deliver all ordnance in the area assigned to them—no aircraft could drop anything without specific clearance and directions to do that from the Candlestick.

By giving the fighter the direction to approach the target, the aircraft commander could position the C-123 on the orbit side away from the fighter's entry direction, because the attacking fighter would have to descend through the Candlestick's altitude to release his bombs at a very low altitude for accuracy.

By the time the first strike aircraft would release bombs, the C-123 would be where the striking fighter entered his bombing dive (on his entry side of the orbit), and could see the explosion of the bombs to use for correction to the second aircraft. This would put the C-123 on the opposite side of the orbit from the next strike fighter. Communications between the pilot and the fighters dropping bombs continued throughout each strike, because the fighter would drop their bombs or napalm below the Candlestick's altitude and then climb back up through the Candle's altitude to its starting altitude above Candle.

The second fighter would stay at that original orbit altitude and would usually roll upside-down (inverted) to better see the bomb explosion of the lead aircraft's bomb delivery in relation to the burning logs on the ground.

The Candlestick would then give a bombing correction to the second aircraft, as well as an entry and exit direction. The first aircraft would then roll inverted to see where his wingman's bomb went off, so he could correct his bombing run on the next go-round.

We called it the "carousel," because three aircraft would be circling over the target and the fighters would be descending and climbing on the opposite side of the orbit from the Candlestick C-123. Most Candlesticks conducted their control in this way. However, in some instances and special circumstances, the Candle would drop the logs, make a pass over the logs to see where they were in relation to the target, then move away from the target to allow the fighters to conduct their ordnance drops in any sequence. I preferred to orbit directly above the target during each fighter strike, in order to get a better idea of the target, the effectiveness of the ordinance delivery, and better handle all of the multiple inputs necessary to maintain a clear orientation and absolute situational awareness.

All during the carousel, there was usually enemy ground fire—anti-aircraft artillery fire, also known as AAA ("triple-A")—to contend with. These guns shot large artillery shells of various sizes at us. The warheads would explode in a flower of shrapnel at the different altitudes set by the enemy gunners. The enemy liked to park trucks and to store materiel (military supplies) very near AAA batteries. Those batteries liked to shoot at U.S. airplanes. A 37mm AAA battery was anywhere from one to four guns in one emplacement. Each 37mm gun shot a "clip" or magazine of seven rounds—all of them tracer rounds (so they could see the rounds going up and we could see them coming at us). There were lots and lots of 37mm guns on the Trail, almost everywhere. There were also 57mm and 85mm AAA batteries.

Exploding artillery rounds were called "flak." Some of the older guys in the squadron called it "archie," a World War I term for AAA. One of the older guys in the squadron and one of my instructors and mentors named Al Vivona, liked to say that he'd been "walking the archie" on a mission, meaning that the flak or AAA was so thick he could almost walk on it.

Any time a Candle crew member identified a round headed for the aircraft, he would shout the direction the round was coming from, and a direction to fly to as quickly as possible (called a "break") to avoid those rounds. For example, a loadmaster on the left side of the cargo compartment might yell, "Clip of 37mm at 9 o'clock, break right."

There were usually a lot of "breaks" during each flight. Sometimes there was no place to go to avoid the ground fire coming up at us. It was not unusual for a crew member on the left of the cargo compartment to shout "break right" while a crew member on the right called out "break left" at the same time. Each of us knew that in those circumstances, it was just going to be a matter of luck. Most of those times, the AC would merely continue to fly the carousel and hope that the multiple rounds rising toward the aircraft would miss.

It's hard to describe glowing anti-aircraft tracer rounds coming up at you at night. Every time a gun battery fired, we would first see the ground flash. After that, we could see the rounds with burning tracer coming upwards toward us. At first, all rounds seemed to move very slowly. As each round got higher, they tended to arc toward down if they were aimed at an angle. Rounds shot straight up seemed slow at first also, but they didn't arc, so all we could see was the bright tracer getting brighter and bigger and larger and larger as it came nearer. As each round got closer, it appeared to speed up. And when they went past the aircraft, they flashed past like lightning. If they passed close by, we could hear them "zip."

A 23mm round looked about the size of a glowing softball going past. When they burst, it looked like fireworks on the Fourth of July. All 20 rounds from a 23mm clip would explode close together, forming black balls of smoke with intensely white centers.

The 37mm rounds looked to be the size of a glowing basketball, and a 57mm round looked like a glowing medicine ball. When either of those rounds burst, they would make a much larger ball of white light with dark edges and the entire explosion looked like it was 20 or 30 feet in diameter.

When any round exploded near the aircraft, the broken shell (called "shrapnel") would be blown out in all directions and sometimes hit the aircraft. The shrapnel sounded like hard hail striking the aluminum skin of the plane. I always flew with my window to my left open and my headset covering my left ear to block the sound of the radial engine just outside that window and my right ear uncovered so I could hear the crew members yelling in the back. I could sometimes hear the sounds of flak bursts around the aircraft and the pinging sound when shrapnel hit the aircraft skin.

When flak burst close enough to hear, it sounded like a huge firecracker. We could sometimes hear the shrapnel penetrate the aircraft skin and go ricocheting around the inside of the cargo compartment. When rounds went off in front of the aircraft, we would hear the hail sound on the nose in front of the cockpit, then smell burnt cordite and smoke as we flew through the flak burst —"walking the archie." Anytime flak burst near us, I would hear crew yelling in the back, so I would always call on the intercom to see if anyone was injured. Each crewmember would respond that he was OK and continue to watch out their assigned window, open door, or open back ramp for more triple-A coming our way.

Sometimes, we would have flak going off all around us. We knew they were experienced gunners and were setting their rounds to explode at different altitudes to adjust for their difficulty in seeing or hearing us.

Barrage fire, with lots of guns shooting at us from different batteries below, seemed to occur more often during full moon and clear and bright moonlit nights. We called every full moon a "gunner's moon," because that's when they shot everything into the air at us they could.

There were a lot of nights like that for every Candle. Every airstrike directed was something like a complex dance on the carousel —with bullets.

MISSION ACCOMPLISHED

After about four hours, most of which was flown over the Trail, we flew back to the southwest toward Thailand. Once we crossed over the Mekong River, we were in Thailand and safe. Pilots would turn the navigation lights back on and everyone would heave a huge sigh of relief.

Even after that first mission, my dollar ride, I recognized the relief from tension that the crew displayed. I thought then, and always thought after each of the missions, that the pilots of World War I might have felt like I did coming back to NKP. Returning after a raid over enemy territory in their Sopwith Camel, they must have felt that same way when they flew back over friendly lines and arrived back at their aerodromes—silk scarves blowing back from the open cockpit, over the top of the fuselage, grinning because they had survived the mission, and knowing that a chilled glass of wine or a cold beer was waiting for them in the drawing room of the commandeered castle located well back from the frontlines. Returning to Thailand and NKP felt that way to me. When I sighed with relief after each mission, I always smiled at the thought of those early pilots in their rickety flying machines returning safely to their castles. Thailand became my safe haven.

LIMA SITE 20

★

After I had started flying as copilot with the 606th, I had *my first opportunity to fly to Long Tien (the primary base for the Air America operations in Laos, which was also called Lima Site 20A, or LS 20 Alternate, or just "Alternate") and see the sights there. I managed to take a few pictures of the area with my "spy" camera (a Minolta 35 mm half-frame) before leaving.*

I asked my Aircraft Commander that day a lot of questions about the landing site, the village, and Vang Pao, the Laotian General who was in command of all of the Laotian military efforts in Laos, including the Hmong warriors. When I returned to the squadron area that evening, I asked other "old heads" about the site and learned that many of them had gone there on a day off, as a passenger on one of the few squadron supply missions, in order to buy a gun, jewelry, gold, or other stuff the employees there were selling. I decided to go there as soon as possible to buy a gun of some kind, to take home as a souvenir of my year in Thailand.

It wasn't long before my opportunity to ride along to LS 20A came up. I made all the necessary arrangements and jumped on the daytime flight that was scheduled for a quick turnaround and return to NKP.

When I arrived at the site, I went up to a mechanic looking at our C-123 and asked him if he worked there. He said he did. I chit-chatted with him a bit, trying to find out more about the site, his contract period (a year), his pay (over $30,000 a year, including "fringe benefits" that he wouldn't describe), and what guns or other items might be for sale there.

He told me that he didn't have any guns, but his buddy did. He said, "Follow me and we'll go look him up and see what he has." So I did. We walked off the flight line, down a slight slope, and onto a somewhat level area where there were small buildings, Quonset huts, and a few tents. He walked into a tent, pulled out a large-size trunk from the corner, and tried to open it. No luck—there was a padlock on a hasp on the wooden lid. So he pulled a large screwdriver out of his back pocket, inserted it between the trunk and the hasp, and proceeded to rip the lock and hasp clear off. "He won't mind," he said. "He's my buddy and I'll fix the trunk when he comes back."

I looked into the trunk. There were 20 or more guns in that trunk, of every variety, size, shape, age, and make. Most of the weapons were submachine guns. I recognized a German Schmeisser, a French make, an American Thompson, an M-2 carbine (still in a cosmoline sleeve), several AK-47s, a Russian PPSh, and several others. There were a few rifles and pistols as well.

I thought hard about buying a submachine gun, because they were so cool, but knew that I couldn't take one home—legally. I also looked at the pistols and decided they might be too tricky to get home too. There was one Russian bolt-action rifle in the box, still in a cosmoline sleeve, and I thought that I could get that one home as a souvenir. So I asked the mechanic "How much?" He said, "Well, I don't really know, but $15 should be enough." I pulled out three fives, gave them to him, and ran back to the C-123. I could hear radial engines firing in that special sound that they had as they were started—huffing and chuffing and sometimes a small backfire when they finally caught. I hoped that I didn't bump into the guy who used to own that rifle, as I ran back to the aircraft as fast as I could. I also didn't want to be left behind in that WWII-looking base.

I jumped into the back of the open cargo compartment, glad that I was getting out of there before the mechanic's buddy came back, discovered the broken lock, and came looking for anybody trying to get out of town carrying one of his guns. I was really relieved when we finally took off. I never returned to LS 20A, although I overflew it one night when I had to shut down one engine for a massive oil leak, just in case I needed a friendly airfield to land on, rather than a rice paddy out in the boondocks.

The Alternate was a strange-looking place. The runway ended in a mountain. All airplanes had to land toward the mountain and take off away from it, regardless of the wind direction. The runway itself was very narrow and a little wavy. There were huts, buildings, tents, and other structures situated along the side of the runway, just a little distance off from the landing strip and a large, palace-looking structure off to one side. It was down the slope from the runway and halfway up another hillside. That must have been General Vang Pao's place. There were unpainted aircraft parked just beside the mountain on a hammerhead turn-around and ramp area. There were T-28s, A1s, a C-46, a C-47 "Goony Bird," several Piper Cubs, some O-1 Birddogs, and several helicopters, including a UH-1 Huey. All of the aircraft were shiny metal, which seemed strange for a "secret" airfield for a secret Laotian army. The place looked like it had just dropped out of 1944.

AIRCRAFT COMMANDER COMBAT CHECK RIDE

After about six months in the squadron, depending on the number and mix of missions each copilot experienced, he would be recommended for an upgrade to Aircraft Commander. I had been with the unit about five months when my turn came up, the first of the five "volunteers" who had come to NKP together in September, to have a chance to become an AC.

For the next few rides as AC trainee, sitting in the left seat, with an instructor pilot in the right seat, I had to perform the entire mission in command of the aircraft, crew, and mission. During that series of practice rides, I was given some time to attend ground school, which ended with a serious written exam and a verbal examination conducted by the three highest-ranking officers in the unit, including the chief navigator. Most of the daytime flights included practiced emergency procedures, like loss of engine on takeoff or landing, fire in flight, loss of electrical or hydraulic power, and touch-and-go's that seemed to go on forever. But it was daylight, and it was a lot like being back at Hurlburt Field in beautiful Fort Walton Beach, Florida. These flights went without a hitch and ended soon. It was kind of nice seeing the ground during flight and not having to worry about someone shooting glowing basketballs at me.

After passing that phase, I had to take a few more flights around the base, at night, to show an instructor pilot that I was proficient with all of the necessary emergency procedures, both by saying the steps to correct or reduce the emergency situation and by action in the cockpit. These procedures had a way of causing more stress at night than during the day. The final step in the upgrade process was a check ride, flying from the left seat as the aircraft commander, with a check pilot sitting and acting as the copilot in the right seat. This check ride had to be on an actual mission, at night, over the Trail.

On the night of my AC check-ride, everything went perfectly all the way through takeoff. Even though I was a little nervous at first, things were going well, and I started to settle down as we crossed the Mekong, heading east into Laos. I turned off the navigation lights and aimed for our assigned mission area in Steel Tiger. Just when I thought everything was going OK, the flight engineer called on the intercom and told me we had an oil leak in one of the engines. I asked the other flight engineer to confirm there was oil coming out of the engine (which was sometimes hard to see at night, even with a flashlight, because of the amount of liquids generally puked out of that big radial engine during normal operations, the color of the oil, and the darkness). Both flight engineers agreed—if I continued eastbound, we were going to run out of oil somewhere too far away to be able to walk home. Getting home on just one engine, even with the jet pods at 100%, didn't guarantee that the airplane could get all the way back from the AO in Laos.

So I turned back, taking the necessary precautionary procedures recommended in the aircraft operator's manual and returned to base. It was too late to pick up another aircraft (a spare plane was always kept ready to fly), so we scratched the mission and called it a night. I would have to do the check ride mission all over again.

Several nights later, I got a second chance for the upgrade check-ride. Again, everything went great during the ground briefings and pre-flight checklists. We told the tower that we were ready to go and taxied into position on the takeoff end of the runway. I ran our radial engines to max power to make sure the engines were performing as required, checked those engine instruments, then started the jets and ran them up to 100 percent power to check their operation. Finally, I released the brakes for takeoff. The C-123 was light, so the takeoff distance wasn't very long. Just as we got about 50 feet in the air, with the landing gear coming up, one of the loadmasters yelled in the intercom: "Fire on number one engine!"

(which was the left radial). Oh boy, I thought, the left engine is on fire—big time. Here we go again.

On takeoff, at low altitude, an engine fire makes the life of the pilot a very busy one. I had the flight engineer confirm the fire visually as I talked to the tower to get permission to return to the runway and make an emergency landing. The flight engineer informed me that the engine was sparking and flashing fire and that he could see pieces that looked like molten material dropping out of the bottom of the engine cowl and flowing into the air stream out behind the wing.

The main fuel tanks for the C-123 are located directly behind each engine. Each tank holds about 730 gallons of aviation fuel and is only an aluminum skin-width away from any engine fire. These fuel tanks were attached to the aft side of the engine framework by four explosive bolts. In case of a massive, uncontrollable engine fire, the pilot can blow those bolts and drop the fuel tank away from the aircraft. All of our instructors said that blowing explosive bolts attached to a fuel cell in the vicinity of a burning engine might not be a good idea. So I didn't jettison the tank, but I did shut down the flaming engine, kept the left-side jet engine screaming at max power, toggled the right jet to idle (in case the right radial engine decided to quit), and headed around the pattern for the runway.

Although everyone in the crew was sweating bullets during the landing, there was no panic, only haste. I taxied the airplane to the end of the ramp area furthest from any other airplane, fuel truck, or anything else valuable that could be destroyed if our airplane blew up. Since the crew exit door was just a few feet away from where burning material was dripping onto the ramp below, I ordered the back ramp lowered as I taxied in and instructed everyone to get out of the airplane as fast as they could in that direction when I stopped. I was the last man out—I thought that was the aircraft commander's job, much like the captain of a ship.

I got out just as the fire trucks were approaching. Behind the fire trucks was a crew bus—it was time to quit for the night, again. We checked our equipment back in at ALSE, stopped by the Tactical

Units Operations Center (TUOC) to tell them we scrubbed the mission because of an aircraft emergency, and headed to the Club for a cool drink (or five).

After things settled down, I called the maintenance office to find out what had caused the fire. After a short pause and a heavy sigh, the chief master sergeant in charge of aircraft maintenance said: "There wasn't anything wrong with your engine. One of my maintenance guys left his fiberglass flashlight lying on an exhaust manifold while he was working on the engine that afternoon. He forgot to pick it up after he was through. It was the flashlight that was burning, melting, and dripping stuff all over the place. The engine's OK." Thank God I hadn't blown that 700-gallon fuel tank off the aircraft.

The next night, I was again scheduled for a check ride. It went without a hitch. I put in several air strikes and we killed a few trucks. When I got back to base, the check pilot told me I had done a great job all three nights and he was going to recommend my upgrade to Aircraft Commander. It was a great feeling. But I knew the problems I had had during the first two attempts could occur any night. Worse things than that could also happen at any time. I was glad I had upgraded before any of my contemporaries, but I was really scared about being responsible for nine other guys riding along with me in dangerous territory. From then on, things could get serious.

NAVY AIR STRIKE— ALMOST

While I was still a copilot, I was flying with my aircraft *commander, Glen McNutt. Glen was an older guy, probably 45 or so, with at least 20 years or so in the Air Force. He had flown during the Korean War, but most recently was assigned to a stateside base as an aeronautical engineer. He was a very good pilot, a very smart man, and a great teacher and mentor to me.*

Glen had just completed putting in an airstrike with two Navy fighters (A-7s). We couldn't see them after their last bombing run—they were "black out" (still flying with their exterior lights off) and "Winchester" (out of ordnance and ammunition). Candlestick FACs always instructed strike aircraft to turn on their navigation lights after each bomb or gun run, when they were safely above small-arms lethal range and before they passed up through our altitude. That way, we could see them in their climb. After we got verbal confirmation of their position as they climbed through our altitude, we could then release them to go back to their ship. But these fighters didn't turn on their lights when they should have.

Glen asked the strike leader over the radio where they were. The lead pilot responded that they were "joining up," meaning they were trying to find each other so they could fly out of the area together, in formation. When Glen tried again, he was told to "wait one," meaning to standby and they would respond again shortly. Glen then told them we did not have them in sight and that they must turn on their navigation lights as quickly as possible to avoid a mid-air collision. The lead pilot acknowledged Glen's call and told his wingman over the radio to go "Christmas tree," meaning to turn on all navigation lights to their brightest position.

Both Glen and I saw the lights go on in both aircraft at the same time—they were filling Glen's side window on the left side of the cockpit.

Glen and I both pushed down on the control yoke at the same time, as hard as we could. The two Navy jets passed so closely in front of us I could clearly see the face of the pilot in the second aircraft by the light from his instrument panel—a very low, red glow.

Unfortunately, the abrupt dropping of the nose of our aircraft resulted in an equally abrupt rise at the rear. One of our loadmasters went weightless at the far back end and was thrown very hard against the overhead of the cargo compartment. When we stopped our nose-down push, and started pulling "Gs" to level off, he came unglued from the overhead and crashed to the floor, a fall of about 7 feet. He was badly injured, with a broken collarbone, a severely injured leg, and a twisted back.

We returned to the base as fast as we could, where a ground ambulance met us as soon as we turned off the runway. After the injured crewmember was loaded into the waiting ambulance, Glen and I finished our post-mission chores as fast as we could, both of us trembling the whole time, and rushed to the Officers' Club for a stiff drink (or ten).

In addition to putting in an air strike that night, we were almost the victim of an air strike of our own—by Navy fighter pilots. In the club, Glen estimated that the wingtip of the closest jet had missed us by less than three feet and that if we both hadn't pushed the nose down as soon and as fast as we did, that particular Navy plane would be wearing a C-123 Candlestick as a hood ornament. Combat can be dangerous I guess?

COUSIN ROGER AND I
TACKLE R&R IN BANGKOK

Communications between me and the home front were slow, because we only had letters to write back and forth. Mail would usually take 10 days to two weeks to go both ways. During my year, I wrote a lot of letters to Vicki and to my parents. Sometime during the first part of my tour, my parents and Vicki started sending cassette tapes in addition to their letters, so I could hear their voices and the voices of my family—especially the mewing and bleating and gurgling of my newborn daughter, Kelli. I bought a small tape recorder at the BX and re-recorded over the tapes sent to me with ramblings of my own and sent them home.

After I had been in-country for several months, my Mother wrote and told me that my cousin Roger Bonebrake of Wichita (oldest son of Mom's brother Gene—who we all called "Jeep") had joined the Army and had just been sent to Vietnam. She wanted to know if I could ever see him there, since I was "close." Since I had always told my parents that I was stationed in Thailand and doing just "routine" flying duties there, they weren't aware (that I knew of) that I was flying over Laos and getting shot at every night. So I told her that I would try to contact him, if she could get his address.

After several back and forth letters, I learned that he was in Vietnam, and was due for an R&R (a rest-and-recreation) leave soon. I wrote Mom and asked her to write Roger and to tell him to take his 10-day R&R in Bangkok and I would try to meet him there. Mom was concerned about Roger, because he was only 19 years old and had never been out of Wichita in his life. He was the oldest of seven boys, in a not too stable household. Uncle Gene worked for Beech Aircraft Company and had to leave town occasionally "on business." Roger was in charge whenever Gene went off on one of his occasional mystery trips. Mom thought that Roger was the one who raised his 6 brothers, some of whom had spent summers at our house in past years or at Grandma Bonebrake's house in Concordia.

One of the "perks" of being stationed in Thailand was the King of that wonderful country. The King had been educated in the U.S. and was known to be a proficient jazz saxophonist. He had decreed that every soldier or airman assigned to a Thai base would be entitled to three days off every month, designated "combat time off" (which we called CTO), and an additional two weeks R&R anywhere we wanted. Air Force policy granted one two-week R&R for AF officers in any other combat area, but the King insisted that we get three days CTO each month and an additional two weeks of R&R. The Air Force wanted bases in Thailand, so they had to agree to the King's wishes.

An additional perk for pilots assigned to the 606th Special Operations Squadron was that we had the capability with the C-123K airplanes to carry CTO troops back and forth between Nakhon Phanom and Don Muang Airport in Bangkok on a regular basis. So we did. About once a month or so, two pilots from the 606th would take a planeload of CTO troops down to Bangkok, off-load the troops, then go on CTO themselves. Two pilots just finishing their CTO in Bangkok would pick up the airplane at the military ramp at Don Muang, go pick up a planeload of troops returning from their three days off, and fly themselves and their passengers back to NKP. It was a sweet deal. And most pilots took advantage of their CTO in Bangkok rather than at NKP, just to have a little fun off base now and again. Besides, Bangkok in wartime was a very interesting place.

I told Mom in a letter that I could probably pick a trip to Bangkok anytime I wanted, if Roger was going there for R&R, and I knew when to meet him. After more back and forth letters, I learned that Roger had chosen to go to Bangkok and the day he would be arriving there. That day would be a couple of months in the future. I arranged to take my CTO on the day of his arrival. We had passed enough letters back and forth that I knew when he was arriving in Bangkok and even had the opportunity to ask where we could meet. He didn't have a hotel picked out yet, so he told Mom for me to meet him just outside of the arrival area at Bangkok Airport. Every soldier on R&R to Bangkok had to go through an arrival briefing and lectures before entering Thailand. Each military person had to attend a series of lectures after arrival and before being set loose on the local economy.

Important information was given to the arriving soldiers at these lectures, like changing the military script (called "MPC" or "script") that was required in Vietnam (American money was illegal in Vietnam) back into U.S. currency (called "green") for spending in Thailand (where script was illegal). Other important information given there included where to stay while there, what to avoid, how to treat the local population, when to report back to the military departure area, and other minor tidbits. Everyone called the building where these lectures were given the "VD hut," since a lecture on VD or sexually transmitted diseases was given there, including graphic photos of "after" a military person had contracted any VD, literally ad nauseam. It was a scare tactic that didn't seem to work on anyone I ever talked to.

On the required day and at the required time, I met Roger outside of the fence at the VD hut. He was walking with a Thai man. Roger told me that he had hired the man as his personal taxi driver for the next 10 days. He told me that the taxi driver was on call for any of Roger's whims, 24 hours a day, the full 10 days of his R&R. He also told me that the taxi driver had charged him a reasonable fee for this service, plus had given him some discount coupons at local restaurants, bars, jewelry stores, souvenir shops, and various other places of shopping and entertainment. We rode together to the fairly nice hotel near the center of the city that Roger said the taxi driver had already arranged for his stay, all included in the taxi driver's one-charge fee.

We arrived at Roger's hotel in the City. Roger said that he wanted to take a shower and change from his uniform into "civvies" so we could go out. It was still early in the day, so we had time to do a little sightseeing with his ever-ready taxicab-driver-cum-guide during daylight. He asked me to wait in the lobby while he got changed. I agreed and headed for the bar.

After about an hour, Roger came strolling down the long, wide staircase from the mezzanine, dressed in casual civilian clothes, and holding the waist of a very pretty, short-skirted Thai girl. He walked up to me and introduced me to the young girl and told me that she was part of his "package." He said that he had paid the taxi driver for her. Just like the taxicab, the girl was his, 24/7, for the full 10 days of his R&R. I knew that I'd never be able to tell my Mom about Roger's R&R "package," but I did tell her in a later letter that I had met Roger in Bangkok and that he had been well taken care of during his R&R there.

Roger and I buddied around together for two days. We went to all of the tourist attractions that his taxi driver/guide recommended. We went to several restaurants together and several bars. Roger's companion went with us everywhere. She spoke a little English and was very nice to Roger in my presence and in public. No one gave Roger and his date a glance. Everyone was polite to both of them, even recognizing instantly that Roger was an American soldier and the short, cute Thai girl was a "short-time girlfriend." We had a pleasant time together during those few days. I let them explore new places alone together at night. I didn't want to interfere with Roger's relaxation and recreation.

At one time during the second day, we decided to go into a nice hotel restaurant and have lunch. We had been sightseeing and we were all a little hot and tired. The restaurant was a nice one. There were few diners present when we arrived in the middle of the afternoon, so we had most of the place to ourselves. We continued to talk and to share stories about Wichita, the Bonebrake boys, Grandma Bonebrake, the Army, Vietnam, Bangkok, and other tidbits about our lives.

Somewhere in the middle of our conversation over beer, Roger decided to go to the restroom. He got up from the table and walked away and left me sitting directly across the small, damask-covered table from the young Thai girl. There was silverware on the table and a single red rose in a clear glass vase in the center of the round table. I didn't know what to say to Roger's girl, and since I had been carrying my new Asahi Pentax 35mm camera around the entire time, I decided that I might kill a little time by taking a close-up, portrait-style picture of the cute girl sitting across the table from me. It was a white tablecloth, a red rose, and a brown-skinned and pretty Thai girl wearing an orange dress. I took one picture, hoping it would come out OK with the great lens on my camera.

Roger came back to the table and we resumed our lunch and chit-chat. It was a pleasant afternoon. At the end of that day, I bid Roger and his girlfriend goodbye, and returned to my hotel. I had an early take off the next day at Don Muang, taking another load of troops back to NKP. It was another CTO under my belt. But this time was different—I had spent two great days with my cousin Roger and his short-time girlfriend in Bangkok. I had enjoyed it immensely and I hoped Roger enjoyed his R&R too.

I usually sent my undeveloped film back home to Vicki to develop. It always seemed easier that way. So, without thinking about my two days with Roger, other than to write in the letter with the film canister that I had met with him and spent two days with him sightseeing in Bangkok, I sent the undeveloped roll of film back home.

Vicki developed it and previewed the pictures. My next letter from home was a short one—one question—"who was the cute Thai girl in the orange dress?" My next letter home was a long one. Thankfully, I had sent all of the rolls of film that I had taken with Roger back home together, so Roger and I and the young Thai girl appeared in lots of them. And there were lots of just Roger and the young girl. I think my explanation was accepted—that I had taken a picture of Roger's girl to test the close-up capabilities of my new camera. I was very careful after that to get my pictures developed at the base exchange (BX) at NKP, just in case I had taken something that would appear improper to my family back home. Even with that close encounter of the worst kind, I had enjoyed being with my cousin Roger on part of his R&R from South Vietnam.

Cousin Roger Bonebrake, Bangkok

Cousin Roger's date for his R&R

FATAL TARGET FOCUS

On one of my night missions, I watched another night *forward air controller put in an air strike of fast-moving bombers right on the Laotian/North Vietnamese border in another AO. Each jet had made several bombing runs without incident. There was a lot of ground fire at the attacking aircraft. We could see a lot of AAA tracer rounds climbing skyward in the vicinity of the strike and exploding at various altitudes. While one of my crewmembers was looking out a window in that direction, he saw a bomb go off near an earlier bomb drop, then a much larger explosion in the same place.*

One of the jets then began to call on the emergency frequency, saying that his wingman had just followed his own bomb onto the target, apparently because of target fixation. There was no chance of any surviving pilot or radar intercept officer from that aircraft, he said. We kept a close radio watch on our emergency frequency for the rest of our mission that night, hoping to hear someone call for help from the ground, but no one did.

We had just lost two Air Force Officers, a pilot and a radar intercept office (RIO) or GIB (guy in back), in an F-4. The crew got pretty quiet after that. I had been lucky so far. I hadn't seen anyone killed in combat where I was flying. But somehow, this loss seemed personal to me. I thought that what happened to that F-4 crew could happen to me and my crew at any time. A very sobering thought.

BLIND BAT—CREW COUNT

There were several layers of control aircraft flying over Thailand and Vietnam 24 hours a day. These aircraft controlled friendly aircraft coming and going into the various areas of both countries. The aircraft flying the highest was usually a C-121, which was the old four-engine airliner called the "Constellation" in the civilian world. This aircraft had radar and could "see" aircraft coming and going from a long distance away. At night, the call sign of this control aircraft was "Moonbeam" or sometimes "Alley Cat." It was also responsible for watching North Vietnam and warning us if any enemy MIGs left a North Vietnam airbase and headed our way.

The next aircraft below Moonbeam was a C-130 four-turbine engine cargo plane, whose call sign at night was "Blind Bat." This aircraft had no radar, but sufficient crew on board to monitor radio traffic to and from aircraft cleared into specific areas of Laos by Moonbeam. In addition to those radio crewmembers, there were also loadmasters and flight engineers, who were responsible for operating the aircraft during each mission. They usually wore parachutes and were tied into the cargo compartment with safety harnesses during most of the flight. Occasionally, one or more of these men were compelled to unhook their tethers long enough to check some distant portion of the cargo hold or wander elsewhere in the airplane. These aircraft flew above our altitude, but were sometimes low enough to have the larger anti-aircraft artillery rounds climb toward them and burst at or near their orbit altitude.

One night a Blind Bat was flying in an area of fairly heavy flak and on the edge of a fairly significant monsoon thunderstorm. One burst of anti-aircraft fire was climbing right toward the airplane, so it did a "break turn" fairly steeply and apparently unannounced. During the turn, the plane encountered some turbulence from the nearby thunderstorms, further upending the plane. One of the untethered loadmasters was bumped right out the open rear door of the cargo compartment—and the plane flew on!!

Finally, someone noticed one of the loadmasters wasn't anywhere in the cargo compartment where he belonged. The pilot called for the loadmaster on the intercom, then ordered the other crew members to search throughout the inside of the airplane.

Then the pilots heard an emergency radio start its recognizable beeping, telling them a parachute had opened. The signal was loud and clear, which indicated the radio was nearby. Not a good sign. Maybe they did lose a crewman.

The pilot turned on all the plane's exterior lights, including the bright landing lights, turned around and headed back the way they had come. After several minutes of flying on the reverse course, someone called that they could see the faint outline of a white parachute, glowing slightly below, in the landing lights of the airplane. The C-130 flew toward the slowly descending parachute, which was drifting down toward the dark, enemy-infested jungle below.

Suddenly the emergency beacon stopped broadcasting its beeping. The pilot turned to the emergency frequency, which was being monitored by every aircraft within a few miles of their location, and said: "Beeper, beeper, come up voice." The reply came quickly: "Pilot, pilot, this is your loadmaster. You are shining your lights on me so every gomer gunner within 20 miles can see my parachute coming down to them. Turn off your lights or I'll shoot you myself with my very own pistol."

Blind Bat turned off its lights and returned the call by saying: "Loadmaster, this is the pilot, we have rescue aircraft in the air and headed your way. Hang on, we'll get you out as soon as possible. We'll stay close until the Jolly Greens get here. Blind Bat out."

For the next month or so, every Blind Bat crew had to put up with unknown pranksters calling on Guard, the emergency frequency monitored by all military aircraft: "Blind Bat, Blind Bat, this is Mother Bat on Guard—crew count!" We all thought it was funny, but Blind Bat didn't. The lost loadmaster was rescued the next day without incident. No one was sure whether or not he returned to the crew that had lost him that night and then returned to shine on him for the enemy gunners below. "Crew count!"

FOOD POISONING

★

NKP was a Thai Air Force Base. Its official name was "Nakhon Phanom Royal Thai Air Force Base." Technically, the base belonged to the Thais. There were 1 or 2 Thai aircraft stationed at the base, but in reality, the base looked and operated just like any other U.S. Air Force Base in America, from Maine to Texas or Florida to California. The exception to the "US look" were the few civilian stores and restaurants located within the base perimeter, most located near the Thai Headquarters Building—an unimposing teak structure of two stories located at the northernmost end of the base. These civilian enterprises were allowed to operate by direct order and authority of the Thai Base Commander (we always wondered if he got a cut of the income from each shop).

One such shop was an Indian jewelry store, which specialized in Laotian gold items and Burmese star sapphires. Many US Air Force crewmembers purchased large-link gold bracelets from the jeweler, since the soft, gold links could be taken off one at a time and used for barter or payment in the local economy. Many flight crew carried these gold bracelets in their survival vests, along with the "blood chit" and gold coins that were included in the vests, to be used to help them avoid capture by enemy troops if they got shot down. The gold links of the local bracelets were thought to have a special value to any natives in Laos who might not recognize nor understand the value of the gold coins.

Another of the shops on base was an Indian restaurant, famous for its hot curry dishes. Although I flew an average of 6 nights each week, I occasionally had a night or two off. We always flew late, usually starting as early as 10 p.m. and as late as 2 a.m. When we had nights off, we always tried to sleep during the day and be awake during our usual mission hours at night. By doing this, we managed our internal clocks to accommodate our usual night missions. On one such night off, I decided to have dinner at the Indian restaurant instead of our usual fare at the Officer's Club. The Club was located directly across the street from our squadron's living area and most of our meals throughout the day were taken there. Sometimes that got very tiresome.

I don't remember exactly what I ordered, but I do remember having a lettuce salad prior to the main course. Because I was off that night and the restaurant closed rather early in the evening, I had completed my meal by about 6 p.m. By 8 p.m. that same evening, I began having severe stomach cramps, severe diarrhea, and vomiting. It came on so quickly that I had no choice but to walk the several blocks to the Air Force hospital between bouts of sitting on the toilet or bowing over it. When I got to the hospital, I asked the Airman at the desk to call the Flight Surgeon on call (officially the Medical Officer of the Day or MOD), as quickly as possible, because of the sudden onset of my symptoms and their severity. The Airman asked me to sit down in the waiting area because the doctor (an officer, doctor and Flight Surgeon) was out of the office, but "should return very soon." By 8:30 or so I had already become very well acquainted with the bathroom adjoining the waiting area—but still no doctor. I asked the Airman several times during that period if he could call the doctor, either by telephone or on the radio (which I knew he carried, because every officer "on call" carried the hand-held radio that we all affectionately nicknamed "the brick"). I asked him to tell the MOD of my severe abdominal pain, violent vomiting, explosive diarrhea, and intestinal distress. The Airman continued to tell me that the doctor should return very soon, but that he was on a "very important call."

Finally, about 9 p.m., after I had come out of the hospital restroom for the umpteenth time, almost crawling, very pale and hot, and sweating through my eyelids, the Airman agreed to call the doctor on the radio, since, he said: "You don't look so good." At that point, I had nothing left to throw up or discharge from the other end and I was too weak to stand up at the counter (and much too weak to go around the counter and physically assault the idiot). When the Airman finally called the doctor (again), he told him what was going on. The doctor replied that he was in a meeting and should be available very soon. I asked the Airman to try the radio again about 30 minutes later, because of my continued pain. The Airman called on the radio again. This time, when the doctor responded, I could hear the dialog of a movie in the background. I recognized the movie lines, since I had attended that same "spaghetti western" the night before at the outdoor theater on base. The doctor responded that "he would be there very soon." Having attended that same movie the night before, I knew that it ended about 10. Sure enough, at about ten after ten, the doctor showed up asking "what's the problem here?" I wasn't encouraged—here was a doctor barely older than me, trying to look and sound important, and still reeking of popcorn and soda pop from the outdoor movie. As soon as the doctor heard the Airman's verbal report and saw me sprawled horizontally on three chairs in the waiting area, he called an orderly to bring a gurney—"Stat!"

The doctor, Airman and an orderly managed to get me onto the gurney and into a bed in very quick order. I passed out as soon as I hit the gurney. The doctor then began several IV's to restore all of the water in my system that had been lost during the previous two harrowing hours.

When I finally came to consciousness in the hospital bed, it was early morning the next day. The doctor who had admitted me saw me on his rounds and told me that I was very lucky and that he was very worried that "he might lose me because of my severe dehydration." I said that I hoped Clint Eastwood was worth it. The doctor could tell that even though I was still very weak, I was very angry at his failure to respond to the hospital when called, as he is required by AF regulations as MOD. In fact, if I could have, I would have jumped out of bed and strangled him with his own stupid stethoscope, which he was wearing looped around his neck in a nonchalant and irritating manner.

Later the second day, the doctor came by and apologized to

me. Being my mother's son, I couldn't let him get away with that scott-free. So I read him the riot act—telling him that even though he was a new doctor that he had real responsibilities, especially to those of us combat pilots (chest puffing here) that were saving the world from the wicked Communists, etc. etc. etc. Anyway, I got that off my chest and he had the opportunity to take very special care of me for another 2 days or so.

During those recovering days, we talked several times and got to know each other better. He really was a nice guy, but had been stationed at NKP long enough that he hadn't had any "real" emergencies to deal with since he had arrived. Life at the hospital had become an unending round of dinners at the club, a movie, and early to bed. But as I got to know him better, I invited him to come visit our squadron and fly with us on less risky missions (after all, he was a Flight Surgeon), which he professed he wanted to do "someday." By the time I was discharged from the hospital, we had had several good conversations about our personal backgrounds, our university experiences, and other things in general. We didn't become real friends, but we did earn mutual respect for each other. After my release from the hospital, I felt like he had become a better doctor because of his professional failure with my serious illness (which he diagnosed as food poisoning, probably due to contaminated lettuce from the Indian restaurant).

BOONDOGGLE TO HONG KONG

A short time after my recovery from food poisoning I was in the rotation to take a C-123 to Taipei, Taiwan, for refit. These were regular-occurring missions. The pilots who were assigned to fly were usually selected only once during their one-year tour. Pilots were selected by each person's time in country. Its purpose was to take a C-123 to Taiwan for extensive repair and refit (called an "IRAN") and to bring back a C-123 that had completed that repair and refurbishment process. This boondoggle was a favorite for the pilots of the squadron, since it was an interesting over-water flight from Thailand to Taipei and back. Also, it meant that we would spend at least one night in Taipei and a night or two in Hong Kong on the return trip. We considered this brief interlude in our nightly FAC missions as a short R&R opportunity.

Hong Kong in 1969 was "the place!" There were semi-nude (and nude) dancing Chinese girls, good restaurants, round-eyed tourists, lots of bars, cheap hand-made custom suits and shoes, and porno films. Every pilot who rotated on this trip was given a list of things to pick up for other members of the squadron. Flying my own aircraft as AC to Taipei was a very interesting and fun experience. Although I was very tired after the long flight to Taiwan, I did manage to see a little of Taipei soon after my arrival and eat in a "civilian" restaurant (hopefully one that had clean lettuce).

Flying into Hong Kong airport was also very interesting and exciting. On the day that we arrived, the weather was foggy, with low ceilings. As a result, I was cleared by Approach Control to fly the "Checkerboard" approach into the international airport along the shore of the island. Not knowing what the heck that type of approach was, my copilot and I quickly scanned the approach plates for Hong Kong and found one appropriately marked "Checkerboard." The instructions on the approach plate were clear, except the part that stated that "upon approaching Hong Kong harbor at XXX feet, for XX number of minutes, at the checkerboard, you should make a sharp right turn and a rapid descent in the landing configuration to the airport." We still didn't understand, but being truly intrepid pilots, we flew the approach exactly as depicted on the instrument depiction. Lo and behold, when we reached the approach altitude and flew it for the directed number of minutes, we saw a big checkerboard sign on the side of a mountain directly in front of us.

That hill was much higher than our approach altitude and was completely covered by ramshackle houses, lean-tos, cardboard boxes, and other hovels. When we saw the sign, we made a quick right turn and started our landing descent. The hovels and ramshackle dwellings descended the side of that same mountain at about the same rate as we were descending. Throughout that part of the approach, we were about 200 feet above the shacks all the way down the side of the mountain. When we reached the base of the mountain we could see Hong Kong International Airport stretching out before us, extending out into the bay. I made a good landing and really impressed the crew with the approach and landing. I even impressed myself!

Since it was early May (1970) and my mind was on the prospect of golf when I returned to the land of the BIG BX (the BX is the Base Exchange—the store on every Air Force Base where a person can buy almost anything he wants at a relatively low price). The Big BX was the local slang for home, the US, and comfort. So while I was in Hong Kong, I had a pair of green alligator golf shoes made for me. All I had to do was stand on a piece of white butcher paper and have the shoemaker draw a line around each foot. He promised to send me the shoes within 2 weeks, so I paid him the $15 he was asking, in advance. I picked out a "wing-tip" style for the shoes. I told him that another AF pilot would pick up the completed shoes in about a month.

I looked around to find a new suit or something that I would like to take home "after the war." I didn't see any suit that I wanted, but I did see a great assortment of leather coats. I went into a shop and asked about the ones displayed in the window. "I make," the man in the shop responded when I asked him, "How much?" I asked. He gave me a range of prices based on the particular style that I liked. I picked out a double-breasted, car-length coat. He measured me, wrote down the numbers on a piece of scrap paper, and brought me a bunch of leather samples to choose from. "The green one," I chose. He told me how long it would take, but since it would be finished after I left, I had him write down my name and unit number, and told him that someone from my unit would drop by to pick it up sometime the next month. He said he would embroider my name on the inside of the coat, on the lining near the inside pocket, so it wouldn't get lost. About a month later, another 606th pilot picked it up for me when he took his turn to Taipei and a brief R & R in Hong Kong and brought it back to me at NKP. It was a great coat. It fit perfectly. I wore it a lot after returning home to the land of the Big BX.

During the time in Hong Kong, I also did the tourist bit by taking the ferry across the harbor to Kowloon, wandered the streets of Hong Kong (accidentally finding myself on Susie Wong Street—the famous street of prostitutes and fast-action bars), took a tram to the top of the mountain on Hong Kong Island, and had a gin and tonic at a British-looking bar at the hotel where I stayed. During my 2 days there, I did pick up the usual stuff for the guys at the squadron. Altogether, it was a fun and interesting trip.

I spent two wonderful days and nights exploring Hong Kong, buying new clothes, new LP records, movies for the guys in the squadron, presents for home, and trying to drink the island dry, before we had to fly back to NKP and face the AAA music again. "Another day, another dollar," as my Dad used to say.

MY SECOND COURT MARTIAL

---   ★   ---

When I returned to NKP, I was summoned to the squadron *commander's office. This was the same Commander who I had pissed off with the low engine torque episode. As soon as I got into his office and formally presented myself with a salute and a "Lieutenant Hyland reporting as ordered, sir," he gleefully announced "I've got you now, smartass!" This didn't sound like it was going to be a fun meeting.*

He wanted to know why the hell I had taken the Hong Kong rotation when I knew that I had to complete a flight physical before the end of May. I responded that it was only early May then, that the physical could be performed at the base hospital, and shouldn't take more than a day or two. "Oh no," he said, "flight physicals take more than 3 weeks because of the time required to obtain the laboratory results from the various blood and urine samples," he said. The samples have to be sent to another base for analysis. You don't have enough time to complete your flight physical before the end of the month," he said.

He then pulled out a book of Air Force Regulations and read me what I expected was his favorite regulation: "any person on flight status, in a combat environment, who does not complete a required annual flight physical before the end of his birth month, unless waived by the appropriate commander, shall be given a court martial for dereliction of duty in the face of combat."

The Commander was gloating and I was really scared. I asked him if he would give me a letter of waiver. He said "NO!" He told me that I had again exercised bad judgment. He told me that I should have turned down my Hong Kong rotation in order to complete my flight physical on time. He also told me that my failure to do so showed him

AGAIN that I was just a smart-ass and not real "Air Force Officer" material. I told him that I would try to complete my flight physical on time by starting right away. I hoped that some miracle would help me finish my flight physical in the 20 days or so remaining in the month of my birth, May.

As soon as I could get away from the gloating squadron commander, I literally ran to the hospital and asked for the Flight Surgeon that I had gotten to know from my bout with food poisoning. Luckily he was there. I explained my predicament. He said "No sweat." He said he would personally do my flight physical and that he would hand-carry my blood and urine samples to the laboratory at the other base in Thailand and wait there for the results. He told me he could do that because of the fact that he was a Flight Surgeon and could get on any airplane leaving NKP that he wanted and return at his discretion.

So we started the physical, which took about half a day. He then took the necessary blood and urine specimens from me and called the Operations Building to find out about aircraft leaving NKP for the other base (Udorn or Ubon, Thailand, I can't remember which). A C-130 aircraft was leaving NKP for the appropriate base that afternoon and would return in 2 days. The Flight Surgeon made a reservation on that flight and drove immediately to the operations building to board the airplane, carrying my blood and urine. I stayed at NKP, continuing my night missions as usual, and saying my prayers that the Doctor's plane wouldn't crash either going to or coming from the lab. I called the hospital in a couple of days and learned that the Doctor had returned, but he did not have the lab results needed to complete my physical. But he continued to say "No sweat." I sweated anyway.

About May 25th, my now friendly and caring doctor called me to his office and handed me my completed flight physical. I then personally carried it to Flight Operations at my squadron building to have it officially entered into my flight records. I then took a copy of the completed flight physical to the squadron commander's office, attached a note saying that I had completed my flight physical before the end of the month, and left both with the commander's secretary.

I checked to make sure that my new flight physical was entered into my official flight and personnel records at my squadron office.

I never again heard from that squadron commander. I continued to fly and he continued to work during the day—flying his desk. I'm sure he still considered me a "smart ass lieutenant."

Although I still bore the scars of the IV's that had been placed in the back of my hands during my food poisoning episode, I thanked my lucky stars that the Flight Surgeon had decided to watch Clint Eastwood rather than respond more quickly to my calls for help from the hospital waiting room. Otherwise, I would have certainly faced a court martial initiated by the grouchy squadron commander.

It wasn't long before this particular squadron commander received orders to a new unit and left NKP (the usual AF procedure to rotate higher-ranking pilots into a combat command to get their files appropriately stamped before sending them on to another unit and promotion). The court-martial king was gone. I was still free! I was sure that I would never have to face the possibility of another threatened court martial from anyone, ever again. And, of course, I was wrong!

BLINDED BY THE NIGHT

⎯⎯⎯ ★ ⎯⎯⎯

My friend Jim Johnson was flying co-pilot one night during the usual crap-storm over the Trail, when a 37mm shell hit the bottom left side of the aircraft, right under the Aircraft Commander's seat. Directly under the AC was an oxygen compartment roughly four feet square that held three or four bottles of oxygen. The compartment had a hatch into it from the cargo compartment. The hatch opening itself was a round-oblong entry about two-feet wide by four-feet tall.

Since we never flew high enough to need oxygen, the policy for the maintenance people was to leave a small amount of oxygen in each bottle to keep the seals tight and to keep positive pressure on the lines. Because the oxygen compartment wasn't needed at all, the hatch opening was covered by a fitted piece of black canvas snapped around the perimeter of the opening.

The 37mm shell hit that compartment and exploded among the oxygen bottles. The explosion blew a three-foot hole in the bottom of the airplane and threw shrapnel and pieces of oxygen bottles straight up into the bottom of the pilot's bullet-proof seat and out through the compartment entry hatch.

When the shell exploded in the compartment, it also blew the black canvas hatch cover out into the cargo compartment. It flew several feet into the cargo area before wrapping itself around the head of one of the flight engineers, who began to scream, "I'm hit, I'm blind." Of course, the entire cargo area was dark, with an open crew entry door right beside the damaged oxygen compartment. The flight engineer who had been struck by the canvas cover began to run around and thrash about, trying to get the object off of his head that was trying to suffocate him. Finally, the other flight engineer jumped down from engineer's space near the cockpit onto the cargo floor, grabbed the attacking canvas cover and yanked it off of his partner's head, who then began to shout: "I can see—it's a miracle—I can see!"

It wasn't until things calmed down a bit that the rescuing flight engineer noticed that the other engineer had been just a short step away from walking out the open crew door. Jim told me that everyone started laughing, obviously with nervous relief. Even the "blind" engineer started laughing.

Then the crew went to work getting the aircraft checked and ready to fly back to NKP, with a gaping and dripping hole under the cockpit. No other aircraft damage occurred and no crewmember was injured in the direct hit. The explosion did blow down the nose gear. The AC decided to leave it down and fly directly back to NKP. Jim also told me that it seemed to him to be a long flight home.

As they neared the base, they declared an emergency, not knowing whether the nose gear would collapse on landing. They landed without further incident, with fire trucks following them all the way down the runway to a parking area on the ramp. Everyone was back safe.

The next day, everyone in the squadron went down to see the damaged aircraft. There were lots of holes and pieces of shrapnel in the bottom of the pilot's bulletproof seat, and a few holes in the floor of the cockpit, but neither pilot had been scratched.

Three days later, I flew that same aircraft down to another AF base in Thailand so it could be repaired. We flew the entire way with all of our landing gear down and pinned to prevent collapse on landing and we flew it very, very slowly, to keep from causing more damage to the bottom of the aircraft, where the aluminum skin was protruding out into the air stream, like the petals of a flower.

Jim was always a little jumpy after that flight, even after his upgrade from co-pilot to Aircraft Commander. He never volunteered for "extra" missions after that and tended to spend more of his off-duty hours in the evenings tucked away in a little bar on the Mekong River, in the downtown area of NKP City.

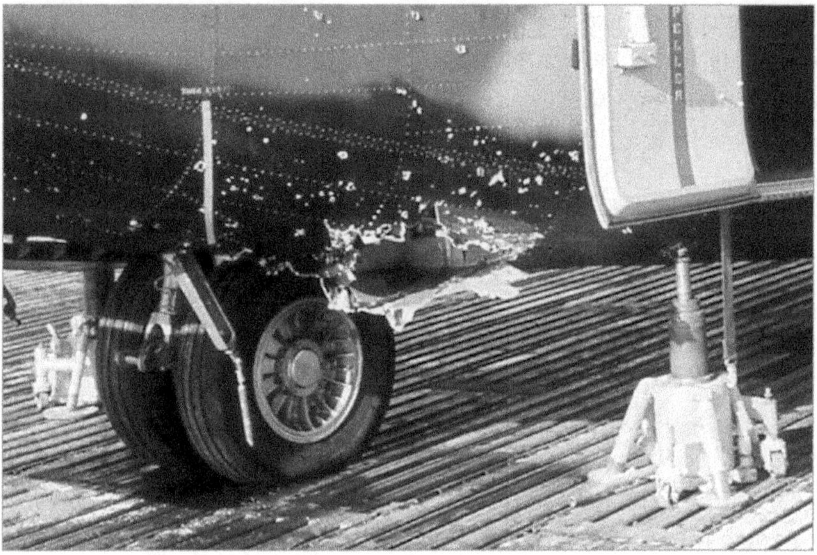

PARACHUTE PANTIES

--- ★ ---

One night on our way out to the Barrel Roll, we had a call *that a friendly soldier on the ground needed our candlelight (parachute flares). So we flew as fast as we could to the coordinates given to us by the Airborne Command aircraft flying in the area, which had taken the panic calls from the friendly Laotian soldier on the ground.*

We were going to be the second Candlestick to drop flares for this group of Laotian soldiers. When we got to the area, we called and talked to that soldier, who informed us that enemy soldiers were surrounding his encampment, and that the only way to keep them away was to have light all night. So we initiated our delivery orbit and began dropping parachute flares one at a time over his position. Every once in a while, our navigator would call him on the radio and ask for corrections of the flare drops and to ask how the soldiers on the ground were doing. Each time we received the response that we were doing a good job and that we should continue as long as possible ("you do numba 1," he always said).

And so we stayed, dropping the flares so that the flare just dropped would ignite just as the previous flare went out. Occasionally we could see ground flashes and tracer fire going both directions—into and out of the camp. But the soldier on the radio would always report that they were keeping the enemy outside of their perimeter wire. It was a long night, and one that had started at the last shift, which meant that we had left NKP a little after midnight and were due to return a little after 4 a.m.

But we stayed as long as we could—until it was just beginning to become light, just as our last flare went out the delivery chute in the back. We told the soldier on the ground that we were out of flares. We also told him that there would be no more Candlesticks coming his way this night, because it was getting light and very dangerous for aircraft painted green on the top and black on the bottom. He said "OK, You numba one. We OK, you go home." So we did.

As we were leaving after the last flare went out, it was just getting light on the ground among the jungle trees and around the camp below. But it was light enough for us to see several hundred bright-white parachutes littering almost every inch of ground for several hundred yards all around the camp. One of our loadmasters, who had helped and supervised the loading and releasing of flares for more than 2 hours, was as tired as both flare kickers. But he was awake enough to tell us over the intercom: "I figure we've dropped enough parachutes on that one position tonight to make enough white nylon panties for every enemy and friendly female within the surrounding 100 miles."

We all had a laugh at that and everyone relaxed and joked during the hour flight home over brightening jungle below. We were done, but not out of the woods yet. As the dawn grew brighter, we were still a long way from home. I managed to take out the half-frame Minolta camera I always carried and took a few pictures of the jungle below. This was no place for 10 tired AF guys to be. It was way too bright and we were way too tired.

PAPER BOMBERS

Every once in a while, some genius at headquarters would decide to send a Candlestick out over the toughest and most hostile part of Laos to drop leaflets enticing the multitudes of enemy soldiers on the ground in those areas to surrender. In Vietnam, they were called "Chieu Hoi" leaflets. In Thailand, in the 606th, they were called "litter."

I had two of those missions during my year at NKP. On both occasions, our orders were to deploy the leaflets over a certain hostile area and return to base, since our mission for the night would be complete. Usually, the area assigned to us for these missions covered 10 square miles or so. Headquarters obviously wanted us to drop leaflets along the Trail and in the jungle nearby to give every enemy soldier the chance to surrender or thank us for all the new toilet paper we provided.

On both occasions, we flew as fast as we could to the assigned leaflet area. While doing so, we had the crewmembers in the back work together to stack the boxes of leaflets in piles near all three entry/exit doors and along the open ramp in the rear. Just as soon as the navigator told us we had crossed over the boundary line of our assigned leaflet-dropping area, I ordered the crew to throw the full boxes of leaflets out of the airplane as fast as possible. The loadmasters would always laugh about the fact that it took us about an hour to load the boxes into the airplane and about six seconds to throw all of them—full and unopened—over the Trail.

I'm not sure any single leaflet ever escaped the boxes on the way down. All of us always hoped we had crushed some poor, unlucky gomer on the ground below with about a thousand pounds of boxed

leaflets. We called those flights "paper bombers."

MY FIRST R&R IN HAWAII

About seven months into my tour, my R&R came up. Vicki and I had decided to spend those two weeks in Hawaii, since that was where most of the married couples in the squadron went—and all liked it. I made reservations through facilities at NKP to stay at a hotel near Waikiki Beach called the Surf Rider Hotel. Vicki would fly over and join me on Oahu on the day I was scheduled to fly there from Saigon.

I left NKP on a C-130 going to Don Muang Airport in Bangkok, then hopped a C-47 "Goonie Bird"—an old WWII two-engine tail-dragger—from there to Saigon. On the outside of the cargo door, the pilot had stenciled his name "Captain Braniff." The sign just inside the bare, nylon-seated cargo compartment said: "Welcome to Braniff Airlines." That was a slow, hot and bumpy trip. I was glad to get out of Captain Braniff's contraption. It might have been a boon in WWII, but it was a hot, slow and bumpy bus in Vietnam.

In Saigon, I had to spend a day at Camp Alpha, where everyone going into or coming out of Vietnam had to register, get or give copies of orders, and spend a few hours in a hot tent watching "R&R" films with great titles like: "VD, Your Worst Enemy" or "Incurable VD, Don't End Up Living in Vietnam the Rest of Your Life" or "Call Girls in Vietnam have Razor Blades Where You Can't See" etc., etc., etc.

Since I had to spend the night there, I was assigned a barrack, which was an open-bay building with wooden walls up four feet, screen walls above that, metal roof, and sandbags all around the wood portion outside. The single room, with one latrine outside at the end, housed about 50 men. Army guys staying there said it was pretty good—us Air Force types with our own air-conditioned trailers thought it was a pig pen, and a hot one at that. Somehow, I survived the night like a true jungle stalker and managed to get to the airplane leaving Saigon on time.

In Honolulu, our first stop was Ford Island to see the U.S.S. Arizona memorial. This was my first time there. I wanted to pay my respects to my Uncle Buford Bonebrake, my mother's brother, who was an engine room snipe on that ship on the day the Japanese bombed the Arizona and the rest of Pearl Harbor on December 7, 1941. We were taken to the memorial on the shuttle boat. When we arrived, I walked immediately to the wall with the names of the sailors still entombed below us. There was Uncle Buford's name, along with all of the other sailors remaining on the sunken ship. We looked down at the pieces of the ship that were still visible just above or below the water, and each of us said a short prayer to the uncle I had never met.

After Pearl Harbor, we strolled the beach, casually dropped into three or four hotels with lanais (patios) on the beach, and listened to famous bands performing to packed ballrooms of other R&R revelers. We rented a car and drove out of Honolulu and went to the Culture Center on the north end of the island. We saw the famous "Blow Hole" on the north coast.

About half way through the two weeks, we flew to Kauai, rented a car, and stayed at a large, fancy and famous hotel on the north end of the island across from a small bay where the movie "South Pacific" had been filmed. The rate for the cottage we stayed in was $200 per night, but military personnel on R&R got a 50 percent discount. It was a great room and well worth the hundred bucks.

After a few days at the fancy hotel, we flew back to Honolulu and spent a few more days in the city doing tourist things. Then it was time for me to get back to night flying.

It was a nice R&R, but Laos did get between us a couple times. Neither of us could forget for long that I had to go back and get shot at for another four months or so.

I flew out of Hickam Air Force Base that evening and arrived back in Saigon very early the next morning. I was given a bed in the bug palace again, but was able to catch a ride on a C-130 going to Bangkok shortly after checking back in at Camp Alpha. By that evening, I was back at NKP, back in the war, and back in the flying rotation for the next night. I stayed up as late as I could to get back in the "night-owl rotation," went to bed just after midnight, and was back flying the next night. Honolulu seemed so far away—it was like I had never been there and that I had never left NKP.

MY SECOND R&R IN KANSAS

Because I was stationed in Thailand, the King gave us a second two-week R&R (unlike those stationed in Vietnam). I decided to return to Topeka and surprise Vicki at her apartment there. I wanted to see her and my 10-month-old baby daughter.

I decided that I could spend about ten days in Topeka. I caught a Freedom Bird out of Saigon to Travis Air Force Base near San Francisco. I then jumped a "stand by" flight to Wichita. To get back to Vietnam, I would have to catch an Air Force flight back to Travis AFB then on to Saigon. Since I was flying "stand by" and on special R&R orders, I would have to wait in Travis until I could find an open seat on a contract carrier or Air Force flight. So I didn't have the full two weeks to spend in Kansas.

Back home in Kansas, Vicki and I tried to make the best of the week or so that I had there. We invited John and Janette Gelvin and their kids to Topeka from Grand Island, Nebraska. We had a great picnic together at the Topeka Zoo. John was my friend at Kansas University where we were both trumpet players in the KU Men's Marching Band for 2 years. He carried Kelli most of the time we were together. I also had the chance to look up my Pilot Training Section Leader Banks Prevatt, who was stationed at Forbes Field in Topeka. I found Banks to say "Hello" to him and his wife Trudy. Banks had been my anchor at pilot training. He was an "old head" and former enlisted AF guy, who had cared for all of us in pilot training class 69-07 at Laredo. I appreciated Banks' steadfast and unequivocal help at Laredo, as both a member of the class and a role model for us "90 day wonder officers."

There wasn't any grand hotel or beach near Topeka, but there

Candlestick: Night FAC over Laos 199

was a lot of peace and quiet. In the few days that I had in Topeka, I worried about my squadron mates at NKP during all of my quiet times. I couldn't sleep at night. I had bad dreams most nights and would wake up with shouts or grunts or by suddenly jumping out of bed. I talked too much about what was going on over Laos at night. I scared Vicki more than once. I worried about being able to get back to NKP on time.

Finally, with some relief to both of us, it was time for me to get back to Travis and try to catch a flight to Saigon. I caught a flight out of McConnell Air Force Base in Wichita that took me straight to Travis. There I got on the waiting list for any flight, of any kind, going anywhere near Vietnam. I spent the next three days sitting in a hard chair and sleeping on the linoleum floor of the waiting area. To leave the space meant that I might miss a chance to get on a last-minute flight or take advantage of a last-minute cancellation by someone else on stand-by status. It began to look like I wouldn't be able to get back on any flight, in time. Being Absent Without Leave (AWOL) from a combat assignment was not a fun possibility. Finally, I talked to the Air Force people there about other ways to return to Saigon.

They told me that the only other way to get back to Vietnam was by commercial airline and that it would cost me about $1,000. I didn't have that much. The Air Force people told me that I could get the Air Force to buy my ticket if I signed a statement that I didn't have the money and couldn't return to Vietnam any other way. I signed the papers. They bought me a ticket on a flight leaving that day via Hong Kong to Saigon. It looked like I could get back to NKP about a day early.

I got on the airline that day. It was a TWA flight and very comfortable, even in economy class. As we arrived in Hong Kong, the pilot announced that the airplane was having mechanical problems and that everyone would have to stay in Hong Kong until it was fixed. "No problem," he said, "TWA will pick up the hotel room charges until we leave." I had to get back to NKP on time or I'd be shot as a deserter.

I checked with the ticket counter when we exited the plane and entered the terminal, but there were no flights going to Saigon that day or the next—I would have to wait for maintenance on the plane that I arrived on. So I got in line with the rest of the passengers on my flight, got into a van, and rode to the hotel where we were being hosted for the night. I spent the rest of the day exploring Hong Kong, taking a water taxi ride, and generally worrying about getting back to NKP on time. The TWA representatives had told us to report to the lobby the next morning by 8 a.m. to see if our plane was serviceable. I went to sleep that night with my fingers and toes crossed—I was too young to die in front of a firing squad at Fort Leavenworth, Kansas.

The next morning, we were told that the plane was fixed and that we would be taken to the airport after a short breakfast. Yeah!

But it was still going to be close.

When I arrived in Saigon, I knew what I had to do to make flight arrangements at Tan Son Nhut Airport and get out of there as soon as possible (I had done this before). I made those arrangements, caught a C-130 going directly to NKP, and arrived "home" with about five hours to spare. I had until midnight to check in and I made it back about dinnertime.

I checked the flight schedule in the squadron operations building, learned that I was not flying for two nights, and went right to the Officer's Club for a drink or three in celebration of my just-missed firing squad. I was glad to be back, but sorry that my R&R in Topeka had not been the dream that I had invented nor the relaxation that I expected. That short time in Topeka was not a vacation, but it was reality. I hoped that married life with a child would be somewhat better when I wasn't so preoccupied with flying over the Trail. I thought that maybe when I finished my tour flying over Laos, I would have every day to learn about my new life with my wife and baby girl. I was looking forward to that day when I could have a "normal" life.

My biggest worry during both R&Rs was when I couldn't get Laos and my Candlestick buddies out of my head, even when I was trying to relax. I was sure that I wouldn't let that happen to me when I returned home for good, after my tour. I was sure! I was sure!

But first, I had to finish my tour as a night FAC over Laos.

OTHER CTOS

Combat Time Off in Bangkok was a great stress reliever from the rigors of NKP. Most of us went to Bangkok for the CTO, except for a few of the more adventurous pilots who took as much time off as they could in NKP City.

NKP City was located on the banks of the Mekong River several miles from the airbase. Lots of the people stationed at NKP went there to visit special friends and girlfriends, or just to have a good time. I had accompanied a couple of my friends on a taxi ride to NKP City one day when I had a break in missions. I wanted to see what went on there and what these two friends of mine—J.L. Hunter and Jim Johnson—found so interesting.

There were three of us—me, J.L., and Jim. We walked together to the front gate of the base wearing our civvies and hired a taxi waiting there. There were always a few taxis waiting at the gate, probably because of our 24-hour a day schedule. There was always someone going to the main gate wanting a ride downtown, regardless of the time. So we grabbed the cab, haggled a minute to get the fare as low as possible, and jumped in for the 20-minute ride into town.

When we got there, Jim and J.L. wanted to show me all the sights. They took me to various and sundry bars, restaurants, a few hotels, and up and down several popular and populated streets in center city.

On one street, we walked through the town bazaar or market. There were lots of stalls and stands with lots of people at each one, haggling in Thai and Lao, and lots of things to buy. The oddest thing I saw were the live animals tied, wired, and nailed to the wooden counters so they wouldn't get away and still be fresh for the consummate NKP Thai cook. Most of these animals were unhappy and making noise about it. Snakes, monkeys, various birds, and other critters were caged. There was almost-fresh meat hanging from the rafters and support beams of the stalls. Food was being cooked in some of the open areas. Men were drinking out of cups and jars from common vats or basins holding some amber-colored liquid. It was colorful, different, noisy, interesting, loud, and very, very smelly. I was glad to finally get out of there.

After we walked awhile, we came to one of Jim's favorite bars. It was along the Mekong and had a deck overhanging the water. We sat down to enjoy a Singha beer, almost cold, and still smelling of the formaldehyde used to make it. J.L. said it wasn't like his Texas beer, but it did quench the thirst. So I tried a few. But I couldn't drink as much or as fast as they did. The best beer in NKP gave me the worst headache.

I talked with them a while longer, then decided to catch a cab back to the base to take some aspirin and get rid of the pain in my head. I didn't tell them what I really thought of NKP City, which was that it was hot, humid, ugly, and smelly. I would just as soon be in Bangkok on CTO than hanging out over the dirtiest river in the world, drinking formaldehyde beer. I never went back into NKP City.

But I did go back to Bangkok for CTO six or seven times. Sometimes I acted like a tourist and went to some of the cultural attractions in the city. I went to a Thai dancing program, a Thai boxing match (where the boxers demonstrated fighting with fists, feet, and homemade swords), and the Thai Cultural Center (where I watched elephants moving teak logs and Thai women dressed in native clothing spinning and weaving silk). In that center, I watched a man standing at the bottom of a 10 foot deep pit swatting the 20 or so cobras that were in there with him, using a stick so they would hiss and fan out their necks. I went to several of the better restaurants and hotels to eat and just to look around. I walked to and through many of the temples (called "Wats"), including the one with the statue of the English woman who had come to Siam to teach the King's children (the basis for the book and movie "The King and I"). I walked along the canals laced throughout the city (called "klongs") and watched the shallow, canoe-like boats race through the town canals using naked V-8 auto engines and a long propeller shaft.

Most of the good bars and restaurants were in the party district of the city, called Pat Pong Street. It was more of an area than a street, but everyone knew where you were going if you said "Pat Pong Street." You could buy anything there. The bars were cheap, there was always excitement, and there were always different kinds of entertainment available by just walking in the door. In 1969, it was a little like the Old West, when the cattlemen came to town after a long drive. Bangkok was interesting, colorful, and very much alive.

On most of my CTOs, I took a cab from the airport to the Chao Phrya Hotel. This was a six-story hotel that the American military had taken over for the Officer's Club and Bachelor Officers' Quarters (BOQ). Since I was a bachelor here for the duration of my tour, I usually got a room there. The hamburgers there were usually cow meat and not monkey or water buffalo.

The bar on the main floor was the meeting and greeting place for all of the military personnel serving in southeast Asia. It was the place all officers eventually gravitated to when visiting Bangkok on R&R or CTO. They had a great bar, cheap drinks, snacks from the kitchen, a nice, big dining room, a massage parlor in the basement, and clean and cheap rooms upstairs. It was my favorite base of operations when I was in town.

One day when I walked into the bar at the hotel and saw my old Training Instructor (TI) from Officer Training School (OTS) at Lackland AFB, in San Antonio, Texas. He was still a Captain and I was now a First Lieutenant. He hadn't been a bad guy at OTS, but he was usually on our cases and he didn't cut us much slack. It always seemed like he was bragging about how good he was and how awful and ugly we Officer Candidates were—a kind of holier-than-thou guy. But I walked up to him, re-introduced myself to him as one of his trainees at Lackland, and asked him what he was doing in Bangkok. He told me that he was assigned as a Petroleum, Oil and Lubricant (POL) Officer in Vietnam (a really nowhere job,

I thought) and that he was on his R&R. He asked me what I was doing and I told him that I was flying for a top secret outfit and that I couldn't discuss it with anyone except those cleared for Top Secret information (a kind of holier-than-thou statement, which I enjoyed immensely). I walked off. It was a great bar. It was a brief meeting. It made me feel really good.

Sometimes, when a group of us went on CTO together, we would take a taxi out to a restaurant to try different kinds of food, rather than the always-familiar hamburger. I tried lots of different kinds of restaurants in Bangkok, but my personal favorite was a Kobe Beef House in the international part of town. This restaurant featured Kobe beef, which were cut as filet mignons, about two inches thick. Because the cows were fed beer and hand-massaged daily, the lightly fat-ribboned meat was so tender you could just separate the bites with the edge of your fork. The steaks came with or without a light brandy-and-mushroom sauce, potatoes, salad, veggies, and other American-usual sides. The meat was tender, tasty and not very expensive. I probably went to that restaurant the most—since I was a meat-and-potatoes kind of Kansas boy.

One night, my squadron mates and I joined another group of Americans at a large, round table at the Kobe house. We all introduced ourselves, ordered drinks for our companions, and sat down together to eat Kobe beef and tell lies.

At some point in the evening, after a great dinner, the group broke up to go their separate ways for entertainment. Since I wasn't much into the nightclub life, and neither was another of those newly-acquainted brothers at the table, he and I decided to go to a place that he liked—a Greek bar. His name was Nick something and his family was Greek. He was American-born, but his parents had immigrated from the old country. He liked the old ways and wanted to take me to this favorite Greek bar, so off we went.

All during my conversations with Nick, I was never able to learn exactly what he did in Thailand or neighboring countries (Laos, Cambodia, Vietnam, China, etc.). He was a little mysterious about that, but on one occasion he mentioned the "Company" (which we all knew meant the Central Intelligence Agency, the CIA, the spooks). It could have been make-believe or true. I didn't know, nor care.

I really liked his favorite Greek bar. I liked the food they had (I recall something wrapped in grape leaves) and after a couple of shots of ouzo, I even liked that. I danced with strangers, I drank with new friends, and toasted anything and everything we could think of. I tried to get Nick to teach me Greek, but all he would teach me were a few Greek swear words. We threw plates—an old Greek custom. We drank more ouzo. We danced some more. I had a great time.

Somewhere, sometime during the early morning hours, I became aware that Nick and I were dancing down the middle of an unknown Bangkok street, arms over each other's shoulders, humming Greek tunes, and cussing in Greek (I think it was the same word over and over again). We were someplace in the city where there were no street lights, no moving cars, no nearby taxis or taxi stands, and no other living human beings (awake, that is). We had no idea where we were and no idea how to get back to civilization.

So we cunningly looked around—nothing. We looked up to try to see stars and find the North Star—totally clouded over. We looked at each other to see if either of us had a compass—not here. We were lost.

Finally, one of us decided that the glow of lights on the horizon over the tops of the side-by-side hovels along both sides of our dancing street might indicate where there was a place where others were still awake. So, we started walking that way. Eventually, we found moving cars and a taxi willing to stop and pick us up. We took the cab to the Chao Phrya, got out, and shook hands. I never saw Nick again. It was an exciting evening in Bangkok.

I sometimes went to other hotels, like the Intercontinental or some of the larger and famous ones of the city, just to sip tea or have a bite of lunch with the privileged and washed folks of the world. Some nights I would go with other squadron members to Thai nightclubs, just to see that side of the local culture. I didn't enjoy that very much and didn't want to participate in the usual shenanigans going on there (although I sometimes did have a beer or three).

Nights on CTOs were tough. I knew that someone else in the unit was flying my mission and might be getting his butt shot off. I didn't like that feeling. I was away from NKP but I couldn't get it out of my head. If I enjoyed myself too much, I knew I had to go back to the Trail in just a few more nights. So usually, I stayed in my room, wrote letters, and read lots of books. It was one way to relax and I tried to do just that.

I appreciated the gift of CTO's that the King of Thailand had given us. I appreciated the recognition that we received from the King as soldiers and airmen in combat. I really liked Bangkok, in all its foreignness. It was a hopping town, lots of life being lived, a lot of give-and-take from a very friendly people, and comforting. Bangkok was a good place to be on combat time off.

RUNAWAY FLARE PALLET

All of our parachute flares were positioned inside the cargo *compartment on a pallet designed to fit between rails running fore and aft on the floor, from the front end out to the very edge of the ramp in the rear. The rails were set up so that a pallet could be loaded into the aircraft from the rear. The rails had ball bearings built into them so each pallet could be rolled smoothly and easily into any place in the compartment. Once the pallet was located where the loadmaster wanted it, he would lock it down with metal clips to the rails.*

We kept the pallet of 100 flares in the center position of the cargo compartment for all takeoffs and landings. This put the weight of the flares near the aircraft's center of gravity. We could then move the pallet from the center position to the rearmost position, nearest the loading ramp, while flying toward our assigned mission area. We did this when the flares were needed by ground troops wanting illumination. In a flare mission, the loadmasters and flare kickers would move flares from this pallet to the flare dispensing equipment that was moved into the opening of the lowered ramp/cargo floor and the raised ceiling. This flare chute had openings for 6 flares, in open tubes, where the flare kickers would place each flare before pushing them out. Each flare tube had a length of metal wire that was attached to a safety pin on the top. When a flare was placed into the tube, the metal wire would be attached to the aircraft, so when the flare kicker pushed the flare down and out of the chute, the wire would pull out the safety pin as it passed the end of the chute on its way out.

One night, as we were flying over bad guy country, I ordered the loadmasters to reposition the flare pallet to the rear, just as I had a million (or so) times before. A minute later, the loadmaster told me the pallet was jammed. They couldn't move it back into the rails and they didn't have anything to secure it safely in its present position. In other words, we had a pallet full of magnesium flares that could be bumped loose at any time by the motion of normal flight and go anywhere inside the cargo compartment, out of control. Not a good thing.

While holding my breath, I very gently turned the airplane around and headed back to base. I told the controllers in the airport tower about the problem and they scrambled fire trucks to meet us at the touchdown point on the runway. I landed very gently, taxied very slowly, and stopped the aircraft near the end of the airfield even gentler still. After we landed, the fire trucks followed us to the safe area of the ramp, out in the middle of nowhere, where we could try to unstick the pallet, move it, and lock it in the rails at its proper position.

As soon as I stopped, the pallet moved slightly and locked itself into the rails where it belonged. We had used up an hour or so of our four-hour mission, but with the pallet locked up tight, and everything checking out with the rails and the pallet-locking devices, we decided to go out and try again. We did, and completed another mission without further incident. We didn't need the flares that night, but were able to put in an airstrike or two. Another night for a Candlestick.

COURAGE

Sometimes, during the day when I knew I had a mission that night, I would get a little nervous about the next mission. It wasn't so much that I was afraid of being hurt or of getting shot down, it was more like I was afraid that I would make a mistake and kill the other 9 guys on the airplane. I began to wonder about courage and whether I had any or not. I knew that I had completed some missions, and didn't seem to be too bothered by them either during or after. I felt like I had been doing a good job as a FAC, since I had been promoted to Aircraft Commander. I tried to think of times before the Air Force when I had either exhibited courage in civilian circumstances that might help me know and understand whether I was, in fact, a courageous person or a nervous Nellie. Then I remembered the bank job.

THE BANK JOB

December 1967

In the Spring of 1967, my wife, Vicki and I decided that we had had enough of college. She had just earned her undergraduate degree at Kansas University and I had just completed my first, lackluster year of KU Law School. I had finished my undergraduate degree a year earlier and started law school the previous Fall. I thought it was going to be easy. I found out that I was wrong. It was a 3-piece suit, button-down white shirt and tie kind of existence with each evening spent in the law library stacks doing case briefs or reading supplemental texts. Nine months of fear, hoping the Professor of each of the classes wouldn't call on me so I could exhibit my nervousness and uncertainty about any of the material that I had spent the previous nights studying. It was a paper chase. It was college hell.

We decided that we needed to do something exciting before I started my second year of law school the next Fall. We decided to go to Washington, D.C. for the summer, find jobs, explore a new place, and see if we liked living and working in a big city. I had a yen to find out about international law toward the possibility that I could get a job after law school at the State Department. I had 4 years of Russian, an immersion summer school in the language in Finland and the Soviet Union, and I thought I knew a lot about the U.S.S.R. after all those years of study.

We drove there in my 1964 ½ Mustang, with all of our worldly possessions stuffed in the trunk. We got there, found a cheap motel, and started putting our prepared Resumes into various places around town. Vicki accepted a job at a place called The Door Store in downtown Georgetown, a real hippie place that sold doors for folks to make into coffee tables or such. I finally accepted a job as a cashier at the Chevy Chase Branch of the Silver Springs National Bank in Chevy Chase, Maryland. We found an apartment in a 3rd floor walkup in a row of turn of the century homes located in the central city. It was a nice Archie Bunker area and near enough to the various attractions of Washington, D.C. to get to with a short walk or a 15-minute bus ride. Eventually, because of my job, we moved to the 10th floor of an apartment building in Chevy Chase, right above the bank where I worked.

Working at the Chevy Chase Branch in our high-rise apartment building was a pleasant job. All I had to do in the morning was ride the elevator down to the first floor, unlock the bank's lobby door, and start work.

Normally, the hours were 8:30 a.m. to 4:00 p.m. Some days I opened the drive-through window on the backside of the bank, which opened into the parking garage under the building. If I did that, I was at the window at 7:30 a.m. and then I could leave at 3 in the afternoon. I usually had the early shift every other week, unless the Branch Manager stepped in to take it for a week, just to break his and our monotony. Early hours weren't bad just because I lived so close to work.

Most days usually started at 8, when I'd report to work, count money, get carts and forms ready, prepare the marked "robbery" money, and help the Branch Manager or his secretary do housekeeping chores around the small bank facility until we opened for customers at 8:30. Normally, the bank closed business at 4, but both tellers usually stayed until 4:30 or so, just to take care of the paperwork and other items of clean up. On my early days, leaving work at 3:00 p.m. gave me plenty of time to explore the Chevy Chase area or to ride the bus downtown to see the sites there. On days when I got off at 3, I always went downtown to ogle the girls and savor the historical items in one or more of the 14 Smithsonian Museums.

At the bank, I worked with Mrs. Minifee, the other teller. Mrs. Minifee was a pretty, married woman of about my own age, but very pregnant. Her husband was in some way responsible for a Christian prayer breakfast for Congress-people, so he was always busy running around and hobnobbing with the rich and powerful.

Mrs. Minifee usually went home alone, to a small apartment

near downtown. She told me that she ate her dinners alone on most occasions. I first felt very sorry for her, and later, as she became more and more pregnant, all of us at the bank became very protective. We each tried to help her as much as we could, to make her days and life easier. Her husband was a creep. I met him and saw him from time to time, but he always seemed like Uriah Heep; a limp-wristed, hand-wringing, whining type who was so full of himself that he couldn't see the special pearl he had married.

As I said, we all became very protective, and a little bit enamored, of Mrs. Minifee. Although we talked a lot at work, I never called her by her first name for fear that that small piece of familiarity would somehow forever expose my romantic fantasies about her. She was Mrs. Minifee to me and I was Jim to her. I had decided that I was tired of "Pat" and wanted to sound more business-like and mature, so I adopted my grandfather's nickname (my formal first name being James also) and became "Jim" in Washington, D.C.

We weren't the only ones closely interested in Mrs. Minifee's welfare. On most afternoons, several of the older gentlemen who lived in the building, or nearby, would drop by to say hello to her and transact minor bank business—usually changing large bills into smaller ones or smaller bills into larger ones. These old codgers seldom came to my window to let me help. One of these guys looked like George Burns, and smoked large, expensive cigars, and often came in just to tell her a new joke he had heard—evidently riding the movie star image as far as he could—but not making much headway with her, since he was at least 80 years old, if a day.

Another regular to the bank was the man who operated the parking garage just outside our drive-through window. Whenever Mrs. Minifee worked the drive-through, he was usually not far away, stopping often to talk to her through the microphone that was always on, so we could hear customers drive up to the window. He was always polite to me too, but seldom spent much time around the window when I had the early morning duty there. The garage closed at 4, so when the garage guy was through with his paperwork and had put his nightly deposit together, he would often knock on the back window of the drive-through in the parking garage, so he could give us his deposit in the drawer and say a nice thing or two to Mrs. Minifee.

Another of Mrs. Minifee's regulars was the beat cop. This young guy would come strolling in almost every afternoon, say hello to Mr. Ebert, the Branch Manager, stop by his secretary's desk to flirt a bit with her, sashay over to my window to say something about sports, and finally, walk over to Mrs. Minifee's window to linger while she closed her drawer or counted money or did some other routine business. He always asked about her health and how her husband was, but seldom took his eyes off of her while he was in the bank. Obviously, a very dedicated young policeman. Very thoughtful. Serving and protecting.

One late afternoon, a week before Christmas, at about 3:30 p.m. just before closing, a young lady came into the bank and sat down on one of the chairs spaced along the outer window wall. She looked to be mid-twenties, wearing a floppy hat and a long wool or camel's hair coat. Mr. Ebert got up from his desk near the back of the bank, walked past his secretary's desk, and in his usual polite way of speaking, holding one hand within the other in front of him, asked the young lady if he could help her. She told him, "No, not right now, I'm waiting for my husband to come from work so we can open a new account."

Mr. Ebert returned to his desk and continued his usual closing routine of reviewing our daily paperwork and other normal office matters. At about 3:45, Mr. Ebert's secretary, a tall, long-legged, red-haired woman of indeterminate middle-age, walked out to the young lady to again ask if there was anything she could do for her. Again, she said "No, thank you" and turned away. The secretary returned to her desk, near the end of the tellers' line, and continued her day-end routine.

Just before 4, our closing time, Mr. Ebert got up from his desk again, walked over to the glass front door of the building, inserted his key and locked the door. He then went over to the young lady and asked her to leave, since the bank was now closed. Just as he was finishing that announcement, the girl drew a gun from her purse, pointed it at him and very quietly said "this is a holdup, get over to the counter!"

Mr. Ebert had that kind of baldness that looks like a friar's—billiard-ball bare on the top, but a fringe of full grey around the head. His head was like a temperature gauge—when he was cool and in control, his head was smooth and clean, just like he'd shaved it. But when he was upset or angry, like he immediately became when the young lady pointed her pistol at him, his head became beet red and sweaty all over.

We knew we were in trouble. The girl pushed Mr. Ebert toward his desk, then turned to point the gun at the secretary, who also turned the color of her dyed bee's-nest hair—bright red. The girl then pushed both of them back behind the teller's counter, "Where I can watch you" she said, and walked to the front of the counter in front of Mrs. Minifee. She handed her a paper bag and said "Fill it up, lady," and looked at me and said, "Keep both of your hands on the counter where I can see them!" Mrs. Minifee was working about three feet from me, and I saw her put all of the bills from her drawer into the paper bag, including the marked "robbery money" stack.

All of this time, the girl was trying to watch all four of us, making sure she pointed her gun at each of us from time to time, and nervously looking over her shoulder every once in a while to see if she could see anything through the plate-glass windows lining the front of the office.

When her bag was full at the other teller's window, she came to mine. She put the gun, a Western-style pistol that looked like a Colt Single-Action Army (Roy Rodgers' favorite) on the counter in front of me and said "You too, mister, and don't touch that alarm button!" So I did what she said, put all of my bills in the bag, along with the robbery stash, and handed the bag back to her.

She then came around the counter and pushed Mr. Ebert and his secretary toward Mrs. Minifee and me. "What are you going to do now?" Mr. Ebert asked. "I'm putting you in there," the girl said and nodded toward the open walk-in vault with her head. "But once that door closes, it can't be opened until 7:30 tomorrow morning!" Mr. Ebert complained.

"I don't care," the girl said, "you've got air in there, I know you do, and someone will let you out in the morning." Mr. Ebert's secretary then chimed in, with her New Jersey accent showing more clearly than usual, "But we have a pregnant lady here, and she's due any day, and where would we go to the bathroom?"

"I don't care," the girl repeated. "Just get in that vault!" I knew that look in Mrs. Minifee's eyes. It was the one she had several times a day when she would suddenly announce, "I gotta go!" slam her drawer, lock it as fast as she could, and hurry out through the lobby door to the ladies' restroom. Being locked in a vault with her didn't seem like a good idea to me then. Where were the cops when you needed one? I thought.

We all started to move together toward the vault. Miss Robber was standing about six feet away from us and walking backward toward it, with her pistol pointed all the time at Mr. Ebert and me. Someone knocked at the back window of the drive-through in the garage—loudly, several times. The girl looked away from us and to her left toward the sound of the banging.

Several things happened to me in the blink of an eye —I got very, very mad about being locked in a vault all night with Mrs. New Jersey accent, Mr. Prissy Manager, and a pregnant woman. I got an instant adrenalin rush. I was MAD! Angrier than I had ever been before in my life.

Without even thinking about it or even knowing what I was doing, I flew through the air, wrapped my arms around the girl. and slammed her to the floor. The gun was under her, I was on top, and everybody was yelling and screaming, including me. She and I wrestled some, both struggling to free the pistol. She started to swear and kept saying to me, between cuss words, "I'm gonna shoot you, wise guy—I'm gonna pull the trigger and blow you away," while crying and fighting as hard as she could. I said at one point, "Go ahead, sister, you'll just shoot yourself, because I have the gun turned toward your ugly stomach!"

"I'll shoot through me" she said, "I don't care about getting hurt if I can get you off my back!" We struggled for a bit longer.

Finally, I managed to wrestle the gun away from her. When I did, she lost all of her steam and just lay on her stomach on the floor and cried.

I handed the pistol to Mr. Ebert and told both the secretary and Mrs. Minifee to sit on the girl gangster. I ran for the front door leading outside to the sidewalk on the front of the building. I noticed as I ran that Mr. Ebert had left his keys in the lock of the front door, so I didn't need to use mine. I grabbed the keys, turned them as fast as I could, and looked out through the glass door to make sure I wasn't going to run into someone. Who could possibly be coming into the bank then, after closing, didn't even occur to me.

When I got just outside of the front door, I looked up. I saw our old friend, the beat cop, Mrs. Minifee's not-so-secret admirer, standing partially hidden behind a pillar in front of the building. I noticed he was looking at me with a funny look on his face. I held the door open, yelled the cop's name, and took about two steps toward him when he yelled back at me: "Stop!" as loud as he could.

Why was he shouting, I wondered—I was almost standing on top of him. Then he looked away from me, out toward the street, and started waving his arms back and forth, up and down, from high to low in front of him, and continued shouting "Stop!"

Now I was curious. I looked out toward the street too—and saw about five cars stopped in the street in front of the bank and about 20 cops of all sizes, shapes, and manner of dress standing behind those cars and pointing their shotguns, pistols, and tommy guns at little old me. My knees turned to Jello, my stomach flip-flopped, and my mind suddenly went totally blank.

The cop ran up to me, stood very close and asked "What's going on?"

"A robbery" I said. "She's inside. We've got her pinned on the floor. Mr. Ebert has her gun." The young cop grabbed my arm and pulled me away from the door. Twenty cops or so ran past me and into the bank. All I heard was yelling and screaming and crying and Mrs. Minifee shouting, "Let me go—I gotta go!"

I sat down on the steps outside the building and let everyone do

James P. "Pat" Hyland

what they wanted to do. Me, I was just going to sit there and wait for my legs to come back.

At some point, I went back into the bank and watched the FBI guys handcuff the girl bank robber. She had tears in her eyes when she walked by me, but she growled at me as she went past, saying, "I'll come back and get you, you bastard!"

The cops let each of us relax a bit. Then they separated us into different parts of the bank and began taking statements from each of us. I sat in the chair at the front of the office where "she" had waited so patiently before, and gave my whole story to a Chevy Chase detective and an FBI agent.

One offered me a cigarette, which I took. He lit it, I took a serious drag from the first cigarette ever in my life, then became even dizzier than when I had faced all those almost trigger-happy policemen out front. I finally got through my story and they let us all go home. I don't remember much of that night in the apartment, but I do remember asking Vicki to go out to the local market to get cold beer.

About 10 days later, a few days before my final day at work, a gentleman came to the bank to speak to Mr. Ebert and me. He identified himself as the Chief of Security for the main bank. He handed me a letter from the FBI, signed by J. Edgar Hoover, which thanked me for stopping a bank robbery and for being such a good citizen. The Security Chief thanked me, too. He told me: "Frankly, that was a hell of a thing to do and I want to shake your hand for having the guts to do that." He did shake my hand.

He then said: "That's just the way I personally feel, but as Chief of Security of the American National Bank of Silver Springs, it is my duty to inform you that you are officially fired from this job!"

Stunned, I asked why. He said, "The bank policy on robbery, which you read and signed, stated that you were to obey the orders of any bank robber, let them have the money, especially the marked and treated bills, and let them go away. Law enforcement has the job to catch crooks," he said, "not tellers."

"How long do I have?" I asked. "Two weeks," he said.

With some smugness, I then said to the Security Chief, "You can't fire me—I've already quit!" I had turned in my letter of resignation about a week before the robbery.

My final day at work was about a week away. They gave me an extra day or two off. Things were looking up.

[The letter from J. Edgar is framed and hangs in my den.]

I realized from that funny and frightening episode that I displayed some courage, even if it was a direct result of my temper. I believed that if I was in fact a wimp, I wouldn't have reacted so drastically and so impetuously. Maybe I had what it takes to be a great FAC pilot and aircraft commander, after all. I guess I would soon find out.

MU GIA INTERSTATE

One of the primary mountain passes leading out of the southern portion of North Vietnam into east-central Laos is the Mu Gia Pass. There was a trail in the bottom of the pass that went through the karst areas on both sides of the border. Karst formations are limestone mesas or buttes, usually very tall (several hundred feet) and very slender. They generally rise out of the jungle canopy with very steep sides. I had flown near Mu Gia Pass on several night missions and saw the fields of karst, glowing whitely within the darker jungle below. They looked like tall, pale, flat-topped legs sticking up out of the top of jungle. They dotted the area where the Trail exited the pass. The pass itself was a very narrow trail between rather large pieces of the karst formations.

The anti-aircraft artillery fire in the area of the Pass was so intense that most aircraft were prohibited from flying near it. Much of the fire was radar directed from the North Vietnam side of the border. Our Rules of Engagement (ROE) prohibited us from striking those radar or anti-aircraft artillery battery sites because they were in North Vietnam, not Laos. But the Trail was clearly visible coming from North Vietnam, through the Pass, winding its way into the jungle on the Laotian side of the border. The Pass itself was steep and rocky with that same pale color as the karst formations near it. The Trail could only be seen a short distance on the west side of the Pass before it disappeared from sight under the triple-canopy jungle of Laos.

On several occasions, special high-altitude bombers dropped small mines in the Pass to try to slow or stop the large volume of foot and small vehicle traffic going through the Pass on the Trail into Laos. The terrain in the area of the Pass was too steep and rugged to allow the larger types of trucks to use that particular trail. Most of the traffic was on foot or bicycles. The mines most often dropped were called "foot-poppers" or "gravel." These were irregular-shaped pieces of explosive that were colored to match the surrounding terrain and designed to explode and severely wound anyone stepping on them, or disable bike tires if they were run over. But mining the Pass apparently wasn't working—traffic wasn't slowing down or diminishing.

Eventually, the powers somewhere decided to bomb the heck out of the pass and close it to all traffic. So they sent in three formations of B-52's, a total of 9 aircraft, each of which carried a hundred and nine 500-pound bombs. During our intelligence briefing that night, we were told this was going to happen, since we were on our way to the area due west of the Pass. Just before the scheduled bombing, the Airborne Communication and Command Center aircraft called out "Arclight" three times over the emergency frequency, which meant that a flight of B-52s was in the area on a bombing mission. We watched the bombs go off all over the Pass area. The three Arclight missions that night over the Pass, each with three aircraft, carried a total of about 480,000 pounds of bombs.

Another Candle was sent near the Pass the following night to conduct bomb-damage assessment (BDA) for the B-52 raid. When the crew returned later that night, they told us that where the Trail had earlier been a very narrow and twisty path through the karst formations, the Arclight strikes of B-52s had blown up the area so badly it had crushed the karst limestone formations into baseball-sized chunks and spread those chunks throughout the Trail area on both sides of the Pass. It was no longer a narrow trail, suitable for only foot traffic. It was now a smooth, rock-covered highway, with moving trucks, guns, and everything. So, in just one short night, the B-52s had changed a rugged footpath into an interstate highway.

Orders came down a few days later that our squadron was forbidden from flying anywhere near Mu Gia Pass, because of the now heavier concentration of radar-directed (Firecan) AAA in the area. Apparently, the gomers had used the new super highway to bring in guns to protect the trucks and other vehicles now using the newest and finest highway in eastern Laos. Mu Gia Interstate —American made, and nothing but the best!

AN ARCLIGHT ENCOUNTER

One of my night missions was to an area just west of Khe *San, South Vietnam, in Laos, and very near the small Laotian village of Tchepone. We were cruising over the Trail, which ran parallel to the Laos-South Vietnam border, looking for trucks. It was a very dark night and Scope had a difficult time seeing anything on the ground because of the total lack of any ambient light (stars, moon, gunfire, etc.), which caused his Starlight scope to lose resolution and flicker with ghost twinkles. Just as we were starting to get really bored with this mission, Scope cried "ground burst" over the intercom, meaning that he had seen a flash of light on the ground, what we normally associated with the discharge of an AAA weapon. Then the whole world lit up below us with over 300 ground explosions. We could all understand that what we were seeing were bomb explosions, because we could also see the blast ring from each bomb radiate outward from the crater. "Arclight," the Scope called on the intercom—a little too late, since all 10 of us on the Candle recognized what had just occurred directly below us.*

I called Blind Bat on the radio frequency given to us that night and told him that an Arclight strike had just happened below us. Those 500-pound bombs had dropped through our altitude to explode directly below. The Blind Bat operator replied "I'll check on it" and ended his transmission.

A few seconds later, on our Guard frequency, which all Air Force aircraft were required to monitor for emergency radio calls, we heard: "All aircraft in sector XXX (our location at the time of this thrilling episode), be aware that an Arclight strike will occur at XXX o'clock GMT (Greenwich Mean Time)"—which was about 10 minutes ago. The crewmembers had been quiet up to that point. Each was probably reflecting, as I was, that we had just been missed by 300 huge 500 pound bombs that had been dropped, without warning, right through our altitude, and didn't touch us. Everyone on the crew started to talk at once. Everyone was mad about the incompetence of the straphang-

ers and ground pounders who should have told us about the strike coming so we could vacate the area before those bombs were dropped. It was another example of too little, almost too late or being at the wrong place at the wrong time. One of Murphy's Laws.

A-26 IN THE WEEDS

Our "sister squadron," the 609th Special Operations *Squadron, was an A-26 bomber squadron, whose call sign was "Nimrods." The 609th provided bombs and bullets to Candlestick targets. The Nimrods flew only at night too. Their aircraft were painted black all over.*

The first thing that struck me about all these "Nimrod" cats was how old they were. There was a lot of gray hair showing around the black ball caps they all wore. Some of them must have been at least 40 or so—I mean, they looked OLD! What were they doing flying a hot number like the A-26?

The A-26 was a mid-wing fighter-bomber of late World War II vintage. It had started its aviation career as a B-26, but by this time in the Vietnam War, most had been re-built and re-named the A-26.

It was a fast and sleek twin-radial engine airplane. The pilots sat in a greenhouse canopy arrangement just behind the nose of the aircraft, with the aircraft commander in the left seat positioned slightly ahead of the copilot or navigator, depending on the mission. The aircraft had eight .50 caliber machine guns in the nose and 10 hard points under the wings to hold deadly napalm bombs (filled with sticky, jellied gasoline), "funny" bombs (filled with thousands of small but lethal explosive grenades), or other munitions. It was not only fast, but it carried a boatload of bombs, it could shoot, and had fuel tanks large enough to stay on station with the Candles for almost our entire four-hour mission time. Candlestick pilots always used the call sign "Nimrod" with a certain amount of reverence in their voices. We all really liked those guys and appreciated the work they did on the Trail.

But one night I was especially impressed.

It was the middle of the dry season and trucks were running

everywhere, all over the Trail. They were on just about every dusty, hot road threading in and out of the jungle in eastern Laos. All of them were heading south. During that dry season, the usual procedure was for Candlesticks and Nimrods to take off together, on each of the four nightly missions. For each Candle taking off, there were two Nimrods.

I was assigned a mission area over the eastern part of Steel Tiger where the gomer trucks were running heavy. We hadn't been in the area too long when the scope called "Tallyho—trucks on the Trail. I see lots of them heading south. Get me some Nimrods." I called Blind Bat and asked for ordnance. He told me he would be sending just one Nimrod, because the other was busy with another Candle. One was good enough for me.

Soon afterward, the Nimrod called: "Candle 504, Nimrod 22, heading your way from the west. Whatcha' got?"

"Nimrod, Candle. We've got about 10 trucks, running in convoy, with convoy (slit) lights, about three klicks (kilometers) north of the Elephant's Back (a place where the Trail formed a large bow, running in the open, along the river, and easily visible with the naked eye). They're heading south. What are you carrying?"

"Candle, Nim. I've got a little of everything —some hard bombs and some nape (napalm). I'm coming up from the south a little bit, over the Trail, and I'm about over the Elephant's Back. Did you say these guys are running with convoy lights?"

"Roger, Nim. The first truck and a few in between are running with slit lights and the others are blacked out. Why?"

"Candle, Nim. I'm coming in just north of the Elephant's Back right now and I see moving lights on the ground. Mind if I take a look?"

"Go ahead Nim. But our scope tells me that they're still in the jungle and not out in the open yet."

"Roger, Candle. I'll go down a little bit and see what I can see."

A minute or so passed.

"Candle, Nimrod, I've got a visual on trucks. I see them just about a mile north of the Elephant's Back, where it switches to the west a little bit. They're still in jungle, but I can see the lead truck *and a couple of other lights in trail behind. Are these the trucks you're talking about?"*

"Nim, Candle. That's a roger. Those are the ones."

"Candle, Nim. I've got a great visual on these guys. I'd like to take a pistol pass (strafing run with machine guns) on these guys."

"Nim, Candle. You're cleared in hot. Call when you're off target."

"Candle, Nim. Roger."

We waited, but we heard nothing.

Nothing.

Nothing.

I broke the silence. "Scope, pilot. You see Nimrod?"

"Nope, pilot. He was blacked out. I still see the lights of some of the the trucks, but I can't see the Nim…holy shit, pilot! I'm seeing lots of flashes in the trees, tracers running along the trucks, tracers bouncing up through the jungle canopy… now some secondaries … Nim is shooting up these guys pretty bad. Wait, now it's stopped."

Again, we waited. Nothing.

"Nim, Candle." I tried raising the Nimrod on the radio.

Nothing.

"Nimrod, Candle."

Nothing.

Now I was getting a little worried. Nimrod hadn't called off target and he wouldn't answer my calls.

"Nim, Candle."

"Goddamit, Candle," he finally replied. "Gimme a second."

So we waited.

And waited.

And waited.

"Candle, Nim."

"Nim, this is Candle. Go."

"Sorry about that," he said. "It got a little busy there for a minute. I wanted to get a better shot at the gomers, so I went down a little before shooting. You know how that goes—when I light up my eight 50s, it gets almost too bright up front for me to see what I'm shooting at. Then when I started to hit the damn things, they started to blow up and

it trashed my night vision all to hell. After I finished my pistol pass, I got a little busy getting back up above the trees so I could call you."

"Nim, you said 'back up above the trees'"?

"Yep, Candle. I guess I got a little carried away with seeing them up close. I really wanted to shoot for a change. I guess I got a little low."

"Well, Nim, low or not, our scope tells me you killed three of those trucks and stopped the rest, so I guess we'd better get back to work and use some of your other ordnance to get them before they get away."

"OK Candle. Set 'em up. I'm out of bullets anyway."

We killed all of those trucks and a few more before ending our four-hour mission. After landing at NKP and going through the usual post-mission drill, I ended up at our squadron clubhouse to have a drink. I really wanted to find out who that Nimrod pilot was, shooting trucks with his nose-mounted machine guns, flying nose-to-nose with them, below the jungle canopy, AT NIGHT!

I saw one of the Nimrods I had flown with before. "Hey Jack, who was Nimrod 22 tonight?"

"That's the one, over there," he said, pointing. "His name is Steve. He's been here a while, but you may not have flown with him before."

I looked across the room and saw one of the really old guys. He must have been 45—lots of gray hair, sweaty flight suit, and just the beginning of a paunch. I couldn't believe it. An old guy, flying an A-26, at night, down in the weeds, killing trucks with his machine guns—he must have brass cajones as big as basketballs. I had to meet this guy. I walked up to him with a smile on my face, thinking about him being an old guy.

"Hi Nim. I'm Candlestick 504. My name is Pat. Nice job!"

He just smiled.

"Can I buy you a drink?" I asked.

COURT MARTIAL NUMBER THREE

Because NKP had squadrons of C-123's, A-1's, and A-26's, *all of which flew both day and night missions, the Officer's Club ("O Club") had three "happy hours." The first was at 5 pm, and was considered the "straphangers'" time, because they were doing the usual 8-5 jobs in administrative positions. Pilots considered non-flying officers as "straphangers," because even though they were officers in the Air Force, pilots were the real point of the Air Force spear. Pilots drove the bus, all others were merely riding along. Straphangers are those who are riding and holding onto the straps suspended from the overhead rails of the bus, railroad car, or subway car. During that first happy hour, those of us who flew at night usually stayed out of the O Club except to eat dinner in the huge dining area off to one side of the main bar. All in the bar at that happy hour were generally the straphangers and ground pounders, which was no place for real men. These "other" people did not talk with their hands, make engine noises with their lips, or drink like fish. They did not talk about combat, airplanes, close calls, women, or fast cars, in that order of priority. Obviously, they were destined for mere drabness.*

The second happy hour at the Club was at midnight and went to about 2 in the morning. This period was for the pilots and other administrative types who had early evening missions or whose jobs required them to be up late (photo interpreters, intelligence types, next-day mission planners, etc.). This hour also included late supper for those who did not attend the normal dining hour at the O Club. Since there was no mess hall or dining facilities for the officers anywhere on NKP, all officers had to take their meals in the O Club or take their chances at one of the several foreign restaurants located at some distance from the Club on the "Thai" side of the airbase. During this time, everyone mixed together pretty well, since most attending this happy hour were directly involved with the support of the flying effort.

The third happy hour was at 4 a.m. It went to about breakfast time and sometimes longer. This time was for those of us who flew the latest night missions. That was our happy hour. Crewmembers of the 606th, A-1 pilots (call signs "Sandy," "Lobo," and "Spad"), A-26 pilots (call sign "Nimrod"), and sometimes the Search and Rescue guys flying HH-3 helicopters (call sign "Jolly Greens") were the only people up at that hour. Most who attended at that time had returned from combat missions shortly before the start of that particular happy hour. It was the crazy hour. Usually some kind of food was available, at least snacks like chips and dip, or nachos, or sliced meat and bread, etc. But the alcohol was the drawing card. Heineken beer was 15 cents a bottle during that special hour. Each night had a different drink special, like martinis for a dime, or manhattans, gimlets, or gin and tonic, each for a dime.

And there were drinking games like "dead bug" (last one to fall to the floor when anyone yells "dead bug" had to buy a round of drinks for everyone in the bar), or one (name forgotten) where everyone at the bar tipped back on their high bar stools, with a shot of vodka or tequila on the bar in front of each person along that 30 foot bar, and when someone calls "go," everyone falls backward on their stool while drinking their shot. The last one to hit the floor buys the next round at the bar.

Another famous game was "carrier landing," where tables were lined up in a row, liberally dampened with beer or other unnamed and assorted liquids, and people run toward the tables to throw themselves onto the wet tabletops trying to slide all the way down the tables. A good carrier landing brings the "pilot" just up to the far end of the table. A bad landing is either a short one caused by lots of skips and bounces from too much tabletop friction or a long one where the "pilot" dives nose first onto the floor at the end of the "carrier."

Another fun one was "dollar poker." In this game, the players use the serial numbers on dollar bills to make poker hands, drinks are bets, and the loser of each hand has to buy all the players another round of drinks. There were always lots of games. There was always lots of drinking and carrying on. There were usually no females or straphangers or high-ranking officers at this special hour of enchantment. We were back from being shot at, we were alive, we were alone and lonely, we were grateful, and we had a terrible hankering for something to drink and something to do that was "safe."

Sometimes things got out of hand at that time of the morning. This was true if there had been an especially rough night on the Trail, like someone getting shot down, or a rescue effort gone bad, or someone getting wounded while flying a mission, or just a hard, tense, scary, normal night mission over the Ho Chi Minh Trail.

One such night, during the dry season in Laos (which we called "gun season" for obvious reasons), several of us had had a very bad night over the Trail. We usually had 5 aircraft out at one time in different parts of Laos, each flying a 4-hour mission. The North Vietnamese used the dry season to move lots of supplies down the Trail, toward South Vietnam and our troops fighting there, and to supply their soldiers and Viet Cong in South Vietnam, Laos and Cambodia. There were always more anti-aircraft guns on the Trail during the dry season to protect the trucks and walking enemy soldiers (which we affectionately called "gomers").

That particular night, all five aircraft, including mine, had had an unusually high number of anti-aircraft rounds shot at us ("walking the Archie," which an older pilot informed us that the World War I pilots used to call anti-aircraft fire, and which we now officially called "Triple-A"). Many of the 23mm, 37mm, 57mm and 85mm AAA rounds had come very near us as we directed air strikes against trucks and storage areas on the Trail. It was not a fun night, although not unusual. We had directed a lot of strikes with NKP aircraft (A-1's and A-26's) and other aircraft from Air Force, Navy, and Marine units stationed in South Vietnam or on Yankee Station out to sea. The NKP aircraft all ended our de-briefings at just after the start of the 4 a.m. happy hour.

That night martinis were a dime. We started a large table of dollar poker. I was drinking vodka martinis because I didn't particularly like gin (and the bartender would slip a couple of extra olives in each of my martinis). I hoped the two or more olives per martini would somehow serve to weaken the effects of the straight vodka. Others at the bar were doing shots and playing the "bar stool game." The O Club bar was crowded, but there were no straphangers, only combat mission crews. I won a few hands and lost a few hands. Games were going very fast. At one count, the last before losing the capability of counting, I had 9 full martinis in front of me and I had already downed 4 or 5 very quickly after sitting down and starting the game (mostly just to quench my after-mission thirst).

I don't remember much of that night in the Club, after the 4th martini. But I do remember that I had downed all of my martinis like a good little pilot-boy (think of all the poor thirsty children in China). I have no idea how many martinis I finally drained before I tried to leave the O Club to go back to my "hooch." My hooch, at that time, was a 2-man trailer, about 40 feet long by 8 feet wide. A door on each end gave access to each of the two pilot's living quarters. Every trailer had a bathroom, accessible from both rooms, in the middle of the trailer. My trailer, as the others of the squadron, was located directly across the street from the Officer's Club. By walking directly out of the front door of the O Club, crossing a concrete footbridge spanning a "monsoon" ditch (which is a cement-lined ditch about 4 feet across and 3 feet deep), and crossing the asphalt-paved street, a person could make a hard starboard turn (i.e., right turn) and enter the side door of our squadron's day room/club (bar, TV, dart boards, card tables, reading library, etc.). If, after crossing the street, I would make a hard port turn (left turn) after passing the squadron club, after just a few more steps, I would find myself in front of my green trailer door (under the sagging frond of a nearby banana tree).

After this particular night of serious poker and silly sipping games, I decided to leave the O Club with my friend and fellow Candlestick pilot, J.R. Hunter. J.R. (a hard drinking Texas boy) and I had been drinking together all night at our poker table. He had been one of the other Candlestick birds that had taken so much "flak" that night. When we tried to leave the bar of the Club, we both found out that our legs wouldn't work. So we talked that little problem over in clear and logical fashion and decided to crawl out of the Officer's Club—out the front door, down the front sidewalk, over the monsoon ditch, and across the street—the most direct route to our respective trailers.

When we pushed open the front double doors with our heads, we found out that it was already daylight, a mighty hurtful discovery considering the condition of our heads. It was so bright out and we were pretty tired from having crawled at least 30 or 40 feet or so from the bar, we decided to rest just a bit on the front sidewalk. Prone, of course, both on our bellies, semi-conscious, so we could resume crawling upon finding strength and direction. Suddenly, we were both awakened by the amplified bugle call that accompanied the raising of the flag on the base every morning at 8 a.m. During that bugle call, the military custom is for everyone, including those in vehicles, to stop, face the direction of the base flag, and salute.

Because we had been so rudely awakened there on the front sidewalk of the Club, all J.R. and I could do was salute the bugs beneath our eyes while laying face down on the concrete. When the bugle call ended, several sets of well-polished black shoes appeared directly in our crawling path. Lots of them—and very shiny. We both rolled over onto our backs to see what herd of people could have such shiny shoes so early in the morning. We quickly discovered that the closest set of shiny shoes belonged to the *Wing Commander* (the highest Air Force Officer on the base and commander of all units stationed there) and his entourage. Crap!

It seemed logical at the time—it was 8 a.m., the flag had just been raised, and the straphangers were on their way to breakfast with The Big Kahuna. Being the well-trained pilots and Air Force Officers that we were, both J.R. and I saluted the Colonel while lying on our backs. Apparently, Colonel Crosby didn't think that was very funny, because he asked us both of our names (which were already clearly marked on the flight suits we were wearing) and our assigned squadron. We both said "Candlesticks, Sir!" The Colonel then asked his aide to make a note of our names and unit and the circumstances that occasioned his attention. Someone asked what they should do about us, and the response, apparently from the Wing Commander, was "leave them there" or words to that effect. All of the very tall officers in their best Class A, blue uniforms, then marched smartly past us, leaving us still in the middle of the sidewalk giving our best salute. J.R. and I both laughed about the straphangers and their funny ways and began again to crawl toward our hooches.

Apparently, we had some difficulty navigating that distance, since I awoke sometime around noon, lying in the concrete-lined monsoon ditch that bordered the road in front of the O Club. I hadn't even made it to the other side of the road before falling into the ditch and going to sleep. J.R. must have evaporated, since I couldn't find him in the ditch. There weren't any fresh smears on the asphalt road and nobody was lying in the shade of our palm and banana trees near our trailers. I guessed that J.R. had made it home. Finally, I was able to walk, somewhat disjointedly, to my trailer and collapse into my bunk.

About 3 p.m. that afternoon, an Airman knocked on my door, waking me up again, to tell me that my Squadron Commander wanted to see me as soon as possible (ASAP). So I took a quick shower, put on my flight suit, took several aspirin (which didn't help much), put on my darkest sunglasses, and walked to our squadron operations room. I found J.R. there also. He too had a really bad hangover. We both knocked on the commander's door and formally presented ourselves to him when he told us to enter.

This Squadron Commander was a good one. He had been a fighter jock sometime in his past. He flew as many missions with us as he could, rather than doing all of his commanding from his desk, even though he was a Lieutenant Colonel and rather ancient (past 40). His name was Firebaugh. Most pilots liked him. I liked him. I had flown with him several times. Some of those times he was the Aircraft Commander (AC) and I the copilot and sometimes I was the AC and he was my copilot. There were never any difficulties either way, and I trusted his flying ability and his combat operational capabilities.

Overall, he was a pilot's pilot.

After putting us "at ease," he asked us to sit down and tell him the story about our encounter with the Wing Commander earlier that day. Of course, we told him everything. He had on his desk the de-briefing sheets from both of our flights the previous night and he reviewed each of them with us. We couldn't lie—he was one of "us," not one of "them" i.e., the straphangers. After hearing our story, and our apologies for getting him into trouble, he told us he would take care of the Wing Commander and dismissed us. Neither J.R. nor I heard anything further about the episode in the next few days.

Then one day I read on the flight status board that I was going to fly with the Squadron Commander, with me as Aircraft Commander, the following night. We were assigned to a very hot area of northern Laos, in "the Barrel Roll". The XO saw me and told me that the Squadron Commander wanted to brief me on that flight as soon as possible. I reported immediately to the Commander. He told me that he had had a long conversation with the Wing Commander about our sidewalk-saluting stunt. He said that he tried to explain to the Wing Commander just how hard our missions were and how dangerous. He said that he told him that Candlestick pilots need to let off a little steam after particularly "strenuous" missions. He said that the Wing Commander bragged that he was a "true" fighter pilot, was currently combat qualified in the A-1 Skyraider, and that he had flown a number of times in the same areas as Candlesticks—even a "few" times at night. He also said that fighter pilots had it tougher than "trash-hauling C-123 types" and therefore Candlestick pilots didn't have it rough enough to justify such "unofficerly" conduct. He said that he could understand fighter pilots acting that way, but not pilots who had easier jobs.

Our Commander, being a cool kind of guy, even though he later told me that he was really hot at the Wing Commander's attitude, suggested that the Colonel might want to ride along with us some night in order to see just how "easy" we "trash-haulers" in the Candlestick squadron had it each night. He also suggested that if the Colonel still thought that our squadron was merely a group of "trash-haulers," with cushy missions, after seeing us actually perform one night, he would agree to cooperate with the Colonel in his reprimand of J.R. and me. Our Commander didn't actually say the words "court martial," but we both thought that we were in a lot of hot water if the Wing Commander couldn't be convinced that we "deserved" to act like "fighter pilots."

All of the pilots in the Candlestick squadron believed that at least the Air Force knew that we had an extra-hazardous job, since we were awarded an Air Medal for every 10 missions and the A-1 pilots were awarded the same Air Medal for every 12 missions. We thought that proved that our missions were tougher than theirs, especially considering that A-1 missions lasted only long enough for them to drop their bombs and go home (usually less than 30 minutes). We had to stay on station as long as 4 hours and put in as many as 10 to 15 air strikes over the same target, getting shot at by AAA the whole 4 hours, not just 30 minutes.

The Wing Commander agreed with our Squadron Commander to give us a chance to show him what we did. After all, he conceded, he had not yet had the opportunity to fly with our squadron and he felt it his duty to do so, as he had already done with every other flight squadron assigned to NKP.

And so my Squadron Commander informed me the afternoon before our mission that we would be going to the hottest part of the Barrel Roll, in northernmost Laos, over a major highway (Highway 7) that led directly from North Vietnam into and through Laos. This was the area of Laos that had the most enemy troops, the most AAA guns, and therefore the best targets for our air strike birds. I was not a happy camper. I agreed with my Commander that the Wing Commander had to be shown our mission and to see it in such a way as to leave us in peace in the future and not press charges of any kind against J.R. or me.

So on that fateful night, my Squadron Commander and I took the Wing Commander on a ride into the Barrel Roll. I was to be the AC and my Squadron Commander was going to be my copilot (CP). I was going to be in charge. This was going to be interesting.

We flew our aircraft with all movable windows open and all

doors removed. This allowed the crewmembers to stay cooler in the hotter, lower altitudes of Laos and also provided easier exit should any of us need to bail out of a fatally damaged airplane. Everyone wore backpack parachutes during all of every mission, without fail. The pilot and copilot wore their parachutes, which fit into the back of each armor-plated seat. If crewmembers in the back of the plane were seated or not moving for any length of time, they tied themselves to the airframe in order to keep from being "bumped" out by turbulence. Some of the newer crewmembers even wore their body armor (which we called "chicken plates," because they were generally canvas or nylon vests with an oblong plate of steel inserted in the front and back) in addition to parachutes. We always thought the plates were old manhole covers, but couldn't be sure.

Because we wanted the Colonel to see "real good," we had asked the ground crew to bolt a steel chair at the very edge of the open troop door on the left side of the cargo compartment, near the front end of that section, and directly behind and below the pilot's cockpit station. The chair was bolted to the floor, had its own safety belt and harness, and was specially designed and fitted to allow him to use the same 5-inch, 4 power Starlight scope used by the Scope navigator to see targets on the ground. The only difference between the Colonel and the Navigator acting as the Scope was that the Scope was lying on a mattress on top of a 7 foot by 3 foot sheet of steel plating and the Colonel was strapped into a steel chair in front of an open doorway. The chair was so close to that open door that if the Colonel looked down between the toes of his flight boots, all he would see would be dark space. When we entered a left bank to begin to the carousel target, he would be leaning into the open doorway and restrained in his chair only by the strength of his 4-point safety belt. During a strike, the only thing between the Colonel and the dangers that would lurk outside that door when we started a FAC mission would be his green cotton flight suit.

That night we flew to the Barrel Roll and then on to Route 7. It took us about an hour to get there, it was so far from NKP. During that entire time we did not see one light on the ground, indicating that we were over hostile territory the whole route of flight. The Colonel also knew from his training "in theater" in the A-1, that all of the darkness below was a "free-fire zone," which meant that we could direct air-strikes anywhere within the zone because it was all considered "enemy territory." It also meant that any lights, vehicles, storage sites, or movement of any kind of vehicle that we might see in the zone were to be considered hostile. We called it "Indian country."

Most of our missions were flown about 3000 feet above the ground, which would generally keep us out of lethal range of small arms fire, but keep us near enough to the ground to provide the best visibility for our Starlight scopes. That altitude did not keep us out of AAA range or protect us in any way from the explosive rounds fired at us by the 23mm, 37mm, 57mm or 85mm enemy anti-aircraft gunners.

On this night, by tacit agreement between me and my copilot (the Squadron Commander), we flew a little lower. Also, we usually flew "blackout," that is, with all of our navigation lights off. The Commander and I had discussed before flight that we might turn on our navigation lights at sometime during the mission to attract AAA gunfire, if needed—all the better to impress the Wing Commander.

But this night, once we arrived at our assigned AO and over Route 7, we didn't need to stimulate the gunfire. It was everywhere. Every time we flew over or near the highway, we were fired on by 23mm, 37mm and 57mm guns. Every once in a while they would shoot a larger 85mm at us just to see if they could scare us away. It was the dry season, there was lots of truck traffic on Route 7 heading out of North Vietnam toward the Trail, the Plain of Jars, Steel Tiger area, and South Vietnam. There was enough moon in the clear sky above to give the gomer gunners confidence that they could see our moving, darkened shape against the starlit sky. They all shot at us—a lot.

Every round of 23mm, 37mm and 57mm anti-aircraft batteries are tracers. The 23mm shoots 20 rounds at a time and looks like glowing baseballs when they are heading toward us at night. The 37mm gun shoots 7 tracer rounds at a time and they look like glowing/burning soccer balls coming up. 57mm tracer rounds come 5 at a time and look like glowing basketballs. Usually, we can see the weapons fire each time, by the flash on the ground, as the rounds are shot out of the cannon. The rounds appear to float upward, very slowly at first, on a slightly curved path as gravity exerts its influence on a round fired at any angle to the ground. It's only when rounds get close that they seem to speed up and turn toward the aircraft. Rounds going past nearby have a cracking sound. Really close shots have a zipping sound, with a hissing note. Rounds that go past the plane continue upward until they explode, at the altitude set by the enemy gunners, throwing pieces of steel (shrapnel) in every direction outward from the explosion.

That night, some rounds exploded below the aircraft; some exploded at the same altitude as we were flying, both in front and behind us; and some went by us to explode slightly above. Sometimes the "flak bursts" were so close that the shrapnel pelted the outside of the fuselage like hail. When flak breaks directly in front of the aircraft, it's very easy to see the bright white and yellow ball at the center of the explosion, with a redder ring around the middle, and the black smoke at the edge of the burst that is generated by the exploding material inside each shell.

Every tracer round fired at us looked like it would hit us dead on. There's a knack to knowing where each round is really going to go, as soon as the trajectory can be seen. All of our crewmembers were experienced and could determine very quickly which AAA rounds were going to intersect our flight course and which ones would miss. If a round or series of rounds looked like they were going to hit us, a crewmember would tell us to turn away from the oncoming rounds. If a crewmember thought that we were headed for a hit, he would shout: "Break right! or "Break left!" to get us to turn away from the approaching rounds. We had crewmembers stationed on both sides of the cargo compartment of the aircraft looking out 3 different windows on each side.

Every crewmember was on intercom so he would communicate with the pilots. The Colonel also was on intercom so he would hear everything being said in the aircraft. He was also in the left door, strapped to a chair, and looking at the AAA coming up at the aircraft through a 5-power Starlight scope. Burning basketballs coming at the airplane at the speed of sound look much larger and much quicker with magnification than with the naked eye. On most of the shouts of "Break" from any crewmember, we had time to start a steep bank toward the coming rounds, which kept them in sight by the crewmembers for later adjustments in flight path, if needed. Sometimes it was necessary to turn away from the oncoming rounds because of the number of them or their location, which put all crewmembers in the "black zone," belly of the aircraft toward those rounds, and unable to see where the rounds would really go in relation to our changing position.

But on this occasion, there was so much flak in the air that the crewman on the right would shout "Break left!" and the crewman on the left would shout "Break right!" and we would have nowhere to go. At those times, we merely had to wait and see if the rounds coming at us were going to miss, go through the aircraft, or explode on contact. Although we usually didn't have to wait long, the seconds seemed to slow down during those straight and level waiting periods. While waiting, most crewmen tended to go quiet, pull his parachute straps a little tighter, and make sure he knew the closest open exit or window in case he had to bail out after any severe hit.

Many rounds went by the aircraft that night. Every round of AAA was called out by the crewmember seeing it so the Navigator keeping track of our location within Laos could also log the total number of rounds shot at us during each mission. Many rounds exploded in the air either beneath the aircraft or above it. Several rounds exploded near the aircraft and the shrapnel peppered our airplane. Some of that shrapnel penetrated the skin that night, but no one was injured. Each round that exploded near the aircraft was a bright fireball of white, red and yellow. Some could be heard exploding even over the sound of our 2 radial engines and our sound-muffling headsets. We could hear the "hiss" of rounds that closely missed the aircraft as they went by.

We found some trucks going west on Route 7. We called in several flights of fighter/bomber aircraft, so we could direct their bombs onto those trucks. To do that, we had to fly an orbit over the top of the trucks, mark the bombing site with ground-burning flares (about ½ million candlepower each), then visually direct the fighter/bombers onto the trucks by giving a distance and direction to the trucks from the flares burning on the ground. It took about 10 minutes for us to drop the ground-burning flares (which we called "logs") in the right place and about another 10 minutes or so to get into a proper left-hand turning orbit for the AC to be able to see where the trucks are located from the instructions given by Scope in relation to the ground burning flares. I would then direct the fighter-bomber aircraft onto the target by "clearing" the fighters "in hot."

We asked each fighter/bomber to drop one bomb or napalm canister or cluster bomb canister at a time. We would then visually correct the strike aircraft to drop the next bomb a distance and direction from his last bomb strike. Most strike aircraft flew in pairs and it would take about 30 minutes for us to direct an airstrike of 2 aircraft. When each strike aircraft acknowledged that he understood our instructions, he was cleared in "hot" or "wet." The strike aircraft would then descend through our altitude (which we gave to each strike bird while it was inbound to our target site) in a dive and release its bomb or canister. The strike aircraft would then climb back up through our altitude and orbit above us until we could give him a revised bomb aiming point. The second aircraft of each pair of fighter/bombers would then initiate the same action as the leader.

And so, Candlestick and the strike aircraft were on the carousel. The fighters were taking turns dropping bombs on our directed target, which tonight were trucks on the Trail. Every time the strike aircraft started its dive, both of us would receive AAA fire. Every time a bomb went off, we would both receive AAA fire. Any time a ground gunner thought he could tell where either of us were located in our separate orbits, he would fire in the direction of the sound or at our darkened silhouette in the nighttime sky.

Every air strike is hectic. The copilot is flying the plane in a changing bank to compensate for wind and keep the airplane in an orbit over the target so the AC can direct the air strike. The AC tells the copilot the angle of bank needed to maintain the orbit over the target, so he is continually stating on intercom the angle of bank he wants the CP to hold ("30 degrees," "25 degrees," "40 degrees," etc.). The AC is talking on the intercom with the Scope to get target information and on the radio with the strike aircraft to relay the bombing aim point directions and corrections. Strike fighter/bombers inbound to the target area call on a different frequency and the AC responds to hand them off to talk to the Navigator. Command and control aircraft (call signs "Cricket" and "Magic" and "Night Owl," "Alley Cat" and "Moonbeam"), orbiting Laos over "safe" areas, are talking to the inbound strike aircraft and to inform me of other aircraft in the area, not only friendly, but also enemy fighters.

This night we were working within 15 miles of the North Vietnamese border and within 50 miles of the nearest North Vietnamese air base that had fighter-jet aircraft. It was not unusual during an air strike to be using 4 different radio channels at the same time, as well as talking and listening on the aircraft intercom. These air strikes on this night were dazzling. At one point in the mission, after the last bomb had been dropped by a flight of A-1's and both had departed the area out of ordnance (which was called "Winchester") and with just enough gas to get home ("Bingo Fuel"), some AAA rounds came at us leaving us nowhere to turn.

Four or five 37mm rounds went up less than 5 feet from the aircraft fuselage and as close to the Wing Commander as possible without hitting either him or the airplane. I could see those rounds through my side window on the left side of the cockpit. Several of the rounds went between the fuselage and the engine nacelle, not 2 feet in front of the Wing Commander who was leaning into them. The Colonel had evidently seen the rounds coming up at us when a crewmember shouted "7 rounds of 37 at 10 o'clock." The Colonel was sitting at the 10 o'clock position within the aircraft, which is left of the nose of the airplane and toward the front. The Colonel had been using the Starlight scope to watch the rounds come up. When his mind told him that 2 or 3 of them were going to come right up to his eyeballs through the Starlight scope, he tried to back out of the steel chair. One of the Loadmasters saw him trying to lift the steel chair out of the bolts. When that didn't work the Colonel realized that he needed to release the seat belt that was holding him to the chair. Finally, after several seconds of very frantic effort, as reported by one of the loadmasters, he did manage to unstrap himself from the chair and then as quickly as he could he began running toward the tail-end of the cargo compartment, trying to get away from those approaching rounds.

More rounds went by very close to the airplane. The interior of the cargo compartment was illuminated briefly by the light of the closely passing 37mm tracer rounds. The loadmaster called on the intercom to tell us of the Colonel's efforts and to report that he was no longer in the chair in the open door, but standing at the back of the cargo compartment "holding on for dear life."

When I asked the Navigator sitting just behind the copilot on the map board how many rounds we had counted that were fired at us to that point, he replied "just slightly more than 2,000 rounds, sir." When I asked him how long we had been on station, he replied "about 20 minutes." I then asked my flight engineer on the panel how our fuel flow was doing and how long we could remain on station. He told me that we could stay on target for another two hours or so and still return to NKP with more than Bingo fuel.

The Wing Commander slowly returned to the steel chair and retrieved the headphones that he had torn off his head while trying to retreat to the back of the bus. The Colonel said to my Squadron Commander (my copilot on this mission): "Get me the hell away from this place." My copilot, bless his heart, said that it wasn't up to him, he was merely the copilot, but that it was up to me, a mere First Lieutenant, flying as Aircraft Commander of a "trash-hauler." The Colonel said: "This place is too hot, there's no reason to come after targets along this major highway, and there's no reason to put me, as Wing Commander, in such a dangerous position." Of course that's what my Squadron Commander was waiting for. He told the Colonel that this was a typical mission, that all of the pilots in the Candlestick squadron could and did carry out these types of missions on many nights, and that our mission was generally to interdict and destroy trucks and materiel located within Laos. My Commander also said that he would encourage me to leave the area if the Colonel had changed his mind about whether or not Candlestick pilots earned their "right" to drink like fighter jocks. The Colonel agreed that he had not fully realized the extent of our mission and that he was now fully aware of the dangerous nature of them. He then asked me if I would consider returning to NKP, because he was now fully informed about our mission, that overall, he was more important to our mission now that he understood it more clearly.

He candidly stated that he truly didn't want to be exposed to that much more gunfire. I talked it over with Lieutenant Colonel Firebaugh, who said that it was up to me but we still had mission time on station remaining. I then asked the crewmembers what their individual opinions were about returning to base (RTB) now, rather than complete the mission. After every crewman, including our volunteer flare kickers stated that they were willing to stay on Route 7 for the remainder of the mission to kill trucks, but would return to NKP if I decided to do that, I conceded and we returned to NKP.

Luckily, on that mission, no one was injured and we suffered only a few shrapnel holes in the airplane. The Wing Commander learned his lesson and I was never reprimanded or "officially" threatened with court martial. Candlesticks continued to drink and get as rowdy as they wanted in the Officers Club from then on. But still, I was very careful after that little episode to leave the O Club well before 8 o'clock in the morning, when the brass showed up for breakfast. I didn't want to have to go back to Route 7 again, to get my behind shot off, just to prove a point, again, to a has-been fighter jock. I had thought I was smarter than that, but I wasn't so sure anymore.

THE BOB HOPE SHOW

Christmas, 1969

Bob Hope and troupe came to NKP shortly before Christ-mas, 1969. I had some work to do at the squadron building that afternoon, so I got to the outdoor theater a little later than most. I did find a seat, but it was way in the back and I didn't have binoculars like most of those attending.

Bob was there with Les Brown and his Band of Renown. Les had a fairly large stage band and they were really belting it out. I don't remember all who were there, but I do remember The Gold Diggers and their tight, sequined god dresses, Connie Stevens, Neil Armstrong, Miss World of 1969, and Teresa Graves. Teresa was a beautiful black girl who did a dance number that was very athletic and ranged all over that small stage. She was wearing a thin, white billowy dress that allowed the audience to see her dancer's legs (a lot and even from my distance). I could see the darker background of her flesh showing through the filmy white covering. She had the troops speechless. It was a great performance and even though there weren't many black airmen or soldiers attending, everyone gave her a standing ovation at the end of her performance. At the end, Bob made jokes about our Wing Commander, whose last name was Crosby (referring to Bob's old pal, Bing), and we all sang Christmas carols. It was a great show and many cried while they sang the songs of home at the end of the performance.

After all that beautiful music, and all those great performances by the dancers, singers, and band, and all of the jokes by Bob and crew, most of us left the outdoor theater very quiet and sad. I enjoyed the show, but I was saddened too by the fact that I would not be home for Christmas, to be with my family, especially my 6-month old daughter, Kelli.

TAPING RECORDS ON NIGHTS OFF

--- ★ ---

Generally, I flew five or six nights in a row then got a night off. Two nights off together was a rarity. I think my longest run was 12 nights without a night off. I flew as much as I could, for several reasons: at the beginning of my tour, nights off were as bad as flying (worry, fret, shakes, dread, study, etc.); later in my tour, I got to the point where I really enjoyed going out onto the Trail. Throughout my year at NKP there was nothing to do on nights off but eat, drink, and make reel-to-reel tapes of new LP records or other borrowed tapes. Since our entire squadron flew at night, with only a few daytime missions on special occasions, all of the pilots stayed up all night when they weren't flying, just so they could keep their circadian rhythm going. Nights off were generally hard.

On the days when I knew I wouldn't fly that night, I would try to exercise a little more than usual during the day, hoping it would help me relax. I would usually walk around base, just to get better acquainted with the areas that I didn't usually go into. There were several jewelry stores on base. I would try to go there to see what was new and to learn a little more about the sapphire gems that were mined in the area and sold in the Thai store. I sometimes had lunch or dinner at one of the two restaurants on base near the Thai compound. One was an Indian restaurant and the other served Thai food.

On the nights I had off, I would make a BX run and see what was new there to buy. I always looked at the new magazines and would sometimes pick up a trinket or two as presents to send home. We usually heard through the grapevine that there were new records in, so a few of us would get together and decide which records each of us would buy. The agreement in the squadron was that all records would be shared. We were always talking about what came in, what we liked, what we had taped, and what we wanted to borrow. Most of the officers in the squadron bought a new tuner/amplifier, a turntable, a reel-to-reel tape machine, and speakers shortly after they arrived. It was the thing to do. As soon as I had several monthly paychecks under my belt after arriving at NKP, I went to the BX and bought a Sansui tuner, a Sansui turntable, Sansui speakers (four of them), and a TEAC reel-to-reel tape recorder and player. As soon as I had hooked all that equipment together and stuffed it into my metal clothes locker, I was ready to record.

My usual routine was to pick up a few new LP record albums from other members of the unit, take them to my trailer with a 6-pack of beer or a new bottle of scotch (Chivas Regal scotch was $4 per quart), and start to make copies of the records on my tape machine. I think everybody's favorite albums were "airline" albums. These were albums of all kinds of music, from lots of different artists. Each was labeled with the type of music, like "show tunes," "country/western music," "easy listening," or "jazz," or such. These albums were pretty long—most had about an hour of music. So I tried to get two or three hours of albums lined up to tape, just to keep me busy.

Usually, after a night of taping, I would lie in my bunk and listen to the new reel as I went to sleep. Since I lived in a one-man trailer, and the trailer was set back from the road, nights off were pretty quiet. Listening to music seemed to help me relax and not worry as much as usual.

Some nights of taping didn't go as planned. Some of the albums that we passed around were bootleg copies that someone had picked up in Hong Kong, Saigon, or downtown NKP. Some of these copies were good and some were really bad—warped, scratched, partial songs, etc. Also, sometimes my tape recorder would pick up the radar antenna nearby. For some reason, on most nights the radar didn't interfere with my equipment. Every once in a while, I would hear the radar sweep on my tuner/receiver as the radar antenna swept past my trailer. The "wheep" sound would be recorded on my tape every time the antenna swung around its full arc. The "wheeps" would be about 30 seconds apart and were clearly heard both during the recording and on the tape when the recording was done. On those nights, I didn't record, because of that interference. But sometimes, when I was especially tired after too many nights out on the Trail, and maybe after a beer or two, I would fall asleep while the music was being copied on tape. I made a few reels, with lots and lots of songs, where there were lots of skips, jumps, silences, and "wheeps," because I wasn't listening to the tape as the LPs were being recorded.

    I kept them that way, rather than erasing those reels and taping over them, as a reminder of what it was like in my trailer on nights when I didn't fly.

DAYS

On most days, even if I was scheduled to fly at night, I tried to do something constructive rather than just sit around my trailer. I often ran along the base perimeter. I sometimes went to the gym, where a small and really strong-looking Thai man would help us do weights and other exercises. There were handball courts at the gym, which I tried a couple of times with the handball nuts in the unit, but it hurt my hand too much. I quit doing that. I would try to write home several days each week and/or make tape recordings of what was going on at NKP. I always took time to read my mail from home and to listen to any cassette tapes that I received. On some days, after a BX and a post office run and a little jog around the base, I would put on my swimming trunks, grab a good paperback book, and go outside of my trailer to my hammock, which was strung between two palm trees.

Paperbacks were easy to come by. There were shelves in the latrines of the officers' barracks and at the Officer's Club where people put books they had finished reading. Those who liked to read were always buying books or getting them in packages from home. Usually, they would put them on one of the "sharing" shelves in the latrines when they were through reading. I enjoyed the books a lot. A little sun, a little soda (when I was flying, or beer when I wasn't), a little reading, a short nap in my hammock, and I was ready for the evening.

Evenings always started at dinner at the Officer's Club. I would go and eat with the guys even when I wasn't flying. It was the only time that I could see the other people in the squadron or in other units. During the days, most of my squadron mates and I were each going our separate ways. During the nights we were all either flying or trying to keep awake all night so we could go to bed at our usual time of around 4 a.m.

Every time I entered the Officer's Club for dinner, I would check my pockets for change and go to the one-armed bandits to get rich. There were three slot machines there, which we were told had the best odds of any slots anywhere. I stayed away from the quarter machine—too expensive. But I played the nickel and dime machines every night. Although I would hit small bonuses now and again, in my entire tour, I never hit a real winner, which normally paid about $200 or so.

Sometimes there were bands or musicians playing in the dining room or bar, sometimes there were festivities of one sort or another (Halloween, Thanksgiving, Christmas, etc.), but most of the time there was just dinner and then back to my trailer or off to the squadron building to get ready for a mission.

THE OUTDOOR THEATER

NKP had two theaters, a brand-new indoor theater that looked just like the ones on every Air Force Base in the United States (except it wasn't yet air-conditioned) and the outdoor one. I only went to the new theater once, just to see what it was like, but it was too confining, too hot, and too much USA. I liked the outdoor theater best.

The outdoor theater was semi-circular in shape, with a large screen constructed at the bottom of a small depression. It had hard, wooden benches arranged upslope away from the screen. The furthest row of benches was only about 50 feet or so away from the screen and the slope of the benches was just about enough to see over the tops of the heads of those sitting in front of you. There were 15 or 20 rows of seating.

The screen was a standard outdoor-type. It was located at the back of a small stage, where the occasional music groups or other entertainment acts played. Bob Hope and his troupe played on that small stage during the Christmas of 1969.

At the back of the benches, near the entrance to the fenced amphitheater, was a small building that was the cashier's booth and the place that sold popcorn. Cans of beer were available at that stand on most nights, but the theater was only about a block from the BX, so most of us who weren't flying could buy a six-pack of beer and carry it to the outdoor theater to eat with our popcorn purchased there. The movie didn't start until it was dark enough to see the images on the screen

I went to the movies on most of my nights off and many of the nights when I had the late takeoff, usually around midnight. I went just to kill time and get my mind off of the upcoming missions. Since the entrance fee was a buck, I wasn't concerned about the cost of seeing a movie more than once or parts of the same movie over and over again. It was something to do, and besides, after a film had been playing several nights in a row, those in the audience who were seeing it multiple times (like me) could always do the dialog along with the actors. If the movie wasn't very good, the comedians in the crowd would make up their own dialogue and shout it out during the action on screen. There was a lot of good ad lib going on in that theater many nights. Sometimes it was annoying, so we'd throw empty beer cans or popcorn sacks at the comic wannabes. But sometimes it really got funny.

If I wasn't flying at all that night, I usually went to the late, late show. Then, the theater was usually quieter and there were fewer people sitting on the benches. Most of those who attended that late show were others who were trying to stay awake all night on a night off—just like me. Sometimes I would see someone watch part of a movie, then get up and walk around the inside of the theater fence a bit, then sit down a while, then get up and pace a few more laps. I did the same thing sometimes. Movies aren't always a good way to get your mind completely off of bad nights—past or future.

When I went to the movie, I didn't care what was playing or what the weather was. Usually it was hot and humid and clear. But during the monsoon season, it was usually rainy in late afternoon or early evening. Sometimes the storms would break up at dark long enough to see one feature all the way through. On nights when it rained all night, the movie played anyway.

One evening, I had the night off and couldn't stand to be in my trailer taping music or writing letters, so I decided to go to the outdoor theater. I stopped by the BX and bought a six-pack of beer and walked over to the amphitheater. It had just started to rain—the monsoon season was just beginning. I bought a ticket, went to the very back row of benches, which had wooden backs attached, and sat down to watch the movie and have a beer or 6. It started to rain harder. I put on my poncho. The movie started.

It rained harder still. I put my poncho hood up, drew my feet up onto the bench with my knees bent so my legs would be under

MUSTANG

Communication between me and Vicki was always very slow. It was possible to call her and talk to her by MARS, a short-wave radio connection maintained by the military through provide Ham Radio operators in the States. But that required me to go to the MARS shack at NKP, sign up, then go another day to stand in line until the previous person completed his call in the soundproof booth located in that special building. The phone calls could only be a few minutes, were sometimes scratchy, or filled with crackling and sparking sounds, or conversations would come and go as if the participants were each turning to face a different direction while speaking. Each person's conversation had to say "Out," or "Over to you," or somesuch phrase to allow the radio operators to change to the other person's microphone. It was slow, sometimes more painful because it was possible to hear the other person's worry, grief, or anger, and always difficult to find the best time to start and finish the whole process. I did it once, but decided I would rather write a letter and wait the normal two weeks to get a response back than face the frustration of the MARS thing.

The letters back and forth could be a challenge also. Take the Mustang episode and resulting letters.

While I was attending KU, in my sophomore year, my brother Tom decided to get married to his sweetheart, Charlene. Since Tom and I were living in the same fraternity house, we shared the car Dad had bought for us—a 1953 Plymouth, 6 cylinder, 3 on the tree, and general piece of junk (but cheap). We usually didn't fight much about who was using the car each weekend, because Tom pulled rank as older brother (and meaner part-owner) to monopolize it the entire two days for "married stuff" and because his bride Beaner (her family familiar name) wanted to go somewhere. It was getting harder to chase my own girlfriends (or possible girlfriends) without wheels. I merely mentioned the troubles I was having with the Plymouth to Dad a couple of times (probably in the neighborhood of 400 or 500 times).

One day during the week, Dad called to ask me if I could come home the next weekend. That was a surprising occasion, because Dad had carefully told both Tom and I as we were each headed out the door to start our first year of college that we should NOT come home every weekend. He said the same thing to both of us (I heard it when he said it to Tom and again when he was pushing me out the door toward KU): "Son, don't come home every weekend. You'll learn more on weekends, taking care of yourself and doing new things (like laundry, which Mom had done for both of us since we were each zero years old)." Calling me to ask me to come home was a mystery. Maybe something was wrong in good old Washington, Kansas. So the next weekend, I borrowed Tom's car (with lots of griping and grinding of teeth on his part) to go home.

I got to Washington late on a Friday night. The next morning, I barely had time to give Mom my full bag of dirty laundry before Dad said it was time to go downtown "for a surprise." I asked if anything was wrong at home. Mom answered with something like: "No, nothing's wrong. Why do you ask?" Well, if she didn't know if anything was wrong, no one would. So Dad and I went off to town. I expected a doughnut with my morning Folders and nothing more. I was discovering at university that life was a mystery and home was apparently no different.

Dad took me to the Ford dealership. His friend Joe Lundblade was the owner and I knew Joe from the many times he had gone bird hunting with Dad, Tom and I. We went into the shop and Dad asked Joe to "show Pat the something" in the back garage. We walked back into the workshop. There, sitting in the middle of the double-space garage, sat a beautiful, black, convertible sports car. Joe said it was a "1954 MG TF 1500," whatever that was. It really didn't matter—it was a sports car—black, brown fabric top, wood on the dashboard, black seats (only 2), wire-spoke wheels, and

Candlestick: Night FAC over Laos 255

beautiful. Joe said it had been stolen in California, but the driver was caught on a nearby highway, so Joe had it towed to his shop. The California owner said it wasn't worth picking up or shipping back to his home, so he sold it to Joe. Joe said it had cost him $400.00.

Dad asked me if I would like to have this car. Joe said he would sell it for $400.00. I just about fainted.

After recovering enough to make arrangements with Dad and Joe—Dad paying Joe the money and Joe promising to polish it up and check it out, I was supposed to pick it up for myself the following weekend. The folks would ask Tom to bring me home that weekend, so they could see Tom. No mention was made by anyone to Tom about my new ride.

The folks offered to help Tom with some money and getting a trailer house to live in near Lawrence and they said I would be getting another "cheap car." When Tom saw my new black sports car, he was speechless (a condition I hoped to find him in). Rather than spend the whole weekend in Washington, taking multiple opportunities to gloat to my older brother, I drove the car back to KU and stopped to show it to my latest date—a sorority girl named Vicki. Together, we decided to call my new car "Cat," since she was black as.

I drove Cat for about a year before mechanical troubles started to crop up. I was beginning to park her on a hill so I could jump start her when I needed a ride, because her starter had quit and I couldn't find a replacement anywhere. One day, while being pushed on a level street, one of my pushing fraternity brothers slipped and jammed his hand entirely through my thinning and rotting fabric roof. Bummer!

I called Dad and told him my troubles. He told me to sell the Cat and that he would try to find a reasonable alternate as soon as he could. I sold the MG to a local car dealership. I called Dad right away to tell him that I had sold that broken down British piece of junk for $450. I almost broke my arm patting myself on the back for selling it for more than Dad paid for it. I guess a little crowing for supreme intelligence and superior selling prowess was OK at college, wasn't it?

Several weeks later, Dad called to tell me to come home next weekend. He said he had a surprise. This time I had my fingers and toes crossed that my next car would be newer and more mechanically sound. So I cajoled Tom and Beaner into taking me home in their slush-bucket, cheap, Plymouth hand-me-up, saying that Dad asked me to come.

Saturday morning, the next day, Dad and I again went to Joe's Ford dealership. Joe had a brand new 1964 ½ Mustang sitting on the showroom floor. Joe said it was one of the first off the assembly line. It was blue. Dad asked me what I thought. I told him that blue wasn't my best color. Joe suggested I look in the ordering book and see what I liked. I like the red pony with the pony seats, automatic transmission, 289 high-performance engine, and a pin stripe along the side in place of the tacky, fake air intake scoops behind each of the two doors. I picked out all the best parts that I liked from pictures and descriptions in the order book. Dad said to Joe: "Order it." Joe filled out the order slip. Dad gave him a check. I almost fainted again from lack of blood to my brain caused by the ear-to-ear grinning that was severely locked in place. I had a new car.

When I got it—it was primo. A gem! A looker! A wower! And it was mine. And I never allowed Tom to drive it. It was my special gift from my Mom and Dad and was made especially for me.

It was my car when I married Vicki in 1966.

It was my car when I went off to Thailand in 1969.

It was my car when I was writing letters home to Vicki from NKP and she was driving it around Topeka with Kelli while I was gone.

One day a letter from home stated that she was having some problems with the Mustang. I wrote back—"What problems?"

Two weeks later, her letter stated that it was starting to make noises when she drove it. I wrote back—"What noises?"

Two weeks later her response letter said that the noises happened when she was slowing down or stopping. I said: "Take it to the Ford dealer to have it checked."

The next letter— "The brakes need replacing. What should I do?" I responded: "Have the brakes replaced."

The next letter—"There is about 60,000 miles on the Mustang. Is it still safe? Can we trust it to carry our daughter?" I responded that 60,000 miles wasn't much and it wouldn't get many more miles while I was sweating each night in Thailand.

The next letter—"I would feel safer in a newer car." I didn't respond.

The next letter—"The Ford dealer said he would give us a good trade-in price for a new car." I didn't respond on that, but did tell her that I was enjoying a break from flying and was getting a few days off soon.

The next letter—"I would really feel a lot safer with Kelli in a newer car." I told her to look at some and get back to me. In two weeks, she said that she had found a new car, that the Mustang would really help pay for it, and that it was perfect (and safe) for her and Kelli. I told her to buy it.

The next letter told me that she had sold my 1964 ½ Mustang for a 1970 VW travel van and was very happy. She included a picture of the beige outside and beige inside, travel van with vinyl covered seats, a built-in cooler and sink (with water reservoir), stick shift, and tiny, tiny engine. The back, bench seat would fold backwards, flat, to form a small double bed. Kelli was small enough to sleep on the half-seat beside the ice box or on the floor between the two front seats. She was gushy about her new beatnik van. I gushed as well, but mostly with tears of loss and frustration.

Married life was starting to catch up with me. Goodbye red Mustang—Hello beige slow-mobile.

(I still have the original key to my '64 ½ Mustang.)

the protection of the poncho, put my beer beneath my knees, and stayed dry and cozy. The movie continued.

The rain became a flood. Water was rushing under my bench in a huge sheet, which became a small stream by the time it hit the front of the stage at the bottom of the theater. I was still dry. I had a few beers left. Then the rain increased to the point that the projected images were dancing on the wall of rainwater, which was so solid that no projection light was reaching the screen. It was like watching people talk and play on the Northern Lights—almost ghostly. I continued to drink beer and watch the movie in the rain, until a lightning bolt landed nearby, and all of the lights in that part of the base went out. The theater was dark. I was out of beer anyway, so I went back to my trailer to write a few letters. I really liked that theater.

OFFICER OF THE DAY

Every officer at NKP had to serve as Officer of the Day (OOD). This was a 24-hour period when that chosen officer was the Wing Commander's representative for all things occurring on the airfield during that time. Although several of the pilots in the 606th had to pull OOD duty several times, I had the privilege of being assigned that job only once.

The appointed day started with me going to Wing Headquarters and getting a short briefing by the be-striped sergeant assigned to the Commander. At that briefing, I was given a hand-held radio (which we all called "the brick"). I had to carry the radio with me at all times during my 24-hour stint. With it, I could summon the HQ Command Post for help should the need arise. I was supposed to use the landline telephone for routine matters or to obtain information from any one of the ground pounders assigned to Headquarters, if needed.

I was also given the keys to an Air Force pickup truck and told to drive to the control tower to assist the airmen assigned there. The truck was the usual A.F. dark blue, with prominent yellow lettering along the side denoting it as the official vehicle of the OOD (with parking privileges at primo locations like the Officer's Club, the control tower, the enlisted men's mess, and other strategic places around base).

As ordered, I drove the truck to the base of the control tower, parked it in the slot marked for us important personages (OODs), entered the tower, and climbed the bazillion steps to the top. There I introduced myself to the three enlisted airmen controllers on duty (there wasn't another officer in sight), and received a brief explanation of what I was supposed to do in the tower: " Do nothing. Just sit there, read our Playboys, and pay attention if there are any emergencies announced by any of the aircraft flying in our airspace." So, I did as I was told, even though the senior airman present in the tower was an Airman First Class (two stripes), at least six years younger than me, and just a few inches shorter than my 5-foot-10. They had some great magazines, though—and some were almost new.

Several times during the day, I would get bored reading either the magazines or the paperback book I had found, so I would just hop in my personal AF truck and go sightseeing around the base on a "drive-about." Even that got boring by mid-afternoon. The controllers had already told me that the interesting times usually occurred after dark, when the night missions went out (boy, did I know how that went).

Sometime in the late afternoon, after I had climbed back into my familiar hard chair behind the control radio boards, I heard a call come in over the speakers that everyone in the tower listened to. "Mayday, Mayday, Mayday!" I heard." "This is XXX52. Can anybody hear me?"

A "Mayday" call was reserved exclusively for any aircraft in trouble. Pilots or aircrew would only make that kind of call if the aircraft or aircrew member was in severe distress. The call would be made over the "Guard" frequency that every aircraft monitored during every mission. The control tower monitored this emergency frequency all the time as well.

One of the airmen jumped to the console and responded: "Aircraft calling Mayday. This is NKP tower on guard. State your call sign, type of aircraft, and emergency."

"NKP tower. This is XXX52. I'm an F-4. My aircraft was hit by AAA on a mission to the east and I'm in trouble. I can't raise my pilot on the intercom."

"XXX52, This is NKP. State your location."

"NKP tower, 52. I'm somewhere over central Laos, flying west."

"52, NKP. Are you flying the aircraft?"

"NKP, 52. Affirmative. I'm the GIB (guy in back or radar-control officer). I've had a little flight training, but not much, but it seems to be going OK. The pilot would let me fly the plane sometimes when we were going out or coming in from a strike."

"52, NKP. Can you see your pilot?"

"NKP, 52. No. We were on a bombing run and there was AAA everywhere around us. I heard a thump from the bottom of the plane just below me and the inside of the pilot's canopy was suddenly covered with blood. I can't talk to him on intercom. I can't see his helmet. I think he's dead. Can anybody out there help me?"

"52, NKP. Stand by, we'll get help!"

During this conversation, one of the airmen at the console grabbed the landline and called the radar station (call sign "Invert") to see if they had the F-4 on radar (they did). The other airman started dialing out to several other control towers in Thailand, trying to find the base from which the F-4 had taken off (each aircraft squadron in Thailand had their own, unique call sign).

Since all of these radio transmissions both ways had been spoken over the "Guard" frequency, the airman talking to the F-4 started getting calls from other aircraft offering help. But the airman said that NKP would handle it and asked everyone who called to continue monitoring that frequency, just in case.

Suddenly another caller came up on the Guard frequency. "52, this is Ubon Tower (another Air Force base in Thailand, located just south and a little west of NKP—known as a "fighter" base). We have your Squadron Commander on site and ready to help (he was obviously a pilot qualified in the F-4 if he commanded that type of squadron). We'll get you home. An ambulance is standing by to take care of your pilot on landing. Change frequency to xxx.xx. Can you comply?"

"Ubon, 52. Wilco (will comply)."

And I never heard anything more about that GIB, either that day or any time later. I never learned if he landed safely or not, or whether his pilot was dead, or just knocked out.

I finished my day and part of the night in the tower, just sitting, watching and listening to snatches of the war going on as the airmen changed frequencies now and again to pick up the aircraft-to-aircraft transmissions going on by planes flying that night over the Trail. I even heard a Candlestick call or two—but no more emergencies.

I packed it in about 10 p.m., carried my brick to my trailer, put it beside the bed, and crashed on my bed in full flight suit and socks, boots ready beside the bed—just in case. In the morning, I returned the brick to the Noncommissioned Officer (NCO) at HQ who had given it to me 24 hours before. Another young officer from another squadron was there, ready to take the radio and become OOD. Another day in the Air Force at NKP.

THE F-4 GIB AND NEW YEAR'S EVE

On several occasions while at NKP, I heard aircraft get shot down. We always knew when one was down, because we would hear their parachute emergency radios start their particular, blood-freezing sound when a parachute was deployed. If the crew member who ejected or jumped from the damaged plane had enough presence of mind, he would pull out the emergency radio from its pouch on the parachute, turn the frequency knob over to "voice" and tell everyone that he was OK and where he was coming down (if he could see the ground). If we continued to hear the "beeper," it meant that the crewmember didn't think about the radio or that he was unable to shut it off. Many didn't shut it off on their way down, but some would turn it off after they hit the ground, just to tell people where they were.

One night I was on a mission and heard the emergency beeper deploy. Not long afterward, I heard someone say the usual on the emergency frequency that all aircraft monitored: "beeper, beeper, come up voice." Shortly, the beeper went off and a person spoke on the emergency frequency, called "Guard," and said that he was on the ground and OK.

He said he was the back-seater (the "guy in back," or GIB) of an F-4 that got hit by ground fire, (AAA) and that both he and the pilot ejected. He said that he saw his pilot's chute go down just to the east of his landing position. We could only hear his voice and we had only heard the one emergency beacon earlier. No one had heard the pilot's beeper when he was coming down. The aircraft closest to the downed GIB told him to switch to the secondary frequency, so they could talk without interfering with all of the other airplanes in the area monitoring Guard frequency and listening to the conversations. The GIB agreed, and I never heard anything more about him until I returned to NKP after the mission.

While the Air Force was getting the rescue effort together, the GIB told the aircraft circling overhead that he had heard his pilot speaking on his emergency radio. He had said that there were bad guys very near him. The GIB heard several pistol shots toward the east, on the other side of a small river nearby, and then nothing. He couldn't raise his pilot again. And he said that the gomers were making noises across the river that sounded like they were coming after him, so he split.

For the next several days, our intelligence briefing kept us informed about where the GIB was on the ground and the rescue effort that was going on to try to get him out. There were a lot of airplanes and helicopters taking part in that rescue. The GIB was moving a lot because there were enemy soldiers chasing him.

The AF was dropping lots of bombs and bomblet clusters all around the GIB to keep the bad guys away long enough for him to move again. It was getting very tricky, since the more the AF tried to suppress the bad guys, the more bad guys were sent to the area to catch the GIB.

Even though I tried to keep up with what was going on in the rescue effort, I had my own problems to deal with and didn't spend a lot of energy worrying about the GIB.

Finally, after three days, the Jolly Green helicopters managed to pull the GIB out of the jungle right at dusk. It was a good rescue. No one had heard any indication of any kind from the pilot. We all suspected that he was captured or killed at the time he landed.

Air Force policy was that whenever a crewmember spent more than 24 hours on the ground in enemy territory after ejecting or jumping out of a damaged plane, he was entitled to a 30-day home leave. That special leave did not count against his R&R or any other time off. It was a special "survivor's" recuperation time. It usually began just as soon as the rescued airman was released from the care of examining AF doctors. Everyone expected this GIB to go home, since it was only a week or so before Christmas. But not this GIB.

On New Year's Eve, the GIB got off a C-130 at NKP and told the Jolly Green Giant crews and the A-1 "Sandy" pilots who had rescued him that he had requested and received special permission to take his "survivor's" leave after his New Year's Eve celebration at NKP. He told the "Jollys" and the "Sandys" that he was going to buy them champagne all night long.

NKP had an Australian band lined up for the party that night—it even had a round-eyed singer (i.e., a white girl). The main dining room of the Officer's Club was decorated with crepe paper and a few remaining Christmas decorations. There were lots of Christmas lights still up and glowing that night for the party. There were a few early missions that night, but since it was the beginning of the monsoon season, late missions were cancelled so all Officers could participate in the Club's New Year's Eve party.

There were lots of people there that night. The GIB was the center of attention. He tried to buy champagne for the Jollys and the Sandys, but couldn't, because everyone in the house was buying him drinks.

There were drinks everywhere. It became an open bar, with the GIB giving all of the money he had brought with him to the Thai bartender with instructions to "keep pouring until it's all gone." It never went. Too many others were throwing money into the "drinking" pot.

Everyone was drinking, singing with the Aussie band, ogling the blond-headed, round-eyed singer, buying each other drinks, and having a good time. The Candlesticks were having an especially good time too.

At midnight, everyone sang "Auld Lang Syne," then hurried to get in line to kiss the white girl. The Jollys and Sandys who were still able to stand by that time pushed the GIB up to the front of the line for the first midnight kiss. He didn't hesitate—he was AF-trained and a surviving GIB. He stepped up onto the stage in front of hundreds of envious onlookers, looked the singer in the eyes, smiled, and then bent her back with a long, passionate kiss. It seemed to take her breath away. The room was quiet for a moment, then everyone cheered. The next thing anyone knew, the next Jolly Green Giant pilot in line pushed the GIB out of the way and planted his own kiss on the blond singer.

She was a trooper. She kissed every one of us at the party that night—me included. There were several hundred of us by then. It was a good party for all of us—especially the F-4 GIB.

THE CHINESE HIGHWAY

A part of our intelligence briefings included information about a highway that the Chinese were building in the northern border region of Laos, where Laos and China connect. We were told that the Chinese workers were building about a kilometer ("klick") of concrete road each day, and that they were also building fighting positions and AAA bunkers about every quarter-klick all along both sides of the road. No one would say where this road was going or why the Chinese were building it. I continued to ask about the status and purpose of the road throughout my tour, but I was never given a straight answer about the road. We were told never to discuss this road with anyone, ever. Weird!

THE RUSSIAN TALKERS

One night out over the Trail, I heard someone speaking Russian on my FM radio. It was the radio that we used to communicate with friendly soldiers on the ground. In Florida, during our combat crew training, several of the students in the C-123 transition course noticed that we could sometimes hear Highway Patrolmen talking on our FM radios. Also, in Laos, we could sometimes hear what sounded like telephone conversations on these radios or one person on the ground talking to another nearby.

But the night I heard the Russian, it was quite clear and distinctly Russian. When I reported that information to the Intelligence Officer who debriefed us on landing (as they did after every mission) said that he didn't believe me. I told him that I had a degree in that language, but he insisted that I was hearing things that weren't there. So I guess I didn't hear it—even though I did.

BLOTTING OUT THE STARS

Toward the end of my tour, the intelligence officers began to brief crews about mysterious "black helicopters" flying at night in the northern area of Barrel Roll. We were asked to look for any strange aircraft in our areas at night. The only way we would be able to see a darkened aircraft at night would be to see a silhouette or a shape blotting out the background stars.

One night, a particularly nervous loadmaster called me on the intercom and said he thought he saw something blotting out the stars behind us, and it seemed to be moving. Because I had more curiosity than good sense, I quickly turned the aircraft around and descended, so all of the crew could look for any strange shape blotting out the stars. No one saw anything.

We returned to our mission of looking for enemy trucks along the Trail below in the Barrel Roll. Just to try to catch the bad guys off guard, I'd do quick reversals every once in awhile, to see if the crewmembers could see any mysterious aircraft following us. But no one ever did.

Later, we were briefed about a friendly helicopter that had been shot down by a mysterious black helicopter out in the Barrel Roll area. We heard a tape recording of the conversation between the air traffic controllers and the pilot of the American aircraft. The pilot told the controller he was being followed, and then we heard a loud bang from the recorder and some screaming ... then nothing.

CHIEF NAVIGATOR IN A PARTY FLIGHT SUIT

--- ★ ---

Finally, after a lifetime, my 365-day tour in Southeast Asia *was coming to an end. The five of us who had come into the squadron together were scheduled to fly our final missions on the same night. All five of us would be in our respective assigned areas at the same time, the earliest mission period, so we would all finish at the same time and get home early. That was important because the tradition of the unit was that every departing officer received a last mission party at our squadron clubhouse after the last flight.*

What was more important to me, and probably all five of us, was that our instructions for our final mission over the Trail were "to stay out of trouble, don't put in any strikes, and get the hell home in one piece." Good advice. I took it literally. I decided I wasn't going to do anything foolish or dangerous on my last trip over Gomerland.

Like most other pilots and navigators approaching their final month of missions, I was very nervous about flying now. There were lots and lots of legends about pilots shot down on their last mission and being forced to endure the Hanoi Hilton in North Vietnam. And there were always whispers about "last-mission shakes" and last-mission mistakes that caused people to become house guests of the Viet Cong or North Vietnamese Army troops occupying Laos.

Everybody always talked about "getting short," and getting back to the "the land of the big BX." There were even yellow ribbons to wear for the final 30 days of a tour. I passed on that tradition—I think I was superstitious.

Finally the night arrived. We were all briefed together, went to our airplanes together, and took off in a line, one right after the other. Our last mission had begun.

The weather was turning bad now that the rainy season was fast approaching and there were lots of clouds in my assigned mission area in the southern part of Barrel Roll. When we arrived, the gunners below started firing through the clouds at the sound of our engines. We could see the flashes of light as they fired and knew that at least seven rounds of 37 mm anti-aircraft shells would be coming at us out of the tops of the clouds below. It made us nervous, but at least we knew something would be coming up at us, so we prepared to dodge, bob and weave as best we could when the rounds actually appeared.

In the places where the clouds were too thick to give us lead time to break away from the flak, the rounds just suddenly appeared below us, climbing slowly at first, then faster, then really fast. In those cases, my heart stopped, and we'd be all elbows and assholes trying to turn the aircraft away from the rounds as quickly as possible. This was not the night to get popped by a lucky hit from the gomers.

All five of us talked almost the entire mission to each other on our separate squadron frequency. We were all getting shot at through the clouds—we thought it was a conspiracy. We were sure the hooch maids or the Thai waitresses at the club had called their buddies in Laos and told them that five last-mission airplanes would be over Laos that night and they should shoot every one of us down as a lesson to the Yankee Pigs.

Whatever the reason, they were shooting at us, and we were feeling very vulnerable. So we decided to fly just a little higher than usual, fly more toward the quieter parts of our areas, and maybe go home a little early, all together, as a flight of five.

After about three hours of sweating out our missions, we had all had enough. We planned where we would rendezvous on the Thai side of the Mekong, so we could all fly back to NKP together and land in the same string as on take-off.

After we landed and had all parked on the ramp, the fire trucks pulled up in front of all five aircraft. When the aircraft commanders got out of each plane, we were liberally sprayed with the fire hose, in celebration of the successful completion of our year. With the water all around, the steel planking got very slick. By the time I got out of my parked plane, I was easily pushed upside down, and ended on my ass by the pressure of the fire hose and the lack of firm footing on the ramp.

I didn't care and neither did any of the others. It was a great night! We were done!

Now it was time to party.

All of us finished our de-briefing and paperwork as fast as we could after landing. None of us wanted to miss even a second of the big party. Most of the people who had met us at the ramp had already left the flight line area and were probably already at the hooch, pouring booze down their gullets. We didn't want to be left behind, so we hurried.

When we were all ready to leave the flight line, we called a crew bus to take us to the squadron club. We all arrived together and entered our squadron clubhouse together.

Last-mission parties were always held at the squadron club rather than the Officers' Club for obvious reasons—everyone wanted to get real drunk and do stupid things. Nothing in the squadron club could be severely damaged by raucous and ribald officers. The club itself was about 20 feet wide by 40 or so feet long. It was covered inside by split bamboo nailed to the walls, with several screened windows on each side placed higher than normal—about head high for the average pilot. There was a small bamboo bar in the corner furthest from the door, several pictures of planes nailed to the walls, a pin-up poster or two that changed with each new issue of Playboy magazine, a TV tuned to Armed Forces Television Network, several card-playing tables, a half dozen folding metal chairs, a few sway-backed easy chairs, and a dart board. That was it.

The entry door was on the end of our building away from the Officers' Club across the street. Strap hangers going into that club couldn't see us real heros going into our squadron club. The door was a solid double door on the outside, swinging out, and two saloon-style half doors inside that would swing either way, depending on the direction and velocity of the body being hurled through them. It was a nice club, if just a little bit bare (especially after every last mission party).

The night was hot, so the outside double doors had been propped open. I was the third last-mission pilot to enter the club through the swinging doors that night. I felt like a gunslinger walking into the Long Branch Saloon in the middle of a celebration of cow punchers just off the prairie, after a year on the trail behind a herd of cattle. I walked about three steps into the room, stopped and stared (probably with my mouth open).

Thai girls who were waitresses at the Officers' Club during operating hours were now dancing nude on top of the card tables scattered about. The room was almost full of pilots and navigators of all ranks, from both the 606th and the 609th, wearing only underwear and combat boots, dancing in the middle of the room and making flying motions with their hands. Some had tatters of cloth clinging around their ankles, others had tatters of T-shirts still partially covering their chests or backs. Most were almost naked—and a few were as naked as the dancing Thai waitresses.

Then the mob saw us—the cause and center of this very celebration—and they were upon us.

Before we could retreat back out the swinging doors, we were each surrounded by very drunk fellow officers. It took about three seconds for my flight suit and T-shirt to be stripped completely off me in a hundred different pieces. I was standing just inside the door, looking pretty stupid in my underwear and combat boots, but so were the other four guys I walked in with, so I guessed that was all right. The squadron pilots around us handed us a beer, we were pounded on our backs, and were swallowed up by the mass of party animals.

Whoever arranged the party for us also arranged to have two stone jars of Laotian rice wine prepared for us. I was told that the jars, standing about three feet high, could hold about 15 gallons of wine each. I was also told that the locals who made them filled them with rice and fruit and other stuff, buried them for a couple of days to get the alcohol started, then brought them to the club. Each jar had a bamboo straw sticking out from the rice straw covering the top. Before any of us could drink this potion, someone came by and put a gallon or so of water into the top, "to generate more wine," he said.

And then we were told to drink.

I did. It tasted like really bad (but weak) Japanese saki. I didn't think it had much alcohol taste, so it probably wasn't very strong. I had another drink. Throughout the night, I sampled the tasty but weak drink, as did many others celebrating that night. Of course, there was also beer and all kinds of booze available; it was plentiful and cheap. Beer at the Officers' Club was regularly 15 cents a can—a dime on special nights—and martinis were a 15 cents or a dime on special nights. I could buy a quart of Chivas Regal scotch at the BX for four bucks any day of the week (and did just that in lots of weeks). So there was plenty of booze at the party, including that good-but-weak Laotian wine, and lots of reasons for all of us to celebrate, especially the famous fighting five who had finished their tour. Bottoms up!

I had been at the party about an hour before the chief navigator arrived. He was an older lieutenant colonel, probably 40 years old (OLD!), fairly short (about 5' 8" or so), and Irish. It was Lieutenant Colonel James M. Donahue. He spoke with a light Irish brogue. He was one of the bosses, but he was a good navigator, and always took his turn to fly combat missions with us. He wasn't a pansy or a desk jockey or a power-hungry moron—he was a good guy. He was proud of his navigators and proud of the work they were doing in our squadron. Everyone liked and respected him.

There hadn't been many new arrivals since we joined the party, but the ones who came in after us were treated to the same indignity—stripped down to their briefs and boots within six seconds of pushing their way through those swinging saloon doors. When the chief navigator arrived, he stopped just a few steps inside the door to take it all in. By this time, everyone was a little bit drunker than before. The room was more crowded, the noise level had gone up at least a hundred decibels, there were more naked waitresses dancing on the tables, and there were more naked officers parading around the room.

Somehow, the chief navigator hadn't gotten the memo about the dress code for this party. He was dressed in his brand-new, custom-tailored, powder-blue, squadron-authorized party flight suit.

This beautiful ensemble was complete with embroidered command navigator wings, embroidered squadron and wing patches on each shoulder, and embroidered, bright-silver lieutenant colonel leaves on each epaulette. It was form-fitted to his short, but trim, physique. He was also wearing his squadron-authorized, powder blue ball cap, with the squadron patch embroidered on the front. He had donned his squadron-authorized, powder-blue-and-white, polka-dot ascot. He was a vision in party attire. We saw him standing there, vulnerable, in his beautiful, new 606th party suit. We started toward him as a mob, with smiles on our lips and deviltry in our hearts.

Before the mob took more than a few steps, the chief navigator drew himself up to his full height, snapped to attention, threw his chin forward in a challenging way, and threw up his right hand in the classic, open-handed, palm-forward, universal gesture for "stop!" He didn't say a word. We stopped.

He did a perfectly crisp about-face, strode purposefully back through the swinging doors of the club, and was gone. We laughed. I thought he was gone for good, too chicken to come in and join the rest of us and have his flight suit ripped off. I was a little disappointed, because I liked the little lieutenant colonel and thought he was a real cool kind of guy.

About 20 seconds after the swinging doors stopped swinging, they swung open again, only this time more powerfully than before. The chief navigator strode into the room with his shiny new low-cut brogans slamming the floor in parade-ground cadence. He came to a halt where he had stopped before and came to attention. Only this time, he was wearing only his white jockey shorts and those dress-black brogans.

All eyes turned toward him. The room grew suddenly silent. He saluted the room, and while still standing at attention, shouted, "Where's my goddamn beer?" Everyone laughed and the party noise and antics resumed.

Someone handed him a beer. He joined the crowd and I only saw him briefly after that, dancing and drinking and talking as loud as he could, while making flying motions with his hands. Yep, he was *one of us, and I liked and respected him even more.*

Sometime the next day, well after the party ended, someone found his party flight suit neatly folded on the ground just outside the front door of our club, lying on the ascot, and covered by the powder-blue ball cap. He had forgotten to pick them up after the party.

I don't remember much of the party after our chief navigator arrived, but we all had a good time. All the Laotian wine disappeared, including the jugs. Apparently, it was a bit stronger than I thought. Somehow, I managed to get back to my trailer just before dawn and fall asleep on my bunk, even though it was whirling around and around, bucking and trying to throw me off. I was holding on and trying not to throw up.

But it had been a good party.

It was my last mission. I was safe!

I had flown 165 night combat missions over the Trail, and a dozen or so forays for people or cargo into and out of South Vietnam. Now I was going home without a scratch.

I had two weeks to do nothing more than pack, party, and go home. I left the squadron before the end of August, 1970, destined for Camp Alpha at Tan Son Nhut Air Base in Saigon, where I would out-process for a few days. I would fly out on a freedom bird on the first day of September.

I was going home!

Author before a night mission over Laos, 1969

ABOUT THE AUTHOR

Pat served a total of 21 years in the military, first in Vietnam and later in the Army National Guard.

Pat finished his tour in Thailand and returned to an assignment in C-141 heavy-jet aircraft at McGuire Air Force Base in New Jersey. He flew world-wide cargo and passenger missions around the globe, first as copilot, later as Aircraft Commander, and finally as Instructor Pilot. He was offered and accepted a Regular Air Force Commission as one of the "Top 5 Per Cent" in the Air Force while stated at McGuire.

On one occasion, when commanding a round-the-world flight carrying brand new Air Force station wagons to various embassies, he had the opportunity and pleasure to meet and shake hands with Brigadier General Chuck Yeager in Rawapindi, Pakistan. He was selected one of the youngest Instructor Pilots in the Air Force to train new C-141 pilots at the Transition Training Unit in Altus Air Force Base, Oklahoma.

He gave up his commission in December, 1973, to return to law school in Kansas. He finished a three-year J.D. program in two and a half years while working several jobs, including law clerk, legal intern, sheriff's pilot in a DeHaviland Beaver, and pilot for an aircraft broker flying single-and multi-engine private aircraft nationwide.

After he graduated in 1975, he joined a practice that had been started by his grandfather, Jim, and joined by his father, Herb. He practiced law for more than 22 years, including seven years as the County Attorney (State Prosecuting Attorney), both appointed and elected.

In 1989, Pat joined the Army National Guard to fly helicopters. He was assigned to fly air ambulance missions, "MedEvac" in the parlance of the Army. He flew UH-1 Hueys first and then UH-60 Blackhawks. He was mobilized into the active duty Army three times. His first deployment was to Bosnia with NATO, as a part of the Stabilization Force there. Bosnia was his second combat tour. He flew MedEvac missions there with the call sign: "Dustoff." He was later mobilized to Fort Benning, Georgia. Most of his six months in Georgia were spent as a MedEvac Pilot-in-Command, located at the Mountain Ranger Training Camp, Camp Merrill, near Dahlonega, Georgia, very near the southern end of the Appalachian Trail. He was again mobilized two months after returning from Georgia and served 15 months in the Army as the National Guard liaison to one-half of his company deployed to Kuwait.

When Pat was past 60 years old, and not considered "deployable" by Army regulations, he represented his National Guard unit in Cheyenne, Wyoming as Training Officer. He retired at the age of 61, a year beyond U.S. Army mandatory retirement age for helicopter pilots.

For more information, photos and mission audio recordings, visit jamespatrickhyland.com

Printed in the USA
CPSIA information can be obtained
at www.ICGtesting.com
LVHW050748021224
PP18477700002B/2